I0595106

J. S Hurlburt

History of the Rebellion in Bradley County, East Tennessee

J. S Hurlburt

History of the Rebellion in Bradley County, East Tennessee

ISBN/EAN: 9783337209063

Printed in Europe, USA, Canada, Australia, Japan

Cover: Foto ©ninafisch / pixelio.de

More available books at **www.hansebooks.com**

HISTORY

OF THE

Rebellion in Bradley County,

EAST TENNESSEE.

By J. S. HURLBURT.

INDIANAPOLIS:
1866.

TO THE

UNION PEOPLE OF TENNESSEE

AND THEIR POSTERITY,

BY THE AUTHOR.

PREFACE.

THE following work, like many other books is forced into existence by circumstances. Regardless of the previous plans, previous and present wishes or present fears of the author, it arbitrarily assumes its present form. A believer in special Providence, he is compelled to accept it as one of the Providential tasks, if not one of the Providential afflictions of his life.

Having prepared to publish the history of the 9th Indiana, under the present high rates of printing, it was found that upwards of $4,000 were necessary to issue 2,000 copies—a book to be properly illustrated and finished, and to contain 600 pages. Only $1,900 had been contributed for this purpose. The scheme must therefore be abandoned, or some method invented to save it from an entire failure. If the sale of the present work does not obviate the difficulty, the enterprise will be relinquished and the subscriptions refunded to all who desire them. The long and heart-rending delay of this work, more heart-rending to the writer than to all others concerned, is as unavoidable on his part as it is afflicting, and the only present consolation is the hope that the sequel may yet be to some extent an atonement for past disappointment. * * * * * * * * *

In regard to the present work, many things suggest themselves that might be said; but in any case, it is bad taste, bad economy, and in principle very suspicious to re-write a book in its preface. The principles entertained and views expressed in the following pages, morally, politically and socially, as general laws, are principles and views for which our only regret is that circumstances have militated against their being expressed more pungently and more at length. No person is fit to write upon the subject of our great rebellion who does not feel that it was at war with every principle of justice, every principle sacred to God and humanity, and that his pen is a two-edged sword put into his hand to wield in defense of his own life and of the life of posterity, as the sword and the musket were wielded at Shiloh and other battle-fields of the war—wielded to the death—by the friends of God and of human rights.

The mournful and costly victory in the field has been obtained, but the triumph is lost if the principles for which the bloody ordeal was endured are not, hence forward, unequivocally made the basis of our national action; and the unequivocal and unobstructed triumph of

these principles in the nation cannot be maintained, only as writers
and speakers upon the subject write and speak from a corresponding
sense of the moral obligation divinely lain upon us as a people, and
from an undying sympathy with, and an agonizing remembrance of,
the bloody sacrifices which, in the Providence of God, was willingly
poured out upon the field in defense of universal liberty and universal
justice.

The only argument we have for those who think that we have been
too severe with *rebels*, is to ask them to become intimately acquainted
with the feelings of those Union people in East Tennessee who were
the greatest sufferers—whose bereavements were the most terrible
from the rebellion. The trials, sufferings and insults endured, for
instance, by the families of Drs. J. G. Brown and Wm. Hunt of Cleveland, and the persecutions and abuses, for instance, heaped upon the
family of Gov. Brownlow of Knoxville, would not be accepted the
second time by these families for the treasures of the State. These,
with hundreds and thousands of other and similar cases in Tennessee,
with very many still more disastrous and terrible, are the only arguments which we care to offer in justification of the severity that,
by some, will be complained of as attaching to this volume. To ignore
such a state of things in any country, and especially in our country,
would be as false to the legitimate and vital objects of history as the
rebellion itself was monstrous and cruel; and we feel that the spirit
in which rebels are dealt with in the following pages, will be sustained by those who, from bitter experience or from theory alone, are
able to comprehend the depths of the malignancy of the spirit that
originated and sustained the rebellion.

Much of the valuable and interesting matter that was obtained and
prepared for this work, and that many readers in Bradley will expect
it to contain, we have been compelled to lay aside for want of space.
The Gatewood raid through Polk county, and the raids into Bradley
from Georgia, in the winter of '64-'65 we have had to abridge to
infinitesimal statements, while many other very interesting and important incidents, with historic matter relating to the movements of
the two armies in and about Bradley, have necessarily but very
reluctantly, and with deep mortification to the author, been omitted
altogether.

CONTENTS.

CHAPTER I.

INTRODUCTORY.

CHAPTER II.

PRETENSIONS OF THE REBELS TO DIVINE FAVOR.

CHAPTER III.

ELECTION FOR CONVENTION AND NO CONVENTION.

CHAPTER IV.

THE ELECTION FOR SEPARATION AND NO SEPARATION.

CHAPTER V.

UNION FLAG RAISED AND LOWERED.

CONTENTS.

CHAPTER XIII.

THE CLEVELAND BANNER.

CHAPTER XIV.

THE STONECYPHER FAMILY.

CHAPTER XV.

CASE OF MR. WILLIAM HUMBERT.

CHAPTER XVI.

CASE OF LAWYER A. J. TREWHITT.

CHAPTER XVII.

TRIALS AND DEATH OF S. D. RICHMOND.

CHAPTER XVIII.

REV. ELI H. SOUTHERLAND.

CHAPTER XIX.

BRADLEY COUNTY COURT.

CONTENTS.

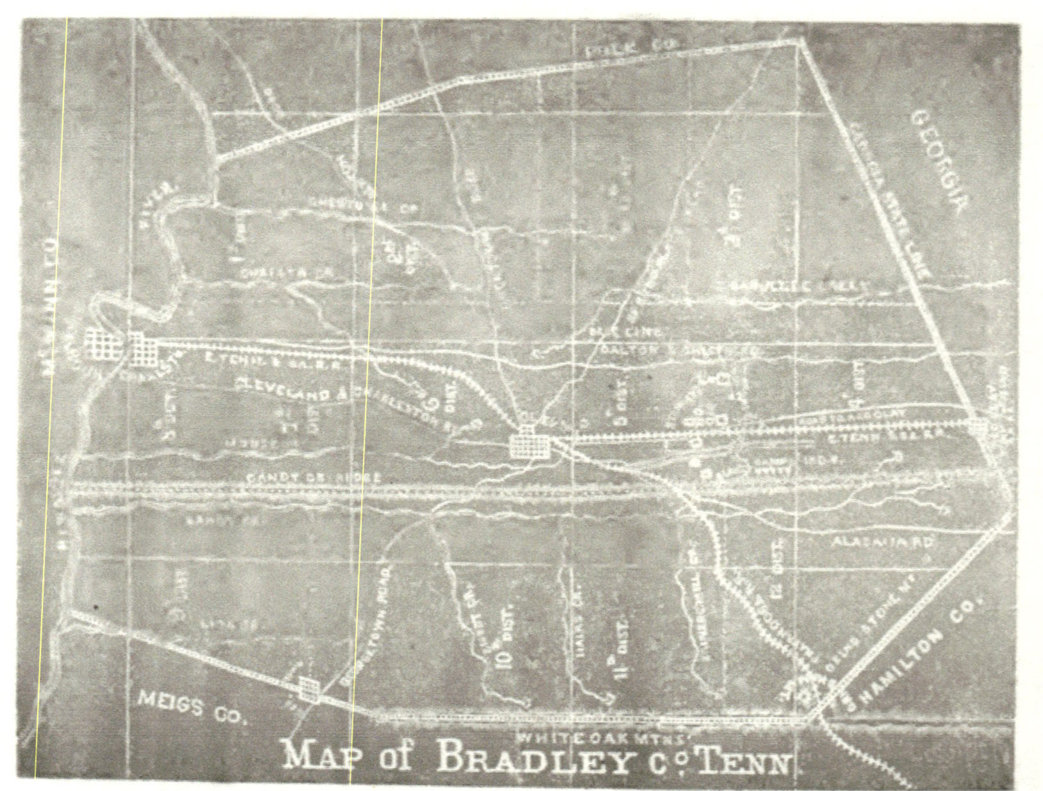

GEORGIA
GEORGIA STATE LINE
POLK CO.
MCMINN CO.
MEIGS CO.
HAMILTON CO.
WHITE OAK MTNS.
RIVER
CHESTNUT CR.
CHRISTY CR.
E. TENN. & GA. R. R.
CLEVELAND & CHARLESTON R. R.
CANDY CR. RIDGE
SANDY CR.
OCOEE
DALTON & CLEVELAND
BRADLEY
BLUE SPRINGS
ALARM YARD
BENTON ROAD
10 DIST.
11 DIST.
HAIR'S CR.
MAP OF BRADLEY Co. TENN

HISTORY OF THE REBELLION

IN

BRADLEY COUNTY, EAST TENNESSEE.

CHAPTER I.

INTRODUCTORY.

BRADLEY is one of the most southern counties of East Tennessee, bordering upon the State of Georgia. It is bounded north by McMinn county, east by Polk, south by Georgia, and west by the counties of Hamilton and Meigs. From Cleveland, the county seat, which is in north latitude. thirty-five, it is by rail, twenty-eight miles west to Chattanooga, one hundred and twenty-eight south to Atlanta, and eighty-two east to Knoxville. The county is twenty-three miles north and south, by nineteen east and west, consequently, it has an area of about four hundred and forty square miles.

The whole surface of the county is decidedly broken and uneven, being thrown into ridges and valleys running generally north and south, consequently, it is very favorable for military operations in those directions. The soil in the valleys is a dark yellow clay with a mixture of loam, having a sub-stratum mostly of red clay and slate formations. The soil of the ridges is substantially the same, but of course more gravelly, with slight scattering ledges of flint, and layers of imperfectly formed slate and sand rock.

About two miles east of Cleveland, or not far from the center of the county, are extensive beds of marble. The product of these quarries, when hewn and chiseled to a polish, present a surface of beautifully variegated colors, denoting the presence of different minerals. A finely worked specimen of this marble is lying within sight while we write, in one of the streets of Cleveland. It is a block or slab about four and a half feet long, by two wide, and from eight to ten inches in thickness. One side is polished, and on the polished surface is beautifully carved, an *ellipse*, or flattened circle, the arc or belt of which is three inches wide, the *ellipse* itself being as large as the surface of the stone will permit. The upper half of this circle is under, arched with thirty-two stars, signifying the number of States in the Union at the time this specimen of art was manufactured. Under these stars is cut the following inscription: "Contributed by the citizens of Bradley County, Tennessee, 1860." Mounting the under half of the *ellipse*, is carved in very expressive characters the following motto: "UNITED WE STAND, DIVIDED WE FALL!"

Thus nationalized, this production was intended by the people of Bradley, to be forwarded and placed in the "Washington Monument," as a token of their fidelity to the Union. But alas! while the loyalty and patriotism of the county were here engraven upon rock, and that rock just ready to occupy an appropriate niche in the most sacred temple of our national liberties, as an evidence that her citizens still loved those principles of National and individual freedom, bequeathed to them by the "Father of his Country," the whirlwind of rebellion, the maddened defection of a traitorous few came upon them, and came just in time to prevent the transportation of this stone to the place for which it was designed.

Traitors and treason did not like the devotion to the Union which it announced as existing in the people of Bradley, consequently, they declared that this stone, though admitted to be an expression of the views and feelings of a majority of the people, should never be sent to the Monument. Accordingly, this little enterprize of marble presentation, as well as all other expressions of national affection by the people here, was, as by mob violence, strangled in an hour; and the neglected and insulted stone now lies as cast-off rubbish in one of the by-ways of Cleveland.

The unimproved portions of Bradley are thinly covered with a medium growth of timber, principally the different kinds of oak, some hickory, a kind of sour wood, the sassafras, a scattering of sugar maple on the creek bottoms, a few other common varieties, with a general inter-spersing of the yellow pine.

The coldest weather here is seldom severer than three degrees below zero, and the warmest is generally from ninety-six to one hundred above it. The seasons, we are informed, are sufficiently uniform that a failure of crops is very rare; and spring and autumn storms and high winds nothing like as vigorous, nor climate changes, it appears, anything like as sudden and disagreeable as with us in the North, nor even as much so here as at an earlier period.

Cotton and tobacco are raised in this county very sparingly. Corn and wheat are now the principal crops. The black oats, however, here a winter grain, produce finely. The seed is sown about the middle of October, the crop being harvested the following June. They usually yield a very solid and heavy berry. The grass of these oats makes, especially for young stock, the finest winter pasture of any grown in the country.

The red and the white wheat are the principal varities raised. The red is sometimes affected with what they call the "*wheat sick.*"

About the time of the Chickamauga battles, a rebel regiment of cavalry was for a short time posted in the vicinity of Cleveland, commanded by Colonel Dibble. Immediately after its arrival the officers as well as the privates spread themselves over the country in quest of supplies. Wheat was to them a desirable commodity; and the farmers—and probably the millers also, as far as possible—secreted their white wheat, turning out the other article to the hungry soldiers, who were, perhaps, ignorant of the difference; at least did not suppose that they were being supplied with a regimental emetic in connection with theirs. After collecting what they thought a supply for the time, Colonel Dibble sent the whole to the mills to be made into flour; after which it was rationed out to the men. The whole regiment partaking pretty heartily of its new bread, it was not long before it found that "death was in the pot"—a strange trouble was in the camp. The men began to sicken at the stomach, and everywhere fell to vomiting as though they had been dosed with arsenic. The Bradley County wheat was at once charged with being the evil demon; and Colonel Dibble forthwith arrested all the millers concerned in making his flour, with as many others as his indignation suggested were accessory in thus poisoning his men. The investigation, however, failed to criminate either any of the millers or of the farmers, it being difficult to prove that these parties knew that the wheat was diseased, even if any such knowledge existed; and Colonel Dibble was compelled to pocket the insult, if such it was, and make the best of the difficulty in applying himself, as soon as possible, to recuperate his men by administering all the anti-arsenicals and gastric disinfectants that his hospital stores contained or his surgeons could manufacture. The difficulty, although it created considerable excitement, did not after all prove to be very serious; yet, serious enough we presume, ever after to impart to Colonel Dibble's men a knowledge of the possible difference between the red and the white wheat of Bradley.

The sweet potato, also the Irish potato if cultivated with care, with almost all other vegetables peculiar to our Northern climate, as well as almost every kind of garden fruit, grow here in abundance. As is the case, perhaps, with the most of East Tennessee, the people of this county have not given that attention to the cultivation of the choice varieties of fruits which their soil and climate, as well as past experience, appear to justify. Peaches, and we believe pears, seldom fail, while plums and cherries are equally sure; and a few years of experienced cultivation of the best varieties in this section, would fill the country with these delicious fruits.

Bradley is emphatically an inland county, no part of it being nearer than sixteen miles to the Tennessee River. The Hiwassee, however, which heads among the mountains of North Carolina, bounds part of it on the north; and, some seasons, is navigable for small boats, twenty or thirty miles from its mouth.

The country is meandered by numerous small streams, affording a profusion of water privileges, most of which are improved by the erection upon them, of flouring and lumber mills, on a scale sufficient for the accommodation of the present inhabitants. In regard to water for all the purposes of life, nature has been lavish in her gifts to East Tennessee. Deep, blue springs, and crystal fountains are everywhere bursting out along the base of the ridges, forming the sources of the numerous silver streams that dance along over their rocky or pebbly bottoms, till lost in the stronger currents of the Tennessee, or the Hiwassee. Had we some of these boiling, gravelly fountains, and leaping, crystal streams, upon the rich and extensive prairies of Indiana and Illinois, we then, most emphatically, might consider ourselves in possession of the gardens of the world.

Cleveland, the county seat, is the principal town of Bradley, is desirably located on slightly elevated ground, is pleasantly arranged as to streets and dwellings, with a suitable central square on which stands the Court House, a respectable brick building surmounted with a dome and spire, which together with its own proportions cause it to loom up in the distance, the most sightly edifice of the place.

At the commencement of the rebellion, Cleveland numbered two thousand inhabitants. It contains four churches, New School and Cumberland Presbyterian, Methodist and Baptist. It also contains an Academy. This, before the war, was under the supervision, as Prinpal, of Mr. —— Blunt, who, at the opening of the rebellion, went North and joined the Federal army. Before the expiration of his enlistment he obtained a Captain's commission, and did good service in the work of putting down the rebellion. Since the war Mr. Blunt has resuscitated his school, and is again at his post as the principal instructor in the county.

Charleston is in the eastern part of the county upon the Hiwassee, and at the point where the East Tennessee and Georgia Railroad crosses that river. It contains about four hundred inhabitants.

Georgetown is a small village located in the north-west part of the county, a portion of it being in Meigs.

Sulphur, coal, iron and leaden ore, exist in some parts of the county, and mines of the latter, containing a significant percentage of silver, were being worked in the eastern portions of it at the commencement of the rebellion. Rich beds of copper have been discovered and opened in the mountains of Polk County, about forty miles from Cleveland. In 1861, an extensive copper foundry or rolling mill was erected in Cleveland by Southern capitalists, their concern being supplied with copper slabs from these Polk County mines.

Some time after the commencement of the Rebel enterprize, a foreigner, probably a Hungarian, an iron monger by profession, and possessed of a good degree of skill in the work of infernalism, had, somewhere, manufactured a large quantity of infernal machines, or as they were familiarly called by the Union people of Cleveland, "Rebel torpedoes." Without the knowledge of Union men, or at least without a general knowledge on their part, of the fact, this Rebel foreigner had brought these destructive missiles and concealed them in a small brick house in the heart of Cleveland.

Immediately after the battle of Missionary Ridge, Colonel Long, with his cavalry, was sent to take possession of Cleveland, and to tear up and destroy the railroad in its vicinity, in order to prevent supplies coming to the rebel army which was then in the vicinity of Dalton. At the news that Long's men were approaching the place, this rebel Zulaski, with six or eight rebel workmen, engaged as his assistants in his peculiar craft, fled in great haste, leaving his black satanic monsters to take care of themselves. Simultaneous with the flight of Zulaski, a nominal rebel Colonel, by the name of Pete, one of the proprietors of the concern, and at that time its manager, threw his books and business documents into a wagon, and hastily fled for Dixie. Colonel Long's men, however, were close upon him, and, although he succeeded in making his own escape, his wagon load of books and papers were captured. Among these papers was found a written contract for the concern to furnish the Southern Confederacy with large quantities of sheet copper, preparatory to being worked into thin plates suitable for gun caps. Also were found among these papers extensive contracts for the concern to furnish the Rebel Government with other ordnance materials.

Acting, perhaps, under orders, and possibly knowing that it was not the intention of our authorities to make an effort then permanently to hold the place, as soon as he had completed the work of demolishing the railroad, Colonel Long, though against the entreaties of some Union men, burned this rebel establishment to the ground. Previously, however, to applying the torch, Colonel Long, at the suggestion of Union citizens, made search for the torpedoes left behind by the defunct Zulaski, and found them in the brick building already alluded to. With a view, doubtless, to destroy them, though possibly not knowing their exact nature, he caused these strange missiles to be placed in this rebel rolling mill, which was situated in the edge of the village about half a mile from its center. This occurred just before the mill was fired. The torch having been applied, as soon as the flames reached the huge pile of these engines, they began to shoot themselves off, leaping about the burning building and darting over the premises, while some went whirling and hissing through the air in the most dangerous and terrific manner conceivable. In the space of half an hour, upwards of sixteen hundred of these nameless, nondescript, rebel inventions burnt themselves loose from the fiery mass, going off with a successive, rattling, crashing noise, and with thundering, cannon-like explosions, enough to make the uninitiated in the vicinity think that a battle decisive of the great contest was being inaugurated in the little village of Cleveland.

These ugly looking projectiles, doubtless of foreign invention, and, in this case, probably, of foreign manufacture also, are malleable cast-iron elongated shells of different sizes, from ten to eighteen inches in length, from two to four in diameter, and when charged and ready for use must weigh from ten to fifteen pounds.

Some days after this mill was destroyed, one of these torpedoes was found, torn to pieces with its own explosive force, full three-fourths of a mile from the mill, having passed nearly over the town. Another, at the time, went smashing through the roof of the dwelling of Mr. W. Crever, at least a quarter of a mile distant.

In regard to the latter case, one is reminded that it might possibly have been a providential rebuke to Mr. Crever; for it is a fact, we believe, not only that his was the only dwelling injured by these shells, but that he was the only rebel inhabitant left in Cleveland who sustained any pecuniary relation whatever to this copperhead establishment.

There is, however, still another circumstance connected with this torpedo affair, which reminds one that good sometimes comes out of evil, and which also indicates that Providence was determined that this violent torpedo dealing of the rebels, should, on the whole, be turned against themselves.

Colonel Long, after destroying the railroads, in obedience to previous orders, was preparing to evacuate Cleveland when he set fire to the mill, and accordingly, commenced to leave while the mill was burning, being at the same time irresolutely attacked by a body of rebel cavalry, assisted with two pieces of artillery. This cavalry came from Charleston on the Hiwassee, consequently approached Cleveland from the east, while the burning mill stood in the south-west part of the town. When near to the place they saw the volumes of smoke ascending from the mill; but as burning dwellings were scenes with which the war had already made both Federals and rebels perfectly familiar, they moved up without suspecting that this conflagration portended anything unusual, and proceeded to distribute and arrange their forces on the east and the south-east of the town, preparatory to an attack. It so happened, however, that by the time they were ready to charge into the place, the fire in the mill had reached the pile of torpedoes, and to the utter bewilderment of the rebels, this torpedo eruption commenced vomiting itself into the sky, and letting off battery after battery in quick succession, so much so, that, not knowing what to make of the strange phenomenon, they came to a halt, held a parley, and as they could account for it in no other way, supposed that Long possibly had artillery and might be using it against some of their own forces unknown to themselves attacking him from the west. This delay of the rebels was time gained to Long, and he doubtless evacuated the place with less fighting and with less loss of life than he otherwise would have done.

Not entirely satisfied with their success, thus far, at torpedo fighting, the rebels of this vicinity concluded to make another attempt, which took place about the first of April, 1864. From a thorough investigation of the case by our military authorities in Cleveland, it appeared that some two or three rebel soldiers stole into the Federal lines, selecting a secesh neighborhood about four miles east of Cleveland as the locality of their operations, and succeeded in placing under the railroad track a torpedo of considerable dimensions, intending, no doubt, to destroy the morning train from Chattanooga, which at that time generally went up heavily loaded with Federal soldiers. Providence, however, again favoring the cause of the just, early the next morning, some two hours before the time for the Chattanooga train, a locomotive and tender ran out of Cleveland to go a few miles east for water. The locomotive passed the torpedo without injury, but the tender was thrown from the track. This, however, was about the extent of the accident, no harm to life or limb occurring to any. A number of rebel citizens fell under suspicion, especially one Mr. Joseph McMillen, and were forthwith arrested, but the inquiry eliciting nothing positive as to their guilt, they were all finally released.

Thus ended the history of rebel torpedoism, at least for a time, in the county of Bradley; and thus ended, in this region, rebel success in this line of warfare. Bringing to their aid the skill and ingenuity of Europe in concocting rebel schemes and in manufacturing infernal machines, with which to blow up Brother Jonathan, establish a negro Confederacy, promising to pay their foreign help with King Cotton, they succeeded in frightening a miserable gang of their own cowards, and in lifting four wheels, loaded with wood, from the track of a Federal railroad.

The settlement of Bradley commenced as early as 1836, with emigrants from North Carolina and Upper East Tennessee. The Cherokee Indians were removed from this and adjoining counties in 1838. Many of the present inhabitants can remember the portly forms of Generals Scott and Wool in the accomplishment of that work.

At the opening of the rebellion Bradley contained about twelve hundred slaves, owned by about one hundred and seventy masters. The free blacks numbered a little more than fifty, and the total inhabitants about fifteen thousand.

The slave trade existed in Bradley to a limited extent. The notorious Wm. L. Brown, of whom we shall speak more hereafter, rebel Congressman Tibbs, John Osment, John Craigmiles, Jacob Tibbs, and Wm. B. Graddy, were, perhaps, the only persons in the county who made the traffic a regular business. Most of these would bring into the county from Richmond, Va., or from some other slave mart, ten or fifteen negroes in a gang, and sometimes more, and dispose of them in the vicinity to the highest bidders. Wm. H. Tibbs, serving in the rebel Congress at Richmond, would avail himself of this opportunity and universally bring home a company of slaves as a matter of speculation.

Any one who takes pains to inform himself of the facts and become acquainted with the people, will see at a glance that the unprecedented rebel brutalities which marked the rebellion throughout the country, never could have been the spontaneous outgrowth of a majority of its present inhabitants. The atrocities, in number and in enormity, committed by the rebels upon the Union people of Bradley, and upon those of other parts of East Tennessee, almost defy belief. The better class of rebel citizens, though living in Bradley during the whole reign of this rebel terror, never fully realized the extent to which the Union people suffered. None but the most abandoned men on earth could have been guilty of the systematic barbarities practiced by the rebels, as a rule, upon the Union people of Bradley.

Judging from the citizens now here, it is impossible to account for the tyranny and heartless oppression that prevailed among them for nearly three years, only upon the supposition that the rebel cause soaked up nearly all the ruffianism of the county, thus compelling the majority to submit to the outlandish rule of the rabble. This rabble, headed and lead on by an upper strata of the same class, unprincipled politicians, and equally unprincipled slave trading, slave driving, money making and speculating characters, reinforced by others of the same sort from southern rebel districts, formed the element which inaugurated and kept alive the rebellion in East Tennessee.

CHAPTER II.

PRETENSIONS OF THE REBELS TO DIVINE FAVOR.

OUR introductory chapter closed with a brief allusion to the cruelties of the rebels in Bradley and other portions of East Tennessee.

The remarkable character of the rebellion in this respect, particularly in East Tennessee, forces upon us even in writing a part of its history, the question of its right or wrong as a national cause.

A history of events or periods of time which presents nothing positively extraordinary, may, with some propriety be superficial, and deal only with the events themselves; but periods or events, the prevailing characteristics of which startle mankind and shock the world with horror, direct our attention to causes and to the investigation of principles for the elucidation of such anomalies, and as a means of obtaining that instruction which no people, especially those most interested, should fail to glean from them.

National as well as individual crimes are aggravated or mitigated by the circumstances under which they are committed, hence an accurate knowledge of all the circumstances in any given case is indispensable to a correct estimate of the guilt of the parties involved; and the more remarkable or unusual the facts or circumstances, the greater becomes the general anxiety for a complete solution of the whole problem.

The truth of these statements has been very strikingly illustrated by our great rebellion, and especially by the rebellion in East Tennessee. This rebellion has been one of the most remarkable events in nature—one of the most astounding things in history, consequently it has awakened a deeper, a more intense feeling among mankind than any other national event of ancient or of modern times, and accordingly, more anxious, struggling inquiry, more intellectual toil and concentration of moral effort, have already been expended upon the profound problem it presents to the world, than was called forth in the same length of time, by any other event transpiring in history.

In presenting a narrative of the occurrences of this rebellion in Bradley County, East Tennessee, we shall attempt, though briefly, to place the tragedy as a whole, so before the public that no doubt can exist as to the parties which were in the wrong at the beginning, upon which basis alone, as we have already seen, can we judge correctly of the guilt or the innocence that attaches to the different actors in the drama.

It is well known, and will not be denied from any quarter, that at the beginning, and as long as the rebels were to any extent able to defy the Government, they did not cease to trumpet abroad in the ears of the Christian world, the assumption that they were nationally and constitutionally, as well as divinely right in striking for the independence of the South.

History presents no other instance of so strong an effort of the kind, as was made by the rebels to convince themselves and the rest of mankind of the justice of their cause. The church and the state, the priest and the politician, the journalist and the slave-driver, were one and inseparable in swaddling their young confederacy as the legitimate offspring of heaven. It was also the beau-ideal of national government, and the quintessence of social humanity. The most talented and influential, if not the most pious and godly, among the clergy of the South, never allowed themselves to doubt for a moment that the cause of the rebels was a child of special Providence, and consequently, embodying a reformation or revolution in the affairs of the world, which having God for its author and protector must be triumphant in the end.

The Southern States, in erecting themselves into an independent nation, had committed no error. They had been guilty of no wrong. They were only the passive instruments of an opening Providence, whose divinity the leaders of the great movement could not deny, dutifully and inoffensively toiling, as directed, to dispense the blessings of that Providence to the world; and as an evidence of their sincerity and their Christian spirit, all the favor they asked of their old connections, in relation to this great work was simply "to be let alone."

Now, all this is historical fact, and as such it is not only our privilege but our province to deal with it. Just here, therefore, we propose to join issue with the rebels. We join issue with them upon this point, their loud profession of being in the Divine favor, to the Divine prejudice against the Northern cause, simply because in making a brief argument it is the best suited to the purpose.

Now, if a Southern Confederacy upon this continent, founded upon the institution of slavery, was plainly depicted in the Providential signs of the times, if it was unmistakably the voice of God as the rebels pretended, and if His hand was so plainly revealed in its inauguration and in its support, even for years, how is it that the rebellion so signally failed? God being the author, the instigator, and the support of the rebellion for so long a time, upon what principle are we to account for the fact, that all at once it met with the most disgraceful overthrow of any revolutionary cause of which history gives us any knowledge? Did the Almighty forsake his own cherished designs, or was he defeated by the mudsills of the North? It is utterly impossible by any fair course of reasoning to reconcile the fact of the sudden and complete failure of the rebellion with the supposition that God was the instigator of it, or that He ever smiled upon the enterprise, or allowed it to exist and progress with any view to its final success.

"For if this counsel or this work be of men, it will come to nought: But if it be of God, ye cannot overthrow it," is a passage of Scripture which all Southern theologians who have expatiated so sweepingly upon the Divine mission of the rebellion, would do well not only to consider in a general sense, but they would do well to consider it particularly in connection with their melancholy reflections upon the disastrous end of their beloved Confederacy.

The simple failure, however, of the rebellion to accomplish what it undertook, is not the only fact under this head that argues against the assumption in question.

The rebels were not only defeated—simple failure of their cause was not the only result, but they were utterly ruined. They not only did not gain anything that they proposed, but they lost everything that they could call their own when they began. Not one stone was left upon another of their old order of things. The result to the rebellion was not merely defeat, but it was annihilation—a visitation of swift destruction. Defeat, destruction, annihilation, and the total loss of all things, were the fruits of that Divine favor that attended them. As well might these political and theological Southern Doctors contend, that God was in the midst of the Cities of the Plain, to befriend and bless the people with His gracious presence, at the very moment when his wrath was causing the earth to open and to swallow them up for their abominable sins, as to contend that a cause with all its principles smitten to the earth and scattered to the four winds like the rebellion, was the cause of God. It is possible, however, that Bishop Pierce and Doctor Palmer can prove that the Almighty was fighting at the head of His people from the walls of Jerusalem, and attempting to defend them against the Roman army, by whom they were finally overcome and destroyed.

The end of the rebellion was unlike the end of any just cause recorded in history. Truth always gains by contact with error, whatever may be the immediate and *apparent* victory against it. Revolutions never go backward. The Commonwealth of Cromwell partially failed at the time of its ostensible objects, but it was far from being a total failure. Its principles *lived* if they did not triumph at the time. It gained much also at the time. The point of its termination was infinitely in advance of the point of its setting out. As Mr. Goldwin Smith remarks, "The principles of Cromwell partially failed in England; but they crossed the Atlantic and perfectly succeeded in America." The principles of Cromwell produced the American Revolution, and fully developed themselves in the fact of our present American Republic. The rebellion, however, it appears, possessed no redeeming or self-sustaining qualities of this nature—qualities that live and grow in spite of defeat, qualities wresting victory from defeat itself; but was, in all respects, a backward movement—a step to the rear, and so far to the rear that the point of its setting out was lost and irrecoverable, never to be seen again; and in an utterly strange land, dying a very strange and singular death, the rebellion found its grave. Not one of its principles are now alive to defend its character or hallow its memory.

The rebellion itself was a strange thing, and everything about it was strange in the extreme. It had strange statesmen, strange politics, a strange religion and strange gods. Strange gods indeed the rebels must have had that could so deceive and mislead them, and false prophets that the Lord did not send.

In viewing the infatuation of the South upon this subject, and especially the infatuation of its Doctors of Divinity, one can hardly avoid being struck with the similarity of their condition with that of the prophets of Baal before Elijah; also, as Elijah did those prophets, one can hardly avoid mocking these Southern Divines by tauntingly enquiring, Why they did not call louder upon their god? For he was a god, but was talking, or pursuing, or was on a journey, or fighting other battles, or peradventure he slept and must be awaked. Why did not more of these prophets leap upon the rebel altars that were made, and cut themselves after their manner with knives and lancets, till the blood gushed out upon them, crying louder and still louder, O Baal, hear us! for thou art a god and will deliver us?

The failure of the Prophets of Baal to persuade their god to answer by fire and consume their sacrifice, and the complete success of Elijah in calling upon his God to come down and consume his offering, instantaneously put an end to all controversy among the people, as to which worshiped the true God. The Prophets of Baal were false prophets, self-condemned by their own failure, and the people slew them at the waters of Gishon.

This subject, however, has another phase which very strongly confirms the position, that Providence never favored the rebellion with any view to its final success.

As a purely worldly scheme, and a purely worldly scheme it was, the one great thing which ruined it, the rebellion did possess all the elements of success. This fact is so manifest that its total failure can be accounted for upon no other principle than that Providence was against it. There was not a moment from the bombardment of Sumter to the fall of Lee, when the preponderance of worldly sentiment and worldly policy not only in our own nation, but in all other ruling nations of Christendom, with one or two exceptions, were not in sympathy with the rebels. Our national triumph is the greatest moral victory ever achieved in so short a time, against such worldly odds. In regard to ourselves, the rebels at heart in the whole country were in the majority a little more than six millions. The Government, therefore, in the contest, was reduced to the ratio of two against three during the war. In other words, the whole country, North and South, contained eighteen millions of rebels, and twelve millions of loyal people; and thus it stood on an average until the end of the contest. Disintegration of the rebel elements was all in a worldly point of view that saved us. Had the rebels in the entire nation been one in locality, as they were one in sentiment, or had rebels in the North been able to combine and organize in the North, as the rebels were able to do in the South, the Government would have been swept with the besom of destruction. The rebellion possessed the numbers, but it lacked in one locality the power of concentration and organization.

In territory also, confining our estimate to the *States*, at the beginning, the Government was inferior to the Southern Confederacy. Leaving the border slave States out of the question, and allowing their conflicting forces to ballance each other, the seceded territory exceeded that left to the Government, about sixty thousand square

3

miles, an area equal to that of the great State of Virginia. In numbers and in territory this was the disproportion in favor of the rebels at home.

Abroad, at the beginning, as well as for two years afterwards, the prospects of the rebels were quite as bright, and ours quite as dark, as they were within our own borders. With one exception, that of Russia, the leading European governments, if not their people, were strongly in sympathy with the rebellion. Fifteen days only elapsed after the dispatch of Lord Lyons announcing to his Government the fall of Sumter, before his Queen issued her proclamation recognizing the rebels as belligerents. France was equally precipitate and ungenerous, and why, contrary to all this, and the eager haste in which it was done, the rebels were ever after disappointed in their expectations of full recognition as an independent nation, is, to-day, upon any principle of their worldly policy alone, as indefinable by the one party as by the other. While the rebels were exhausting every art of diplomacy to hasten the event, these governments were at work with equal industry to get themselves ready, or in other words, to get themselves into a safe position to grant the request, yet, some invisible power retarded every step and mysteriously held back the coveted boon, till an EVENT at the White House; no noise of war in it either, shook the continent, if not the earth, and knelled among European thrones, that the hour of Southern recognition had passed.

Another argument that might be here presented against the assumption in question, is the spirit of the rebellion itself. That instance is not on record where any just National cause, immediately successful or otherwise, characterized itself by those brutalities and studied cruelties, as a rule, practiced by the rebellion, though perhaps not without exceptions, seemingly in a spirit of revenge, and with a view to accomplishing its ends. History does not furnish a more glaring and frightful paradox than exists in this pretension to Divine guidance on the part of the rebels, and the systematic cruelties which they allowed themselves to perpetrate under it.

Our American Revolution is now universally admitted to have commenced in justice, consequently with the Divine approval. It was provoked by grievances and abuses which made it positively unavoidable, or made it indispensably necessary to the success of the Colonists as a people. Theirs was a case infinitely more than that of the Southern rebels, calculated to tempt and provoke revenge; and if such a course had been good policy, much more an inducing cause of resorting to wasting cruelties as a means of defeating their enemies. Like the rebels, our forefathers believed that their cause was right, and more honestly than the rebels, appealed to God for the sincerity of their convictions and the purity of their motives, and as submitting to Him the grievances for which they took up arms, for Him to answer to the justice of their position by giving them victory.

With them this work was real, and brought them upon too sacred ground for the kindlings of revenge or of any other spirit as an element of the contest, only such as was consistent with the Attributes of the Being to whom they applied, such as they felt and professed to be governed by at the start, and saw to be indispensable qualifications for being heard by the Creator and Judge of the world.

Thus our Revolution on the part of our forefathers was not, like the rebellion on the part of the rebels, a *war of the passions*. Their grievances being real and utterly unavoidable only by an appeal to the sword, made their dependence on God a corresponding reality; and they, from the very nature of such dependence, compelled to continue in this frame and fight the battle through upon this principle, there was no room for the spirit of revenge and retalliation, only as the latter was occasionally justified as a means of self-protection; and being no room nor any disposition for these passions, there was, of course, no grounds for a barbarous resort to them as a means of weakening their enemies.

The conclusion is therefore irresistible that had the rebels, as they so loudly professed, been in this same condition, their spirit would have been the same also. The undeniable fact, however, that the general spirit of the rebels was the very reverse of this from the beginning to the end of the war, is evidence conclusive that their extravagant pretensions in this respect were either destructive self-deceptions, mental infatuations to which they were given up that they might be destroyed, or hypocritical and wicked devices to inspire with mistaken enthusiasm the thousands of ignorant soldiery whom the leaders were sacrificing to their own diabolical purposes.

An enlightened and considerate view of the spirit and genius of the rebellion, its fancied and falsely arrayed grievances, its insatiable greed of National power, its determination to rule or ruin, its aristocratic corruption and domineering cruelty, and the social vortex which it was preparing and towards which it was remorselessly driving the people of the whole land, white as well as black, causes every good man to tremble when he reflects how near the terrible effort approximated to a final success.

CHAPTER III.

ELECTION FOR CONVENTION AND NO CONVENTION.

It was stated at the commencement of the second chapter, that the rebel leaders, both in church and state, very positively assumed that the rebellion was politically as well as morally right.

Every person in Bradley County knows that this was the position unequivocally taken by the rebels, not only in this county, but in the whole of East Tennessee, and that this position was maintained during the war. Throughout East Tennessee, as well as in Bradley, the rebels set themselves up as *the loyal party*—the only true patriots in the state. Standing upon this platform, they constantly justified their cruel treatment of Union people on the ground, that these Union people were traitors; and, contended that the sufferings which they were inflicting upon them were not cruelties, but righteous and well deserved punishments for their crimes as tories, traitors, and rebels against their own lawful government. Upon this principle the rebels of Bradley asserted that the Union citizens had forfeited all claim to their homes, that their possessions were no longer theirs, and therefore, that Confederates were justified in robbing Union families, plundering their farms, hunting them through the country like so many wild beasts, and shooting them upon the run like so many robbers and outlaws.

Now, we wonder if it ever occurred to the rebels while they were engaged in all this, that as a theory, this was a wholly false position. Did it ever occur to them that this platform of theirs was, in fact, completely reversed all the time? That they themselves, were the tories, traitors, and robbers, instead of the Union men whom they were murdering? Did it ever occur to the rebels that they were robbing and murdering these Union men, only because they refused to commit the very crimes which they alleged against them? They murdered them, they said, because they were traitors; but the fact is, they murdered them because they were not and would not be traitors. Traitors against the best government in the world, were murdering loyal citizens because they were not traitors like themselves. Men guilty of the highest type of treason, were murdering others for exhibiting the highest type of loyalty. Men guilty of treason, the highest crime known to the law, were murdering their neighbors for their loyalty, the greatest virtue known to society.

The former chapter was devoted to a consideration of this subject as a general question, a question in regard to the rebellion as a whole, and not with especial reference to it in any particular locality. If the rebellion as a whole was wrong—its principles offensive to God, its designs at war with His providence—then, of course, the rebellion was wrong in Tennessee, and the statements just made in regard to the criminality of Bradley rebels, consequently, correct. The question, however, of the false position of the rebels in Bradley, and their criminality in consequence, deduced from the fact, that the whole rebellion was wrong, with the remark just made, we will let pass for the present.

There is another question of importance, less general, bearing upon the subject, to be considered, and which must be considered before the guilt of Tennessee rebels can be accurately measured. Though the rebellion as a whole was fundamentally wrong, yet, if Tennessee had, by a clear majority of her people, decided to go with this rebellion, such action, if it had not palliated the cruelties inflicted by Tennessee rebels upon their Union neighbors, might, at least, have given some show of consistency to the political position which they assumed towards the loyal people. If, however, it can be shown that this majority was exactly the other way—against secession, and was clearly expressed, then, it will not only follow that the position assumed by the Tennessee rebels that they were *the loyal party* was false and inconsistent; but that they stand before the world as that class of men known in history as the *double-headed* traitors—traitors against the general Government, and also traitors against the Government of their own State. In any Republican State, the will of the people clearly expressed, is the *Government* of that State—is the Supreme Law, and whoever rebels against that law is a traitor. Dual treason, however, does not seem to be the only distinguishing characteristic of the Tennessee rebels; nor the only particular brand of infamy with which they will be handed down to posterity. Having perfected this double crime, or rather having committed the crime of treason the second time, first against the general Government, then against the clearly expressed will of a majority of their own people, the course of evil had been sufficiently protracted to harden them for the third and final denouement of indiscriminate blood-letting which followed and crimsoned their footsteps, especially in East Tennessee—a barbarousness not exceeded even by the Andersonville and Belle Island horrors, and which when viewed as a third stride in the career that had already designated them *dual traitors*, forever brands them as the *tripple* and blood-stained *criminals* of the Great Rebellion.

The infidel writer and pamphleteering castigator of John Bull in the days of the Revolution, Thomas Paine, never uttered a sentiment truer, nor one falser than this is true, than when he said, " One bad action creates a calamitous necessity for another." The bloody scale on which Tennessee rebels graduated from one degree of crime to another will remain, to the end of time, a monumental illustration of this proverbial truth. We shall now give a brief statement of facts in regard to the secession of Tennessee—facts the most of which have already been made historical by appearing in official or documentary form, and all of which can be substantiated by living witnesses.

South Carolina broke the way and seceded from the Union family on the 20th of December, 1861. As well as exciting treason in other portions of the South, this also fired the rebel blood in Tennessee. On the 7th of January, only eighteen days after the great sin of South Carolina, Governor Harris convened his Legislature at Nashville. On the 19th, this body appointed a State election for the 9th of February following, at which the people of Tennessee were to decide whether a State Convention should be called to consider the subject of the great Southern movement now commenced in South Carolina. Convention or No Convention on this subject was to be the distinct issue before the people of Tennessee at this election; consequently, those in favor of the measure were to write on their ballots "Convention," those opposed to it were to write on theirs, "No Convention."

In view of the possibility that the people at this election might decide to have this convention, each party, Union and Secession, nominated its candidates to be elected as members of this convention, and voted for them at the same time that they voted for Convention and No Convention. Every county in the State, we believe, on that day elected its members to this convention. The Union candidates were pledged to vote, in case the convention took place, against secession under any circumstances and at all hazards. The rebel candidates were pledged to vote for secession except on certain conditions—a redress of grievances, &c.

The results of the election were No Convention, and a majority of Union candidates. Even the city of Memphis elected its Union candidates by 400 majority. The majority of Union votes cast in electing these members over those cast by the rebel candidates, was 64,114. The Union majority for No Convention was not so large, being only 30,839.

It appears that a great many Union men in the State, who on that day voted for Union candidates, did so under the impression that, although they were thus opposed to secession, yet it was proper to have a State Convention on the subject of existing difficulties. Hence this difference between the majority for these Union candidates, and that for No Convention.

The 8th of February came, and the following is the vote of each county for Convention and No Convention:

EAST TENNESSEE.

COUNTIES.	Convention.	No Convention.	COUNTIES.	Convention.	No Convention.
Anderson	137	1,077	Washington	891	1,353
Bledsoe	130	650	Monroe	723	971
Bradley	242	1,443	Morgan	13	488
Campbell	71	870	McMinn	139	1,457
Cocke	192	1,332	Meigs	328	323
Carter	55	1,055	Blount	450	1,552
Grainger	158	1,675	Claiborne	95	1,030
Green	337	2,618	Hawkins	420	1,338
Hamilton	415	1,145	Hancock	100	746
Jefferson	250	1,929	Johnson	38	631
Knox	394	3,167	Sevier	65	1,243
Marion	108	751	Scott	29	385
Polk	117	1,112	Sequatchee	...	...
Roane	67	1,585			
Rhea	79	573	Total	7,029	34,312
Sullivan	1,180	733			

MIDDLE TENNESSEE.

COUNTIES.	Convention.	No Convention.	COUNTIES.	Convention.	No Convention.
Maury	3,145	628	Dekalb	336	1,009
Wilson	462	2,565	Lawrence	692	351
Smith	363	1,829	Overton	563	863
Warren	821	452	Macon	73	960
Lincoln	1,863	845	Giles	1,531	550
Jackson	169	2,012	Dickson	449	490
Bedford	828	1,656	Hickman	765	298
Montgomery	1,611	389	Lewis	192	84
Stewart	997	96	Van Buren	103	142
Rutherford	1,003	1,539	Robertson	1,611	389
Williamson	430	1,684	Wayne	255	737
Franklin	1,240	206	Marshall	1,186	481
Humphries	385	327	Fentress	334	325
Davidson	2,525	3,083	Grundy	363	58
Sumner	1,408	770	Cheatham		
White	673	976			
Cannon	304	1,038	Total	7,360	27,520
Coffee	613	698			

WEST TENNESSEE.

COUNTIES.	Convention.	No Convention.	COUNTIES.	Convention.	No Convention.
Shelby	5.697	197	Madison	1.757	86
Carroll	618	1.495	Fayette	1,521	19
Henry	1.334	776	Perry	382	232
Benton	621	296	Decatur	251	514
Dyer	876	163	Lauderdale	407	65
Hardin	791	395	McNairy	811	916
Gibson	2.227	533	Weakly	1.472	483
Haywood	816	544	Tipton	700	147
Henderson	619	1.105			
Hardeman	1.694	30	Total	24.328	8.324
Obion	1.672	328			

```
Total for No Convention............................70.156.
Total for Convention ..........................  ...39.317.
Majority for No Convention .......  .. ..........30.839.
```

The above was taken from a number of the "Memphis
Appeal," dated January 27th, 1861.

The following extracts show conclusively, the rebels
themselves being judges, that this election was a fair trial
of the question at issue—an honest and perfectly volun-
tary expression of the will of the people.

The first of these extracts is from the editorial of the
"Cleveland Banner," a bitter rebel sheet, and which was
continued till silenced by the Federal army in the winter
of 1864.

The "Nashville Gazette," the paper from which the
second extract is taken, was also a strong rebel paper.

"THE ELECTION.—The election on Saturday last resulted in the defeat of everybody, in one sense of the word, except "No Convention"
—he run like a scared dog, and beat the field out of sight. In this
county the vote stood. Convention 242. No Convention 1443. Brown
was elected delegate. We have but few returns from the adjoining
counties. and they not full; but one thing is certain, *a Convention has
been voted down by an overwhelming majority,* and those fortunate men
who were elected to a convention. will have the pleasure of remaining at home."

"THE RESULT.—The people of Tennessee yesterday had an opportunity of saying through the ballot-box, whether or not they desired the assembling of a State Convention, as provided for by Legislative enactment. The indications are that a *large majority* voted "No Convention." However much we might have desired a different result, we feel fully satisfied that the proposition to hold a Convention has been defeated. *The people have spoken, and we have naught to say against their decree.* It may bring them no harm, or it may result in evil only—which of the two will be known before the expiration of many days."

Now this election furnishes us with a two-fold expression of the will of the people in regard to the secession of the State. First, we have a clear majority of 64,114 votes, those cast for the Union candidates for membership in this convention, expressing the sovereign will of the people, that Tennessee should not under any circumstances secede from the Union. Second, in the votes at the same time cast, respecting a convention, we have another clear Union majority of nearly 31,000, not only against secession; but, deciding that no cause whatever existed, even for a convention on the subject, that Tennessee had no grievances to complain of, that she had no quarrel with the General Government, and proposed to remain in the Union as she was. This was the legitimate announcement of the people of Tennessee at this election, doubly expressed. That this is so, as well as being a fair and binding expression of the will of the people, is now not only the testimony of every Union man in the State, but is the testimony of the rebels themselves. The following is from the Cleveland Banner, a rebel sheet, from which we have already quoted in this connection, and taken from a number dated February 15th, 1861.

"THE CONVENTION.—The returns leave no reasonable doubt that the Convention has been voted down by an immense majority. This was a result not looked for. This object was gained by a systematic cry, that if you vote for "Convention" you are for *immediate secession*—he who is for the Union must vote "No Convention."

The practical result is, that by voting "No Convention" the people have deprived themselves of the power of having a voice, at this time, in the settlement of the questions at issue—they have for the present taken it from themselves and left it in the hands of the politicians—the last place where it ought to be.

But this is not all. The Legislature, as is well known, sent on commissioners to the Border State Convention, now being held in Washington city, the vote of "No Convention" is equivalent to saying. "*Tennessee asks nothing, she desires no settlement, she wants things to stand as they are.*"

The arm of our Commissioners is paralyzed. The Black Republicans can say to them, 'what are you here for now? Since the Legislature sent you *the people themselves have spoken, they are for standing still; they are content with the existing state of things; your Commissions are revoked;* we are not bound to listen to your declarations that there must be no civil war; that there should be a final and peaceable settlement of all matters in issue; *the verdict of the people is against what you ask—they are for no action—for standing still—for letting things drift on as they are—your people are satisfied with us, and the policy on which we have declared we will administer the Government.*"

It is seen that this rebel editor in this extract himself strongly testifies to the truth of the position we have just taken in regard to this election. Admitting the fact then, why did not he for the future act consistently with his own admission? Admitting that such was the sovereign will of the people, expressed as he says by an "immense majority," why did he, traitor like, fight it for the next three years or as long as he could with all his might? Why did not he, why did not Governor Harris, why did not this rebel Legislature, with whom this proposition for a State Convention originated, and why did not the minority in the whole State submit to this sovereign will of the people, instead of flying together in a foul conspiracy against it and trampling it under their treasonable feet?

One statement in this extract so manifestly betrays either the stupidity or dishonesty, or both, of this editor, that we cannot resist the temptation to give it a passing notice. He says, "The practical result is, that by voting 'No Convention' the people have deprived themselves of the power of having a voice, at this time, in settling the questions at issue—they have for the present taken it from themselves and left it in the hands of the politicians —the last place where it ought to be." Just as though the sovereign voice of the people was no *settlement* of this question at all.

The substance of the above statement amounts to this: The vote of the people of Tennessee which settled and disposed of the question of secession in her case, forever deprived them of the power to settle it. The vote or act of the people which took it *out* of the hands of the politicians put it *into* the hands of the politicians. The self-same vote or act of the people which took the question *into* their hands put it *out* of their hands.

A Supreme Judge from whose bench there is no appeal, receives a difficult case from the lower courts; and after giving it a thorough and impartial trial, delivers his verdict upon it, and this verdict is a final disposition of the case. This Cleveland editor, however, starts up and says. Judge you have committed a grave error! You have forever deprived yourself of the power to settle that question. You have forever taken it out of your own hands and put it in the hands of the lawyers, "the last place where it ought to be." This is exactly the position of this rebel editor in the above statement.

From the fact that this February election was a fair expression of the will of the people, it followed that this dictated and pointed out the subsequent duty of the minority. It was the duty of the minority to submit to this decision, and allow the State to be governed by the principles it announced. Even more than this, it was the duty of the parties and individuals composing this minority to become co-operators with the majority in carrying out these principles, by exerting their influence to resist rebellion and discourage revolt among the people of Tennessee. This was just what the people at this election decided to be the duty of all parties and individuals in the State, particularly those into whose hands they had entrusted the reins of authority from the governor to the lowest municipal officer among the people.

The great misfortune of the majority at this election, and the great misfortune of the State was, that nearly all her politicians and incumbents of office at the time, were among the minority. As another writer remarks, "The secession or rebellion of Tennessee was a rebellion of office-holders and politicians." The people arrayed themselves on the side of the Government; office-holders and politicians arrayed themselves on the side of the rebellion.

As soon as the result of the election was known, the politicians throughout the State, and most of those in authority, conspired with each other in public as well as in private, to defeat the wishes of the people. Hundreds of instances might be given in confirmation of this statement.

The writer of these pages arrived in Nashville five days after that city surrendered to General Buell in the winter of 1862. While there he obtained various items of important information from Union men respecting the secession of Tennessee. It was their universal testimony that the failure of this project for a "Convention" created no little excitement and no little dissatisfaction among the secessionists in Nashville. For days after the election companies of them were seen excitedly conversing upon the subject on the streets and in public places throughout the city. Among one of these companies an individual named More, a very active and strenuous Southern-rights man, was heard to use, in substance, the following language: "This election is a disgrace to the State, and Tennessee is disgracing herself by longer remaining in the Union. We will see Governor Harris, and he shall call an extra session of the Legislature, and d——n the State, we will put her out at all hazards." This remark was heard by Mr. John L. Stewart, a truthful and reliable Union man well known in Nashville, having been a citizen for many years, though now deceased.

The active hostility thus exhibited by More and his rebel crowd to this election will be recognized by Tennessee Union men as the identical spirit that prevailed against it everywhere among rebels throughout the State, and as that feeling which *originated* the measures immediately commenced by those in power to force the people into the vortex of rebellion. Agreeably with his own feelings, and prompted by this spirit among the rebels, Isham G. Harris, then Governor of Tennessee, convened his Legislature on the 25th of April, a little more than two months after this rebel proposition for a convention had been voted down by the people.

The following are the introductory remarks of his message to this body on that occasion:

Executive Department.
Nashville, April 25, 1861.

Gentlemen of the Senate
 and House of Representatives:

The President of the United States—elected according to the forms of the Constitution, but upon principles openly hostile to its provisions—having wantonly inaugurated an internecine war upon the people of the slave and non-slaveholding States, I have convened you again at the seat of Government, for the purpose of enabling you to take such action as will most likely contribute to the defence of our rights, the preservation of our liberties, the sovereignty of the State, and the safety of our people; all of which are now in imminent peril by the usurpations of the authorities at Washington, and the unscrupulous fanaticism which runs riot throughout the Northern States.

The war thus inaugurated is likely to assume an importance nearly, if not fully, equal, to the struggle of our revolutionary fathers, in their patriotic efforts to resist the usurpations and throw off the tyrannical yoke of the English Government; a war the duration of which, and the good or evil which must result from it, depends entirely, in my judgment, upon the readiness with which the citizens of the South harmonize as one people, and the alacrity with which they respond to the demands of patriotism.

I do not think it necessary to recapitulate, at this late hour, the long train of abuses to which the people of Tennessee, and our sister States of the South, have been subjected by the anti-republican spirit that has for many years been manifesting itself in that section, and which has at last declared itself our open and avowed enemy. In the message which I addressed to you at your called session in January last, these things were somewhat elaborately referred to, as constituting, in my judgment, the amplest reason for considering ourselves in imminent danger, and as requiring such action on the part of the Legislature as would place the State in an attitude for defence, whenever the momentous crisis should be forced upon us; and, also, as presenting to the North the strongest argument for peace, and, if possible, securing a reconstruction of the Union, thus already dissolved by the most authoritative, formal, and matured action of a portion of the slaveholding States.

The position of Gov. Harris throughout this message, and particularly those in this extract show the extent to which he disregarded the will, and disobeyed the instructions of the people of Tennessee, delivered to him at this February election. The very first words of this message reveal Gov. Harris as a traitor. He says, "The President of the United States, elected according to the forms of the Constitution, but upon *principles* openly hostile to its provisions." Now, which was the better judge of this matter, Gov. Harris or the people? Who was the final authority upon the subject, he or the people? Mr. Lincoln was elected President on the 8th of November, 1860; and the people had from this time till the 9th of February,

1861, a period of three months, in which to consider and decide for themselves, whether Mr. Lincolns' election was or was not in accordance with the provisions of the Constitution. They did consider this subject, and at the expiration of this period delivered their opinion to the effect that this statement of Gov. Harris is false, deciding that the election of Mr. Lincoln was constitutional and binding upon them as a State; and that they were not only willing but anxious to remain under the old Government, and accept its administration at his hands during the next four years.

There is not on record a more absolute and insulting case of official despotism and grinding usurpation than this act of Gov. Harris, in convening his Legislature and instructing its members as he did in this message.

But Governor Harris proceeds: and in another part of this incendiary document we find the following:

"Therefore, I respectfully recommend the perfecting of an ordinance by the General Assembly, formally declaring the Independence of the State of Tennessee of the Federal Union, renouncing its authority, and reassuming each and every function belonging to a separate sovereignty."

We have seen that this Legislature convened on the 25th of April, 1861. In obedience to the above recommendation respecting an ordinance of secession, among the first acts of this body we find the following:

DECLARATION OF INDEPENDENCE AND ORDINANCE DISSOLVING THE FEDERAL RELATIONS BETWEEN THE STATE OF TENNESSEE AND THE UNITED STATES OF AMERICA.

First. We, the people of the State of Tennessee, waiving any expression of opinion as to the abstract doctrine of secession, but asserting the right, as a free and independent people, to alter, reform, or abolish, our form of Government in such manner as we think proper, do ordain and declare that all the laws and ordinances by which the State of Tennessee became a member of the Federal Union of the United States of America, are hereby abrogated and annulled, and that all obligations on our part be withdrawn therefrom; and we do hereby resume all the rights, functions, and powers, which by any of said laws and ordinances were conveyed to the Government of the United States, and absolve ourselves from all the obligations, restraints, and duties incurred thereto; and do hereby henceforth become a free, sovereign and independent State.

Second. We furthermore declare and ordain that Article X, sections 1 and 2 of the Constitution of the State of Tennessee, which requires members of the General Assembly, and all officers, civil and military, to take an oath to support the Constitution of the United States be, and the same are hereby abrogated and annulled; and all parts of the Constitution of the State of Tennessee, making citizenship of the United States a qualification for office, and recognizing the Constitution of the United States as the supreme law of this State, are in like manner abrogated and annulled.

W. C. WHITTHORNE,
Speaker of the House of Representatives.
B. L. STOVALL,
Speaker of the Senate.

Passed May 6th, 1861.

JOINT RESOLUTION TO APPOINT COMMISSIONERS FROM THE STATE OF TENNESSEE TO CONFER WITH THE AUTHORITIES OF THE CONFEDERATE STATES, IN REGARD TO ENTERING INTO A MILITARY LEAGUE.

Resolved by the General Assembly of the State of Tennessee, That the Governor be, and he is hereby authorized and requested to appoint three Commissioners on the part of Tennessee, to enter into a Military League with the authorities of the Confederate States, and with the authorities of such other slaveholding States as may wish to enter into it; having in view the protection and defence of the entire South against the war that is now being carried on against it.

W. C. WHITTHORNE,
Speaker of the House of Representatives.
B. L. STOVALL,
Speaker of the Senate.

Adopted May 1, 1861.

In accordance with the request of this resolution Governor Harris, in due time, appears with the following message:

MESSAGE OF THE GOVERNOR.

EXECUTIVE DEPARTMENT,
Nashville, May 7, 1861.

Gentlemen of the Senate
and House of Representatives:

By virtue of the authority of your joint resolution, adopted on the 1st day of May inst., I appointed Gustavus A. Henry, of the county of Montgomery, Archibald O. W. Totten, of the county of Madison, and Washington Barrow, of the county of Davidson, "Commissioners on the part of Tennessee, to enter into a Military League with the authorities of the Confederate States, and with the authorities of such other slaveholding States as may wish to enter into it; having in view the protection and the defence of the entire South against the war that is now being carried on against it."

The said Commissioners met the Hon. Henry W. Hilliard, the accredited representative of the Confederate States, at Nashville, on this day, and have agreed upon and executed a Military League between the State of Tennessee and the Confederate States of America, subject, however, to the ratification of the two Governments; one of the duplicate originals of which I herewith transmit for your ratification or rejection. For many cogent and obvious reasons, unneces-

4

sary to be rehearsed to you, I respectfully recommend the ratification of this League at the earliest practicable moment.
          Very Respectfully,

                                   ISHAM G. HARRIS.

The following is the document or League referred to in
the above Message :

CONVENTION BETWEEN THE STATE OF TENNESSEE AND THE CONFEDERATE STATES OF AMERICA.

The State of Tennessee looking to a speedy admission into the Confederacy established by the Confederate States of America, in accordance with the Constitution for the Provisional Government of said
States, enters into the following temporary Convention, Agreement
and Military League, with the Confederate States, for the purpose of
meeting pressing exigencies affecting the common rights, interests,
and safety of said States, and said Confederacy.

First. Until the said State shall become a member of said Confederacy according to the Constitution of both powers, the whole military force, and military operations, offensive and defensive of said
State, in the impending conflict with the United States, shall be under
the chief control and direction of the President of the Confederate
States, upon the same basis, principles and footing, as if said State
were now, and during the interval, a member of said Confederacy,
said force, together with that of the Confederate States, to be employed for the common defence.

Second. The State of Tennessee will, upon becoming a member of
said Confederacy under the permanent constitution of said Confederate States, if the same shall occur, turn over to said Confederate
States, all the public property acquired from the United States, on
the same terms, and in the same manner as the other States of said
Confederacy have done in like cases.

Third. Whatever expenditures of money, if any, the said State of
Tennessee shall make before she becomes a member of said Confederacy, shall be met and provided for by the Confederate States.

This Convention entered into and agreed, in the city of Nashville,
Tennessee, on the seventh day of May, A. D., 1861, by Henry W. Hilliard, the duly authorized commissioner, to act in the matter of the
Confederate States, and Gustavus A. Henry, Archibald O. W. Totten,
and Washington Barrow, commissioners duly authorized in like
manner for the State of Tennessee—the whole subject to the approval
and ratification of the proper authorities of both Governments respectively.

In testimony whereof, the parties aforesaid have herewith set
their hands and seals, the day and year aforesaid, in duplicate originals.

          HENRY W. HILLIARD.   [SEAL.]
      Commissioner for the Confederate States of America.
          GUSTAVUS A. HENRY.   [SEAL.]
          A. O. W. TOTTEN,   [SEAL.]
          WASHINGTON BARROW,   [SEAL.]
              Commissioners on the part of Tennessee.

JOINT RESOLUTION RATIFYING THE LEAGUE.

WHEREAS, A military league, offensive and defensive, was formed
on the 7th of May, 1861, by and between A. O. W. Totten, Gustavus

A. Henry, and Washington Barrow, Commissioners on the part of the State of Tennessee, and H. W. Hilliard, Commissioner on the part of the Confederate States of America, subject to the confirmation of the two Governments:

Be it therefore resolved by the General Assembly of the State of Tennessee, That said league be in all respects ratified and confirmed, and the said General Assembly hereby pledges the faith and honor of the State of Tennessee to the faithful observance of the terms and conditions of said league.

W. C. WHITTHORNE,
Speaker of the House of Representatives.

B. L. STOVALL,
Speaker of the Senate.

Adopted May 7, 1861.

AN ORDINANCE FOR THE ADOPTION OF THE CONSTITUTION OF THE PROVISIONAL GOVERNMENT OF THE CONFEDERATE STATES OF AMERICA.

We, the people of Tennessee, solemnly impressed by the perils which surround us, do hereby adopt and ratify the Constitution of the Provisional Government of the Confederate States of America, ordained and established at Montgomery, Alabama, on the 8th day of February, 1861, to be in force during the existence thereof, or until such a time as we may supersede it by the adoption of a permanent Constitution.

Sec. 6. *Be it further enacted,* That those **in favor of** the adoption of said Provisional Constitution, and thereby securing to Tennessee equal representation in the deliberations and councils of the Confederate States, shall have written or printed on their ballots the word "*Representation*; those opposed, the words "*No Representation.*"

Sec. 7. *Be it further enacted,* That in the event the people shall adopt the Constitution of the Provisional Government of the Confederate States, at the election herein ordered, it shall be the duty of the Governor, forthwith to issue writs of election for delegates to represent the State of Tennessee in the said Provisional Government; that the State shall be represented by as many delegates as it was entitled to members of Congress to the Congress of the United States of America, who shall be elected from the several Congressional Districts as now established by law, in the mode and manner now prescribed for the election of members of the Congress of the United States.

Sec. 8. *Be it further enacted,* That this act take effect from and after its passage.

W. C. WITTHORNE,
Speaker of the House of Representatives.

B. L. STOVALL,
Speaker of the Senate.

Passed May 6th, 1861.

At the commencement of this chapter we assumed that Tennessee rebels were not only rebels against the General Government, but also rebels against the government of their own State.

In confirmation of this position we have seen, first, that on two different ballotings, the people of Tennessee in one case gave a majority of 64,114 forbidding the secession of the State under all circumstances; in the other a majority of nearly 31,000, not only against secession but declaring that no occasion whatever existed for a State Convention on this or any other subject then agitating the country; that Tennessee had no grievances to complain of, was satisfied with the General Government, and proposed to remain in the Union as she was.

Second, we have seen, that those who on the same day were found in the minority, or in other words found to be the rebel element of the State, immediately rebelled against this decision, setting on foot all possible unfair means and measures forcibly to set aside the people's verdict, and officially hurled Tennessee out of the Union. By overwhelming majorities the people of the State declare themselves to be loyal; instantly, however, Gov. Harris and his legislature, in secret conclave, assume themselves to be the people, convert the power entrusted in their hands into a law of brute force, blind and gag every Union man whom they cannot bribe, take the majority by the throat, and in three months from the time the people expressed their will to the contrary, league Tennessee with the rebellion.

Language cannot express facts, nor can facts prove any proposition if the above is not the logical showing of the case of this election. The proposition, therefore, is incontrovertibly made out that the rebels of Tennessee were not only rebels against the General Government, but rebels against the government of their own State.

Viewing the proceedings above described in the same light that we have considered them, the people of East Tennessee, through their delegates, assembled at Greenville, Green county, on the 17th of June, 1861, with a view, among other things, to petition their Legislature for the privilege of East Tennessee to withdraw as a part of the State, and become independent, that she might thereby not only avoid actual conflict between herself and its secession portions, but avoid complicity with their treason, and especially escape being swept with the rest of the State into the vortex of secession and rebellion. The following is substantially an extract from the views of this body expressed in regard to the conduct of **Governor Harris** and his legislature, developed and examined in this chapter:

Resolved, That the action of the State Legislature, in passing a declaration of independence, and forming a military league with the Southern Confederacy, was unconstitutional and *not binding upon the* **loyal** *citizens of the State*.

CHAPTER IV.

ELECTION FOR SEPARATION AND NO SEPARATION.

REBELS in Tennessee will boastingly refer to this election, as an argument against the position we have taken in regard to the secession of their State. Nothing, however, is wanting to demonstrate that this election of June 8th, 1861, an election surreptitiously appointed and tyrannically managed by Governor Harris and his Legislature, that they might cloak their treason under the forced popular suffrage of the people, if possible, was a darker crime in them, as well as a greater farce in itself than their act of ignoring the results of the election of February previous.

The following is another extract from the published views of the Greenville Convention, being a part of an address by its members to the people of the State.

"We, the people of East Tennessee, again assembled in Convention of our delegates, make the following declaration in addition to that heretofore promulgated by us at Knoxville, on the 30th and 31st days of May, last; So far as we can learn, the election held in this State on the 8th day of this month was free, with but few exceptions, in no part of the State other than in East Tennessee. In the larger portions of Middle and West Tennessee, no speeches or discussions in favor of the Union were permitted. Union papers were not allowed to circulate. Measures were taken in some parts of West Tennessee, in defiance of the Constitution and laws, which allow folded tickets, to have the ballots numbered in such manner as to mark and expose the Union voters. A secession paper, the Nashville *Gazette*, in urging the people to vote an open ticket, declared that 'a thief takes a pocket book or effects an entrance into forbidden places by stealthy means—a tory, in voting, usually adopts pretty much the same mode of procedure.' Disunionists, in many places, had charge of the polls; and Union men when voting, were denounced as Lincolnites and abolitionists. The unanimity of the votes in many large counties, where, but a few weeks ago, the Union sentiment was so strong, proves beyond a doubt that Union men were overawed by the tyranny of the military law, and the still greater tyranny of a corrupt and subsidized press. Our meeting was telegraphed to *The New Orleans Delta*, and it was falsely said that we had passed a resolution recommending submission if 70,000 votes were not cast against secession. The dispatch adds that the Southern rights men are determined to hold possession of the State, though they should be in a minority. Volunteers were allowed to vote in and out of the State, in flagrant violation of the Constitution. From the moment the election was over, before any detailed statement of the vote in the different counties had been published, and before it was possible to ascertain the result, it was exultingly proclaimed that separation had been carried by from fifty to seventy thousand votes. This was to prepare the public mind, to enable the secessionists to hold possession of the State, though they should be in the minority. The final result is to be announced by a secession governor, whose existence depends upon the success of secession; and no provision is to be made even for an examination of the vote by disinterested persons, or even for contesting the election. For these and other causes, we do not regard the result of the election as expressive of the will of a majority of the freemen of Tennessee."

Parson Brownlow, in his *Experiences Among the Rebels*, says:

"For Separation and Representation, Richmond, East Tennessee, gave 14,700 votes, *one half of that number* were rebel troops, having no authority under the Constitution to vote at any election. For No Separation and No Representation, East Tennessee gave 33,000 straight out Union votes, with at least 5,000 quiet citizens deterred from coming out by threats of violence, and by the presence of drunken troops at the polls to insult them."

A short time before this June election an attempt was made by the Union people to hold a meeting at Paris, Tennessee, and this attempt resulted in the death of two Union men, both being shot by the secessionists; and a public notice that Emerson Etheridge would speak at Trenton, Tennessee, called forth the following correspondence:

"TRENTON, TENN., April 16th, 1861.

To J. D. C. Atkins and R. G. Payne:

Etheridge speaks here on Friday. Be here Friday or next day."

The above was answered in the following manner:

"MEMPHIS, TENN., April 16th, 1861.

To Messrs. —— ——

I can't find Atkins. Can't come at that time. If Etheridge speaks for the South we have no reply. If against it, our only answer to him and his backers must be cold steel and bullets.

R. G. PAYNE."

In the Louisville Journal of May 13th, 1861, we find the following:

"The spirit of secession appears to have reached its culminating point in Tennessee. Certainly the fell spirit has, as yet, reached no higher point of outrageous tyranny. The whole of the late proceedings in Tennessee has been as gross an outrage as ever was perpetrated by the worst tyrant of all the earth. The whole secession movement on the part of the Legislature of the State has been lawless, violent and tumultuous. The pretense of submitting the Ordinance of Secession to the vote of the people of the State, after placing her military power and resources at the disposal and under the command of the Confederate States without any authority from the people, is as bitter and insolent a mockery of popular rights as the human mind could invent."

The following is the vote of the State at this June election for Separation and No Separation, as taken from the Memphis Appeal of June 27th, 1861:

EAST TENNESSEE.

COUNTIES.	Separation.	No Separation.	COUNTIES.	Separation.	No Separation.
Anderson	97	1278	Washington	1022	1445
Bledsoe	197	500	Monroe	1096	774
Bradley	507	1382	Morgan	50	630
Campbell	59	1000	McMinn	904	1144
Cocke	518	1185	Meigs	481	267
Carter	86	1343	Blount	418	1766
Grainger	586	1492	Claiborne	250	1243
Green	744	2691	Hawkins	908	1460
Hamilton	854	1260	Hancock	279	630
Jefferson	603	1987	Johnson	111	787
Knox	1226	3190	Sevier	60	1528
Marion	414	600	Scott	19	521
Polk	738	317	Sequatchee	153	100
Roane	454	1568			
Rhea	360	202	Total	14780	32923
Sullivan	1586	627			

MIDDLE TENNESSEE.

COUNTIES.	Separation.	No Separation.	COUNTIES.	Separation.	No Separation.
Maury	2731	78	Dekalb	833	642
Wilson	2329	353	Lawrence	1124	75
Smith	1249	671	Overton	1471	364
Warren	1419	12	Macon	447	697
Lincoln	2912		Giles	2458	11
Jackson	1483	714	Dickson	1141	72
Bedford	1595	727	Hickman	1400	5
Montgomery	2631	33	Lewis	223	14
Stewart	1839	99	Van Buren	308	13
Rutherford	2392	73	Robertson	3839	17
Williamson	1945	28	Wayne	409	905
Franklin	1652		Marshall	1642	101
Humphries	1042		Fentress	128	651
Davidson	5635	402	Grundy	528	9
Sumner	6465	69	Cheatham	702	55
White	1370	121			
Cannon	1149	127	Total	58265	8198
Coffee	1276	26			

WEST TENNESSEE.

COUNTIES.	Separation.	No Separation.	COUNTIES.	Separation.	No Separation.
Shelby	7132	5	Madison	2704	20
Carroll	967	1349	Fayette	1364	23
Henry	1746	317	Perry	780	168
Benton	798	228	Decatur	310	550
Dyer	811	110	Lauderdale	763	7
Hardin	498	1051	McNairy	1318	586
Gibson	1999	286	Weakly	1189	1201
Haywood	930	139	Tipton	943	16
Henderson	800	1013			
Hardeman	1516	29	Total	29127	6117
Obion	2936	64			

VOTE IN CAMPS.

Camp Randolph. 3.500; Camp Davis, Va., 506; Camp Duncan, 111; Harpers Ferry, 575; Fort Pickens, Fla., 737; Fort Harris. Tenn., 159; Camp Desoto, Tenn., 15; Camp Hermitage. Tenn., 16; Camp Jackson. Va., 622—Total. 6.241.

The majority for separation appears to be 61,095. Other authorities differ but little from these figures. In *More's Rebellion Record*, and in *The New American Cyclopœdia*, this majority is given as 57,675. Also, Governor Harris in his proclamation of June 24th, 1861, announced this as the majority by which the State had declared her separation from the old Government.

The overwhelming majority for No Convention was at first felt by the rebels as a death-blow to their hopes; while the loyal people correspondingly considered the victory complete and lasting, supposing that they had now ended the secession movement in Tennessee. The leading secessionists in the State, including the rebel portion of the Legislature, were confused and beaten, and even Governor Harris for a short time apparently abandoned the scheme as hopeless. In a few days, however, especially, as the great movement continued rapidly to progress in other sections of the Union, the discouragement of these rebels began to subside, and by means of secret societies, secret plotting, mining and counter-mining, they steadily recovered both spirits and strength, waiting and stealthily preparing to make another spring at the loyalty of the State. In Nashville, the great seething crater of Tennessee rebellion, the secession leaders played the double and deceptive game of friend and enemy, pretending to occupy a medium position, censuring and suspicioning, as well as measurably favoring, both parties. They were opposed to the confederate scheme for dismembering the Union, and equally opposed to coercion to recover South Carolina, already seceded.

Privately driving forward this plan till it would answer to call the people of Davidson county together in convention, by a grand rally on that occasion they succeeded in persuading, a portion of the people at least, to commit themselves to their line of policy, and announce that they, with these leaders, were pledged against coercion. This effected, some of the most sacrificing rebels repaired to Charleston, South Carolina, and encouraged the rebel military authorities there to fire on Fort Sumter, or in any way they could, draw the Federal fire and bring on a battle, to make it appear that coercion was the inaugurated policy of the Government, when Tennessee would be almost a unit for the South, for she was pledged against coercion.

The bombardment of Sumter on the 12th of April, followed by President Lincoln's call for troops on the 15th, three days afterwards, furnished these rising rebels with the very occasions they desired. These events produced an excitement that shook the State from one end to the other. The whole rebel element of the State, especially Governor Harris and the rebel portion of his Legislature, were not only aglow with indignation, but were fired to a high pitch of frenzy at the thought that the Government was going to make war on the seceding States to coerce them into submission. But what was still more unfortunate, the conservative element of the Union or loyal party—the weak-kneed gentlemen—were frightened also, and by the aid of the initiating degrees which this element had already taken in rebellion as just stated, now stumbled over the great bugaboo of coercion into an error that not only sundered and broke up the solid ranks of the loyal party in the State, but bound its scattered fragments hand and foot, and left them a helpless prey to the intriguing venom of their secession enemies.

Excited by the ominous signs of immediate war between the two sections in the fall of Sumter, in connection with their surprise that the Government should call on Tennessee for two regiments of militia to send against their brethren of the South, and to aid in putting down the rebellion by force, a few of the most eminent of these Union conservative leaders, such as Messrs. Neil S. Brown, ex-Governor of the State, Russell Houston, G. H. Ewing, C. Johnson, John Bell, R. J. Meigs, S. D. Morgan, John S. Brien, Andrew Ewing, John H. Callender, and Baylie Peyton, published at Nashville on the 18th of April, a warm and deeply appealing address to the people of the State, expressing their views of the crisis, and of the position that should be taken by Tennessee.

The following is an extract from this probably well-meant but greatly misguided expression of interested patriotism :

"Tennessee is called upon by the President to furnish two regiments; and the State has, through her Executive, refused to comply with the call. This refusal of our State *we warmly approve.* We commend the wisdom, the justice, and the humanity, of the refusal. We unqualifiedly disapprove of secession, both as a constitutional right, and as a remedy for existing evils. We equally condemn the policy of the Administration in reference to the seceded States. But, while we without qualification condemn the policy of coercion, as calculated to dissolve the Union forever, and to dissolve it in the blood of our fellow-citizens, and regard it as sufficient to justify the State in refusing her aid to the Government in its attempt to suppress the revolution in the seceded States, we do not think it our duty, considering her position in the Union, and in view of the great question of the peace of our distracted country, to take sides against the Government. * * * Tennessee ought, as we think, to *decline joining either party.* * * *

"The present duty of Tennessee is to maintain a position of independence, taking sides with the Union and the peace of the country against all assailants, whether from the North or the South. Her position should be to maintain the sanctity of her soil from the hostile tread of any party."

The following is governor Harris' refusal to furnish the two regiments, which the government required at that time of Tennessee :

"*Hon. Simeon Cameron.*

"Sir:—Your dispatch of the 15th inst. informing me that Tennessee is called upon for two regiments of militia for immediate service is received.

"Tennessee will not furnish a man for purposes of coercion, but 50,000 if necessary, for the defence of our rights and those of our Southern brethren."　　　　ISHAM G. HARRIS.
"*Governor of Tennessee.*"

In the winter of 1862, shortly before the battle of Stone River, between Nashville and the Hermitage, the writer was conversing with an intelligent farmer, who explained the cause of his backsliding condition as a Union man by saying: "What could I and such men as myself do, when Neil S. Brown and John Bell went by the board? both, condemning and rebelling against the policy of the Government, Mr. Brown stumping the State against coercion."

The step thus taken by these men was disastrous to the Union cause in Tennessee, in two respects. It helped to break the solidity and compactness of the loyal party in the State, sending bewilderment and hesitation, more or less into its ranks, and starting many Union men upon the high road to secession and rebellion. Particularly did it have this effect in Middle and Western Tennessee. In the second place, this act of these men threw them and the whole conservative element that adhered to them, helplessly into the arms of the rebels. It was just so much strength added to the rebel cause. It was meeting the rebels at least more than half way, which emboldened them to assume that the other half was taken also, dishonestly it is true, yet none the less to their benefit.

Basing themselves thus upon State independence, or State sovereignty, the principle of State secession was virtually admitted, and though they denied the right of secession in any case, yet, what did the rebels care for that, so long as they themselves neutralized this very denial by correspondingly opposing coercion. By taking this position, therefore, these men went completely over to the rebels, and bound themselves and their adherents hand and foot, a helpless, if not a willing prey at their feet. Denying the General Government the power to prevent secession by coercion, was equivalent to admitting the right of secession. With this accession to their strength and this encouragement, the rebels were now not afraid to ask whatever they desired, and to take any steps they pleased, to accomplish their objects. Occupying this position, these men consistently could offer no effectual resistance; and thus dismembered and deserted, the great Union party was measurably discouraged and disheartened, and consequently proportionately weak in their opposition.

Thus while this address was issued on the 18th of April, on the 25th, only seven days afterward, Governor Harris had his rebel Legislature convened and instructed to take steps for immediate secession, which, notwithstanding all the necessary preliminaries, mutual consultation, appointing commissioners, etc., was consummated by the adoption of the secession league on the 7th of May following, a lapse of only twelve days from the first hour of the session.

By this act the State with all her State Institutions, and the people, were officially transferred into the arms of Jeff. Davis. Her militia, with her whole military resources were, from that moment subject to the command of the Southern Confederacy, and were so considered, not only by the South, but by every rebel in the State, who consistently with the change, immediately prepared himself with revolver, bowie-knife, rifle or double-barrel shot gun, insolently assuming, as by authority, an attitude of hostility toward all Union movements and loyal expressions of the people, by which, together with the consciousness on their part, that Southern help was at hand and ready at any time, and would be immediately invoked if necessary, all Union action if not Union sentiment in Middle and West Tennessee, was effectually crushed out long before the 8th of June. In East Tennessee, the Union sentiment was so predominant that it took a little longer and a more persistent application of these means to overcome it.

By an act of this Legislature, convened on the 25th day of April, Governor Harris was authorised to raise, and equip a provisional force for the defense of the State, to consist of 55,000 volunteers—25,000 of whom, or any less number, as demanded by the wants of the service, were to be fitted for the field at the earliest practical moment, the remainder to be held in reserve, ready to move at short notice; and should it become necessary for the safety of the State, the Governor might " call out the whole available military strength of the State ;" and was to determine when this force should serve, and to direct it accordingly.

Thus clothed with a semblance of power, Gov. Harris hastened the organization of the provisional force of 25,000 men, and before the day of election, June 8th, 1861, had the greater part of it on foot, distributing it in camps around Nashville, and in other places, armed and supplied as far as it could be with the munitions of the United States then in possession of Tennessee, and with such as could be obtained from Augusta, Georgia, from where they were brought by General Zollicoffer. Thus on the morning of this election, for the first time in their lives, the people of Tennessee repaired to the polls conscious that they were no longer a free people, aware that the Governor and Legislature with the treasury of the State in their hands, and with all the arms of the State in requisition, and a formidable army in their pay, had already joined the foul conspiracy of the South purposely to overthrow the General Government.

In the same act authorizing the Governor to raise these troops, passed May 6th, 1861, the County Courts of the whole State were empowered to have organized a Home Guard of minute men in companies of not less than ten for each Civil District in their respective counties. It was the duty of the officers of these companies to procure warrants from the Justices, *arrest and bring to trial all suspected persons* before the civil authorities. It was the duty of these companies to assemble for drill at least once a week, to council with each other and take precautionary measures, and to hold themselves momentarily ready for a call to active service. A general commander was appointed in each county whose duty it was, in case of an emergency, to take charge of the Home Guards in his county and superintend their operations.

On the 16th of May, Governor Harris proclaimed to all volunteer organizations in the State who were in possession of State arms and did not hold themselves ready for immediate service at his command, to return the arms forthwith to the State arsenal at Nashville. The object of this was to disarm all bodies and organizations throughout the State who were friendly to the old Government.

Thus for a month previous to the election were the Union people of the State, in every county, if not in every district, awed and guarded by rebel military forces, and subjected to the tyranny, abuse, and proscription of these rebel military organizations in their very midst.

From the 16th to the 24th of April, rebel military operations had so far progressed in the west of the State that there were planted on the Mississippi five or six batteries of heavy guns, including mortars, columbiads, and 32 and 24 pounders, commanding the river from Memphis to the Kentucky line. Under the control of Major General G. J. Pillow, as commander-in-chief, with Brigadier Generals Cheatham and Sneed, were concentrated at the same time not far from fifteen thousand rebel troops in West Tennessee. About eight thousand Mississippi troops of all arms, also, sometime before this election passed up the Mobile and Ohio Railroad to Corinth and Grand Junction, on their way to rendezvous near the Kentucky line, to be commanded by General Clark, acting in concert with General Pillow. With these troops was a command of cavalry with two light batteries. At least seventy-five or one hundred heavy guns had been placed in battery in Tennessee, and other large guns were in the State and ready for use before the election. In addition to these preparations a command under Brigadier General Foster had assembled at Camp Cheatham; and General W. R. Caswell had collected and equipped over a thousand men in East Tennessee ready to repel any hostile movements in that division of the State.

The following is from the Cleveland *Banner*, and from a number dated May 10th, 1861, within two days of one month before the election:

"TENNESSEE MUSTERING HER "BRAVEST AND BEST."—The Nashville *Union and American* says the unparalleled unanimity with which the men of Tennessee are responding to the summons to war, makes the heart of every true Tennessean beat quicker and prouder. The Governor has not yet issued any official call to the volunteers of the State, and yet, in anticipation of such call, 117 companies have already been reported to the Adjutant General, as ready for service. This is exclusive of 44 companies mustered in by General Anderson in West Tennessee, and of Colonel Pete Turney's 1100 men, which have been received into service of the Confederate States and have already gone to Virginia.

We do not overstate the case, when we estimate that 75,000 as good and efficient troops, as ever met an enemy, can easily be raised in Tennessee, and this will not include more than one-half the men capable of bearing arms in the State.

The Black Republican tyrants and Vandals can never make much, in glory or profit, by invading such a State as this. These gallant men are as ready, too, to rush to the defence of their Southern sisters as they are to defend their own homes and soil. Tennessee is marshaling her chivalry for the heroic era into which we have entered. These troops know no such word as defeat. Death is to them far preferable to such a fate.

Under such a condition of things in Tennessee, added to which are the facts that her great lines of railroads were then also at the service and subject to the control of the Confederacy, and even then were alive with her war preparations against the Government; especially the great rail thoroughfare connecting Virginia with the Cotton States, passing through Knoxville and Chattanooga, literally swarming with rebel troops on their way from the South to the rebel army in the East, with other facts that might be given, the appointment of a State election at which her citizens as a free people were to ratify or reject secession, a thing already consummated, and which nothing on earth now but the subjugation of the whole rebellion could fully restore, was a farce, an unmeaning, hypocritical performance, certainly, the like of which had before never been known in the history of the country. Even had no fraudulent votes been cast by the rebels, under these circumstances, the trial would have been but an insulting mockery.

In regard to fraudulent votes, however, a glance at the table of returns given in this chapter will convince any one that rebel fraudulent voting on that day was perpetrated proportionately with the abominableness of the rest of the transaction.

The whole number of rebel votes cast for Convention, according to this table was 39,807, and for Separation 102,172, an increase of rebel votes in four months of 62,855. The whole number of Union votes cast for No Convention was 72,156, and for No Separation 47,307, a decrease of Union votes in four months of 24,918. Now, even admitting that this Union decrease indicates the exact number of Union men that went over to the rebels between these elections, and voted with them for separation, there would still be an increase of rebel votes during this four months of 37,937. It is not the fact, however, that this number of Union men deserted their friends, and voted for Separation. It is admitted, as indicated in another place, that many Union men, by one means and another, especially about the time that Sumter fell, were drawn into the rebellion, and doubtless voted for Separation. Not more, however, than ten thousand, in all probability, during this four months, even in the whole State, made a clear stride to the rebel ranks, and voted with the rebels for Separation. This would leave, this estimate being anything like correct, an increase of rebel votes, during the four months between these elections, of about 52,855. Now, that the rebels made a strenuous effort and polled all the votes in their power for the Convention, on the 9th of February, will not be denied; and the secret that enabled them on the 8th of June following, to exceed their February vote by 52,855 is yet, in all probability, a great deal better known to themselves than to anybody else. If there is any other principle than that of fraudulent voting on which this remarkable difference can be accounted for, the fact has escaped our knowledge, and probably always will escape it.

This fraudulent voting is also shown upon the same principle by reference to the votes cast in some of the counties at different times. Wilson County, Middle Tennessee, for instance, gave for Convention 462 votes; but for Separation 2,329. The same is the case with many other counties. The increase of almost two thousand rebel votes in Wilson County during the short space of four months, to say the least, is a very suspicious circumstance.

CHAPTER V.

UNION FLAG RAISED AND LOWERED.

IMMEDIATELY after the election, on the 9th of June, 1861, from which time the rebels considered that the people had ratified the secession of the State, the clouds of rebellion, more ominously than ever, began to lower upon East Tennessee; and Bradley felt that she was elected for her part of the scathing.

On the 25th of April, 1861, a Union pole was raised upon the Public Square in Cleveland, in front of the Court House. As soon as the pole was erected and firmly placed in the earth, a beautiful Union flag, presented by Miss Sally Shields, was elevated, and soon waved gracefully from its pinnacle, the stars and stripes unfurling themselves in the breeze, a visible evidence that the people of Bradley were yet enthusiastically attached to the government of their fathers. Being previously notified, the people from the different parts of the county assembled to enjoy and participate in the ceremonies, and to listen to an address delivered on the occasion by John L. Hopkins, Esq., of Chattanooga, the whole constituting a scene of Union interest and excitement, not soon to be forgotten by the lovers of true liberty in the village of Cleveland. The pole was a beautiful hickory, and a piece of bark taken from it at the time, and on which are inscribed in legible characters the date of the occasion, the name of the young lady who presented the flag, the name of the orator of the day, etc., is still in possession of Mr. C. M. Gallaher, a merchant of Cleveland.

This flag was permitted to wave above the dwellings and the people of Cleveland, from the time it was raised till June following, either a few days before or a few days after the election just alluded to. About this time a rebel regiment of Mississippians, the first that passed Cleveland from the South, on its way to the eastern rebel army, while the train conveying it stopped at the depot, a quarter of a mile south of the Court House—espied this flag proudly flapping against the northern sky, and soon began preparations to haul it down from its proud position. Some of these Mississippians immediately fired upon the flag, one of the shots taking effect upon the Court House, where the marks of the bullet are yet to be seen on the blind of one of the front windows. A few of the Union people of Cleveland were inclined to resent the insult, and not allow their flag to be disturbed. Others, taking a cooler and more considerate view of the subject, saw it would be impossible for the people to arm and organize in time to meet eight hundred or a thousand rebels, thoroughly equipped, and at that instant ready to march upon them, consequently they submitted with the best grace they could—gently lowered the flag themselves and conveyed it to a place of safety.

As already stated, from this June election, and particularly from the event just narrated, things in Bradley grew worse and worse for the Union cause. Rebel citizens gave their Union neighbors to understand that no more Union flags would be allowed to float above the soil of Bradley. The loyal people, however, thought otherwise. They had faith to believe that the same flag which they had then been compelled to strike at the insulting demands of Southern traitors, would, at some future day, triumphantly wave and unfold its brilliant colors to their gaze in the same spot from which it had just been displaced. No further attempts, however, were immediately made to accomplish this desirable object; but the flag was secreted among Union families at different places in the county, its locality being changed from house to house, as dangers thickened and followed it up, for nearly three years. For two years it was concealed in the house of Mr. John McPherson, of the ninth district. While here, and probably while at other places, when Union neighbors and Union refugees from different parts of the county were present, moved with a desire to see *the old flag*, some of the family would slyly withdraw it from its place of concealment, and after all had sufficiently feasted their eyes upon the sight, and volunteered their remarks naturally suggested by the hazards through which this emblem of national liberty, as well as themselves, were passing, it would be as carefully returned to its seclusion, there to wait in silence, and like all other things noble to abide its time of public glory.

On the 10th of February, 1864, not long after our forces had driven Bragg from before Chattanooga, and taken possession of the State from this place to Knoxville, Gen. Grosse, from Indiana, and Col. Waters, of the 84th Illinois, assisted the Union people of Bradley to raise this same flag which they had concealed and protected with so much devotion, in the same spot from which Mississippi traitors had dislodged it. These gentlemen delivered, each, a patriotic and encouraging address to the people on the occasion.

It was a high day in Cleveland, when the *blue coats* of the North and the *blue coats* of Tennessee, mingling with the crowd of men, women, and children, loyal Bradley sent up the Stars and Stripes, announcing the redemption of their rebel-smitten and traitor-ridden county.

A FALSE ALARM.

On the 6th of July, 1861, from some accidental circumstance, a report spread over Bradley that a rebel regiment, apparently from Chattanooga, had appeared in the vicinity of Georgetown, or near a place called Swafford's Springs, in the north-western part of the county. The report carried the idea that this rebel force meditated some evil against the rights of the Union people of Bradley. Having taken this form it spread like wild-fire till it reached every Union section if not every Union family in the county. This occurred on Saturday, and notwithstanding the people were closing up their week-day affairs, and receding towards the quiet of the Sabbath, this news threw the whole Union element of the county

into commotion, and set it to heaving like a tempest. Mr.
Hiram Smith, of the fifth district, like many more of other
districts, mounted his horse and rode post-haste nearly
the whole night to rally the people to the rescue; and
Sunday morning, instead of finding them at their different
places of worship, found seven or eight hundred of them
armed with every conceivable weapon which in the excitement of the moment they could lay their hands on,
hurrying from their different points, and organizing to
beat back a fancied rebel foe. One point of rendezvous
was Smith's Mills, we believe, in the twelfth district.

Sometime during the day on Sunday, however, it was
ascertained that this report was an utter fabrication;
that no rebel force was or had been in the vicinity of
Georgetown, or anywhere in that direction, consequently,
these Union warriors had nothing to do but enjoy a hearty
laugh at the awkwardness of their position and return to
their homes. The editor of the Cleveland *Banner*, in his
next number after this Union demonstration, devotes to
this subject nearly two columns of burlesque and rebel
censure, from which the following is a short extract:

"The news from the fighting District at this juncture of writing,
is of a rather pacific character. Since the uprising of the Union
men on Saturday night last, the excitement is subsiding and growing
beautiful less by degrees. The warriors, on that memorable occasion, armed with guns, knives, reap hooks, scythe blades, claw-ham-
mers and hand-saws, in the fury of their anger, burnt a foot-log and
blockaded Candy's Creek. Thus appeasing their 'voice for war,'
they dispersed to their homes, and believe now they are perfectly secure, and can maintain their independence and *neutrality*, in spite of
Jeff. Davis, King Harris, the Southern Confederacy, the Devil and
Tom Walker. We hope no straggling Secessionist will get among
them, to disturb their quiet repose, because if they get another *big
scare* they will *ramose* the *ranche*. We don't want them to leave till
corn is laid-by and the wheat is thrashed."

This demonstration illustrates the Union feeling and
determined hostility which at that time existed in Bradley against the rebellion. Unfortunately, however, this
was the last general exhibition of Union sentiment that
was permitted in the county, until it was relieved by the
Government forces in the spring of 1864. Rebel military
power, soon after, was effectually inaugurated to suppress

not only all general expressions of loyalty, but all individual liberty of speech and action. This unlooked for Union opposition to the rebellion, it appears, suggested the necessity of the presence of rebel troops to awe the Union people into submission to the demands of treason. In the same editorial of the *Banner* from which we have quoted, we find the following :

> "On Thursday, before the absurd rumor was put afloat in regard to the Southern troops, nearly all of these thousand Union voters had a meeting at Georgetown, where their regularly organized companies, not less than five or six hundred armed men, had been mustered and drilled under the old Union flags; and had been addressed by Dan Trewhitt, Michael Edwards, and a fellow by the name of Matthews, in a most *inflammatory and rebellious style!*"

In connection with the above, this rebel editor also teaches the Union people of Bradley to understand their duty, and warns them in the following manner of what they may expect in return for disobedience.

> "Our Union friends were greatly exercised on Monday last, for fear that troops from the Confederate States, would be stationed in our midst, in consequence of the uprising of the Union men at Georgetown on Sunday. Could they expect anything else after such a demonstration as that! *We know* that the State does not wish to send them here, and if they are ordered here at all it will be from a feeling of necessity, and not because there is any desire to do so on the part of the State or the Confederate States.
>
> Armed Lincoln men are enemies to the Confederate States, whether they are found in Massachusetts, Virginia or East Tennessee—and such armed men with hostile intentions, if persisted in, must as a matter of course in a state of war expect to be treated as enemies."

We insert the last extract because it reveals the exact point of time when the military power of the rebellion was resorted to, and depended on by Bradley rebels to put an end to expressions of loyalty in the county. We believe that no rebel forces were at that time sent into the county ; but from this moment Union men were given to understand that rebel military power would be applied if all loyal demonstrations in the county did not at once cease. Besides, in a very short time after this, home rebel volunteering commenced, and the presence of military camps in full blast, and acting in combination with Southern rebels formed a power making rebel ascendancy in Bradley complete.

DAMAGES TO BRADLEY COUNTY.

First District	$80,000	Eighth District	80,000
Second District	40,000	Ninth District	80,000
Third District	40,000	Tenth District	80,000
Fourth District	60,000	Eleventh District	80,000
Fifth District	60,000	Twelfth District	90,000
Sixth District	100,000	Thirteenth District	30,000
Seventh District	40,000		

The above estimates do not refer to the *aggregate* losses of Union men in this county occasioned by the war generally, but simply to the amounts of property of all kinds destroyed and taken from them by the rebels during the war. These figures, in every instance except one, are considerably below the respective damages as estimated by good judges. Getting estimates of rebel damages from different individuals living in the several districts of the county, the medium between the highest and the lowest are the figures in each case here given.

The best judges put the Union loss in the first district at $100,000. None put it less than $75,000; and it was put down finally at $80,000. The Union loss in the fourth district by some was estimated at $75,000, or even $80,000, while others judged it as low as $50,000. We have given it at $60,000. This is the rule followed in the case of every district except the eighth, the Union damages of which were calculated by Mr. Benton H. Henneger, of Charleston,—a gentleman whose judgment and candor none will question. Mr. Henneger's own loss in this district was over $5,000. A. J. Cate, Esq., of the first district, lost $25,000. The rebels burned two of his barns with a large amount of property stored in them at the time. Mr. Jesse B. Cleveland, of the seventh district, lost $10,000. Rev. Eli H. Southerland, of the third district, lost $3,500. John McPherson, Esq., of the ninth, and Mr. Samuel Maroon, of the fourth, were equally heavy losers with some of the above. Every Union man in the county, first and last, lost by the rebels nearly everything movable on his premises, especially everything in the shape of stock. A closer and more critical examination of these damages doubtless would increase instead of lessening the foregoing figures.

In some cases, particularly at the commencement of the war, the rebel authorities paid Union people for the property they took from them in Confederate paper money. Generally, however, this proved but a small compensation. Some time in 1863 Mrs. Benton H. Henneger paid $500 in Confederate money for a common feather bed and a common bedstead. In the same year, Mr. Henneger himself paid in this money $3,000 for three boxes of tobacco, being ten dollars per pound. Towards the close of 1863, thirty dollars in Confederate money was frequently paid for a block of cotton thread, which in ordinary times cost perhaps $1.50. During the first year of the war, however, Confederate money was of more value.

A committee of good judges in the ninth district, who lived in Bradley throughout the war, estimated the Confederate money owned by Union men in the county, while it was in circulation, as having been worth to them on an average from twenty to twenty-five cents to the dollar. Individuals, of course, will differ on this subject; yet those who give it a candid and thorough investigation, will probably admit that this committee of the ninth district was not far from the truth.

CHAPTER VI.

THE FIRST CLIFT WAR.

HAVING conducted the reader to the edge of the mael-strom into which Bradley was precipitated, and in which she floundered for nearly three years, we must turn aside for a moment to include a brief sketch of a somewhat remarkable scene, which, though not enacted in Bradley, is nevertheless a part of its war history, and cannot with propriety be separated from it. By way of introduction, we will present another short extract from the editorial of the Cleveland *Banner*. It is found in the issue of September 27th, 1861, and reads as follows:

"Old Clift, down in Hamilton, who has been rather obstrepulous for a few weeks, we learn, has cooled down and concluded to 'ground arms' and demean himself like a loyal citizen hereafter. Sensible conclusion that, and come to just at the nick of time, because it would have been a pity to disgrace the scaffold with such an old imbecile as he has proved himself to be."

Of all the national commotions which the world has ever witnessed, this great Southern Rebellion has developed the greatest variety of characters in its line—characters filling the measure of every human medium, others circumscribing all human extremes excepting *extreme greatness*, executing and leaving for our backward view the most extensive field of scientific and unscientific military maneuvers, tragic events and comic scenes—characters prescribing and proscribing respectively every form of government both for communities and individuals; prescribing and proscribing every form of philosophy, morals and religion—characters presenting or inhering the sublimest ranges of humanity and Christianity, side by side with every evil work produced by other characters, with a lengthened category of cases of the strangest combinations of human weakness and efficient qualities in the same individuals—qualities fitted for accidental and impromptu strokes of power and success, but impossible of adjustment with even, systematic and sure progress; the whole of which during the last four years have moulded the most gigantic mass of facts and forms for the intellect of man—facts and forms which will follow in the realm of thought and tinge the literature of the world for the next thousand years.

As a solitary individual or figure helping to make up this mass of phenomena, one that will be remembered by the people of Bradley, Hamilton, Polk, Reah, Meigs, McMinn, and those of other counties, during the present generation at least, WILLIAM CLIFT stands pre-eminent in East Tennessee, his active individuality in 1861 having given rise to what is known, in that region, as the famous *Clift war*.

This brave and patriotic Tennesseean, at the opening of the rebellion, was living in Hamilton County, on the north-west side of the Tennessee, on a small stream named Soddy, about three miles from where it empties into that noble river, twenty-five miles above Chattanooga. He was an early settler in the country, from which time to the commencement of the war, he had amassed considerable property, was an owner of mills, &c., rather a leading character in his vicinity—known to be honest, industrious, a fair and liberal dealer, a good citizen, prompt, short, direct, outspoken, uncompromising—having not the least of the non-committal or secretiveness in his composition. Being a strong Union man, a worshiper of the flag of his ancestors, he was one of the first in his section to denounce secession—opposing the rebellion in all its features. So decided was his course, and so fearlessly were his Union sentiments expressed from the beginning, that he soon became known not only in his own county but in the adjoining counties, as a more than usually active Union man and vehement friend of the old Government; and was as much dreaded and hated by the rebels as he was favorably regarded by the Union people.

Near the close of the summer of 1861 Union men began to flee from East Tennessee and Northern Georgia through Kentucky to the Federal army. Col. Clift, as just stated, being known throughout the country as an enthusiastic friend to the cause: and living near the Tennessee river, also on the refugee route of travel to the Northern army, the vicinity of his plantation soon became the converging point for crossing the river to those who were thus flying from the fires of rebellion. Refugee pilots acquainted with the country would secretly conduct companies of Union men to the river opposite Clift's premises; when by his aid, or aid which he had previously prepared, they were slyly crossed over and concealed till arrangements could be made for their departure to the Northern lines. This system of operations continued and increased from about the middle of the summer, 1861, the time it commenced, till after the middle of the following September, Col. Clift's plantation being both receiving and distributing refugee headquarters.

For his own convenience and for the comfort of the refugees, Clift took possession of a Cumberland Presbyterian camp ground, situated not far from his own home, and on a small stream called Sails Creek. The refugees now quartered in the board tents left standing upon this ground, while the work of organizing them into companies, fitting them out with pilots and supplies necessary for their trip through Kentucky, could be accomplished.

Not long after Clift took possession of these tents, his numbers so increased that all attempts perhaps at secresy were thrown off; and the premises began to assume the appearances of a military camp, so much so, that the movement was soon interpreted by rebel citizens as incipient rebellion against the Confederate States. News of Clift's Union activities had been spreading for some time through the country; but the erection of this camp gave a new impetus to rebel fears, and the Confederate authorities at Chattanooga, Knoxville and other places thought it quite time to put a stop to the Lincolnite proceedings on Sails Creek. Accordingly Capt. Snow of

Hamilton, Captains Crawford and Guess of Rhea, and Capt. Rogers of Meigs, collectively commanding about three or four hundred men, were ordered to repair to Col. Clifts camp, and if they could not capture, disperse him and his men. This rebel force reached the vicinity of Clift's operations about the 15th of September, 1861. From cowardice or some other cause, the rebels did not make an immediate attack; but halted in Rhea county, at a place called "The Cross Roads," six or eight miles from Clifts' headquarters.

When it became known that this rebel force was ordered to dislodge Col. Clift, many of the leading Union men of Bradley and perhaps a few from other counties, some of whom had sons with Clift, knowing that he was in no condition to make a successful defence, and knowing also that he would not run, but would fight, if attacked, whether the chances were against him or not, thought proper to visit the scene of hostilities and lend their influence to prevent an encounter which would doubtless occasion loss of life, and which could not, whatever the immediate result, benefit the Union cause in the end. These men reached the ground in time to confer with Clift, who, yielding to their advice took advantage of the delay of the rebels to attack him—broke up and vacated his camp, allowing his men to disperse, each one disposing of himself as he thought best. Immediately after this, and while the rebels were yet at "The Cross Roads," the rebel Assistant Inspector General of the State, James W. Gillispie, having been sent from Knoxville to superintend operations against Col. Clift, appeared on the ground. He arrived on the evening of the 18th, and being informed that the Union camp had already been voluntarily abandoned, sought an interview with Col. Clift and his citizen councillors, endeavoring to extort a promise from them, that thereafter they would discourage all Union men in their respective communities from leaving their homes, and especially from going to the Federal Army. He also endeavored, particularly, to obtain a promise from Col. Clift, that he would not again allow his premises to become the rendezvous for Union refugees; and more particularly still, that he would organize no more such camps as that he had just abandoned. Gen. Gillispie, however, found it no easy matter, notwithstanding the presence of three or four hundred rebel troops, to bring Col. Clift and these few Union men to subscribe to his terms.

They argued, that Union men not only had been, but were then being seized at their houses, and oppressively forced into the rebel armies, and compelled to fight against what they conscientiously felt to be their lawful Government, and for a cause which they as conscientiously believed to be treasonable—a cause that must ultimately fail and involve all connected with it in ruin. They contended that Union men had the same right to their political opinions, that rebels had to theirs, and while rebel recruiting officers, and the rebel soldiery were, at the point of the bayonet, compelling Union men to enter their ranks and fight the battles of the rebellion, it was right for these Union men to escape, in any way they could escape, to the Federal army or any where else. These arguments were too consistent, and were too forcibly urged for Gen. Gillispie to make head against them altogether; and he found himself necessitated, before he could effect anything like a settlement on peaceable terms, to yield at last half the contested ground. He therefore obligated himself that Union men should thereafter be unmolested and allowed to remain at their homes in peace—that under no circumstances, would the rebel authorities allow their soldiery to force them into the Confederate ranks to fight against the Government of the United States. Accordingly, he drew up the following singular article of treaty stipulations, as obligatory upon both parties.

WHEREAS, the State of Tennessee has separated from the United States, by a vote of a large majority of the citizens of the State, and adopted the permanent Constitution of the Confederate States of America; and we, as members of the Union party, believing that it becomes necessary for us to make an election between the North and the South, and that our interests and sympathies and feelings are with our countrymen of the South, that any further divisions and dissentions among us, the citizens of East Tennessee, is only calculated to produce war and strife among our homes and families, and desolation of the land, without any material influence upon the contest between the North and the South

We hereby agree, That we will in future conduct ourselves as peaceable and loyal citizens of the State of Tennessee, that we will oppose resistance or rebellion against the Constitution and laws of the State of Tennessee, and will use our influence to prevail upon our neighbors and acquaintances to co-operate with us in this behalf; *We having been assured by the military authorities of the State, that no act of oppression will be allowed toward us or our families, whilst we continue in the peaceable pursuits of our several domestic occupations.* September 19th, 1861.

The general wording of this document did not harmonize with the feelings, either of Col. Clift or any of his citizen advisers. They especially objected to that statement "our interests and sympathies and feelings are with our countrymen of the South." As this document, however, promised immunity to Union men from rebel oppression for the future, upon the authority of the Assistant Inspector General of the State, and as Gen. Gillispie was not disposed to yield more, having the power at hand to enforce his own measures; after a lengthened discussion, without fully committing themselves to the moral position it required of them, Col. Clift and his friends consented to the conditions of the treaty, promising that so far as hostile demonstrations were concerned, its terms, on their part, should be faithfully kept, so long as they were observed by the rebels; and thus, the famous "Cross Roads Treaty," between Gen. Gillispie and Col. Clift terminated the first "Clift War."

When the news of this treaty reached Bradley, and the people became acquainted with its character, dissatisfaction, or rather a disposition to ridicule it, was the result among Union men. Some were disposed to complain because Col. Clift and his friends had submitted to anything of the kind. But a few weeks transpired, however, before it was discovered that "The Cross Roads Treaty," though farcical enough at the beginning, was nevertheless resulting in considerable good. Gen. Gillispie, to his credit, no doubt intended that the provision of this agreement, on the part of the rebels, should be faithfully kept, and exerted himself with the rebel authorities to this end. Rebel abuses in Bradley were so manifestly checked for a season by "The Cross Roads Treaty" that many Union men were heard to say that it was the most fortunate thing for their side that had occurred since the rebellion commenced.

Should this page, at some future day, meet the eye of Gen. Gillispie, he will doubtless wonder at the accidents that preserved and finally gave publicity to his profound diplomatic stipulations upon Sails Creek.

THE SECOND CLIFT WAR.

Whatever were the efforts of certain individuals engaged in the rebellion to conduct it, so far as they were concerned, upon principles of justice, the fact that the great scheme was fundamentally wrong, made it impossible for any of its parts long to remain untainted with the central wickedness.

"The Cross Roads" agreement, so far as Gen. Gillispie was concerned, proposed to secure something like justice to the Union people of the country, and to some extent for a short time had this effect. As the rebellion rose in its might, however, the obligations of this measure were swept away, and Union people soon became the subjects of the same persecutions as before; consequently they again attempted to save themselves by flight to the Northern army. The contract being thus broken by the rebels, Col. Clift felt himself released from its obligations, and immediately opened his house and offered his premises again for the protection of Union refugees.

Upon this renewal of hostilities the refugees flocked in upon Clift in such numbers that he not only found his old camp ground on Sails Creek indispensable to their comfort, but he was induced to institute a system of operations entirely different from any by which he had previously operated.

It was unnecessary in his opinion for Union people to fly to the North either for protection or for an opportunity to fight; and acting upon this principle he proposed to organize his refugee friends into a regiment and prepare for defence, making his premises their base of operations. Whether Col. Clift's plan was altogether approved or otherwise, many if not all that were with him yielded to his solicitations, and the result was that in a few days their camp had assumed quite a formidable appearance as a military post.

At this stage of the proceedings it was rumored that the notorious Wm. Snow, of Hamilton, with his gang of cut-throats, was quartered in a Methodist camp ground in the north-west part of Bradley, recruiting rebel soldiers, and, as usual, arresting Union men and pressing them into the rebel service. Ascertaining this report to be true, Clift proposed to lead his men against Snow, whom he thought it would be easy to dislodge if not capture, with his whole party. For want of arms or from some other cause, this enterprise, notwithstanding its importance, as well as its practicability, was not undertaken, and Snow and his men, after desolating the country and abusing Union people to their satisfaction, left at their own convenience. Although Col. Clift's anxiety of offensive movements against Snow was not gratified, yet his diligence preparatory to defensive operations was not slackened, he and his men making the best of their time and means to strengthen their position. Clift's men, however, were poorly armed, a deficiency which, in his locality and condition, it was difficult to supply. His genius, however, when in a strait, was as strangely inventive as his spirit was brave; and he at once set to work to remedy the serious evil under which he labored. Procuring an old iron pipe, which, perhaps, had formerly been some part of a steam-engine, he improvised it into a heavy ece of ordnance, and, in some way, mounted it behind his breastworks, in readiness to use as artillery in case of an attack. This novel invention, whether it could have been of any service in beating back an enemy or not, had the effect very much to enlarge the fame of Col. Clift as a warrior of determined spirit, and, also, once more to arouse the fears of the rebel authorities, and cause them

6

a second time to turn their attention to their old and vigorous enemy on Sails Creek.

Accordingly, Col. Wood, of Chattanooga, commanding a regiment of Alabama troops, Captains Brown and Hardwick, of Cleveland, Capt. McClellan, of Charleston, Bradley county, Capt. McClary, of Polk, Capt. Smith, of McMinn, Capt. McKinsey, of Meigs, with two other Captains of home guards in Rhea county, with their commands, comprising a rebel force of fifteen hundred or two thousand men, were ordered to concentrate in the vicinity of Clift's operations, and, as soon as possible, make a descent upon his camp that would effectually silence an enemy that had entrenched himself in the very midst of the rebellion, defying the whole Confederacy, and one that had already given the rebel authorities in Tennessee so much trouble.

With the exception of Col. Wood's regiment, this formidable array of troops reached its destination on the morning of the 11th of November, 1861, and went into camp a short distance to the east of Col. Clift's fort. Col. Wood, of Chattanooga, it appears, did not arrive till two days later, the manner of which arrival will appear hereafter. As was the case when Clift was previously assaulted, some of the leading Union men of the country stole the march upon these rebel troops, and on the 12th entered Clift's camp, advised him of his danger, and succeeded in convincing him that with little more than four hundred men, and those without arms, it would be impossible to resist an armed force of nearly two thousand. Fortunately for the cause, Mr. Robert Sullivan, a United States recruiting officer from the North, reached Clift's camp on the same day of the arrival of the rebel troops; and, it being decided to abandon the fort without resistance, a portion of the refugees enlisted, and that night, while the rebels were encamped before them, secretly left with Mr. Sullivan for the Northern army. Mr. John McPherson and C. S. Matthews, two of the Union men who remained till the next day, seeing the fort completely vacated, for some cause, perhaps out of mere curiosity, entered the rebel camp. Attempting to leave that evening or early the next morning, they were very politely informed that they must remain and await further orders.

Not knowing that Clift and his men had fled, on the morning of the 13th, the time appointed by the rebels to bring things to a crisis, they sent out their scouts with instructions to proceed cautiously and reconnoiter Clift's position. Coming within sight of his fortifications, these scouts used every possible means to descry an enemy, but, unable to do so, they ventured forward till they entered the vacant Union camp. After strolling among the deserted tents for a short time, one of their company discovered, at some distance, a body of troops approaching them from the west. Supposing, in the excitement of the moment, that these were Clift's men, who had vacated their camp only to entrap them, they sprang to their animals, and in the act of mounting were fired upon by their supposed enemies. This confirmed their fears that Clift and his men were upon them, and perhaps surrounding them from ambush; consequently they lost no time but retreated towards their own camp, returning the fire as best they could, till their precipitate flight placed them for the moment out of danger, when they halted, but sent one of their number on to camp with information that they had found the enemy and were holding him in check that the main body might be prepared to receive him. This information suddenly created a perfect commotion in the rebel camp. Officers and men hurried to and fro, perfecting arrangements and forming themselves into line of battle preparatory to receiving the renowned scoffer at rebellion from Sails Creek.

Esq. McPherson, however, and his friend Matthews, whom the rebel officers had detained, stood by and looked upon the scene with complacent smiles, enjoying the hurry and alarm of these rebels with a high degree of internal satisfaction, knowing that neither Clift, nor any of his men were anywhere in the vicinity.

After the confusion and bustle of the alarm had a little subsided, these Union men ventured to suggest to one of the rebel officers that some mistake must be at the bottom of the matter, for it could not be the Union refugees who were pressing back their scouts. In a few moments, however, a second messenger rode into camp, and not only confirmed the tidings of the first, but added that Clift and his men were advancing in very heavy force, easily and steadily bearing back their companions, and that everything must be in readiness to receive them. This second intelligence spread quickly through the rebel camp, and left no doubt on the minds of any that they must either fly, or, in a few moments, meet the approaching foe, and preparations were completed for the struggle. The two Union men, however, still insisted that the advancing force could not be Clift's men. But quickly a third messenger dashed into camp, apparently more excited than the others, when anxiety was again on tip-toe; but instead of anything terrific and startling to increase the alarm as before, the first salutation was, "A flag! a flag! We are afraid that we are fighting our own men!" "There!" ejaculated Esq. McPherson, "that sounds to me something like a solution of the mystery." The flag was immediately procured, and the trooper hastened back with it to the scene of conflict in front, where it was elevated—a truce obtained, and instead of old Clift, their mortal enemy, they had been fighting no other than Col. Wood and his Alabama regiment, just arrived from Chattanooga.

Both these rebel parties had been mistaken — both errors centering toward the same object, but, in part, inversely laid in regard to themselves, Col. Wood, supposing that he was fighting and *driving* Col. Clift; the others, that they were fighting and *being driven* by him. The old fox, however, had eluded their spring—stepped out from between them just in time to give them a blind fight among themselves. From the results however, one would judge that they fought at rather a safe distance, for through all this heavy skirmishing but a solitary man was hit—on the foot, a slight scratch—no blood drawn, Col. Woods' party ahead in this respect. This was rather a fortunate out-come from the awkward and somewhat dangerous position the rebels had fallen into.

Recovering a little from their excitement, they began to feel the mortification of their general failure. Notwithstanding all their toil and dangerous fighting among themselves, the Tennessee Lincolnites, and especially the central object of their expedition, Col. Clift, had escaped. With the exception of Col. Wood's regiment, which, we believe, returned to Chattanooga the next morning, these rebels remained in the vicinity for several days, scouring the country, stealing property, and arresting Union men wherever they could find them. A guard-house was erected in which the prisoners were confined as fast as they were brought in. Many of these prisoners were not simply mistreated, but some of them were savagely abused—berated as Lincolnites, threatened to be shot, accused of complicity with Clift, of bridge burning, etc. Col. Clift's premises were laid waste, and other Union plantations besieged and robbed; Capt. Bill Brown particularly distinguishing himself in this business. We were creditably informed that he reached Cleveland richly laden with Union spoils, a desirable portion of which were oppropriated to his own use.

It was reported at the time that, in addition to these general depredations, a number of Union men were shot, some being killed and others wounded. That a great deal of shooting was done by these rebels, in connection with this whole affair, is attested by Union men present from Bradley, some of whom were under arrest at the time, but there is ground to hope, perhaps, that no Union lives were lost.

Utterly failing to capture Col. Clift or obtain any traces of his men, yet satisfactorily avenging themselves by success in much more uncivil villanies—capturing and brutally mistreating every male person in the vicinity suspected of connection with Clift in his operations or of being friendly to the old Government, and after administering suitable threatening and warning to old men and Union women and children, these rebel companies left and returned to their respective home camps. Thus terminated the second "Clift War," an affair which at the time created the most intense excitement throughout the country.

Having given, perhaps a sufficiently detailed account of Col. Clift's early opposition to the rebellion, and his efforts to defend himself against it at his own home, the reader will doubtless desire to know something of his further career in aiding to crush the power, which of all others his very soul hated. Whether he was concealed upon his own premises or somewhere in the country, when both rebel armies were fighting his rear ghost, and when the vandals were trying to scent the track of his physical *reality*, among the rocks and swamps, or whether he fled with Mr. Sullivan, like some of his men, to the North, or escaped in some other direction, we are not informed; but certain it is, that he escaped without personal harm, and it is equally certain that he made no further attempts upon his own plantation, two hundred and fifty miles in front of our lines, to fight the whole Southern Confederacy.

Up to this period, Col. Clift was acting upon his own responsibility, independently of the Government, conducting a war of his own, having no authority to enlist troops or anything of the kind. Being now, however, not only compelled permanently to change his base of operations, but to abandon the idea of whipping the rebellion without the aid of the Government, he repaired to Washington, obtained authority from the War Department to recruit and organize a regiment of which he was to have the colonelcy.

With a view to accomplish this object, early in the spring of 1862, Col. Clift established his headquarters near Huntsville, at the head of Sequatchee valley, Scott county, East Tennessee. Enthusiastically pushing forward his new enterprise, by the following August he had collected and enlisted between four and five hundred men, and prospects appeared so flattering, that in a few months longer he thought he would be able to report his thousand men ready for service. All this, however, was too significant a fact in that part of Tennessee, long to remain a secret from the rebel authorities; consequently, soon being fully advised of the nature and extent of his operations in Scott county, these authorities determined on one more effort to secure this ubiquitous and troublesome enemy. Eighteen hundred cavalry were dispatched from Knoxville for that purpose. Just previous to this, however, Col. Clift's superiors, aware that his position was too advanced for safety, ordered him to retire to some point within or near our lines. Either for want of time, between the arrival of the order and the arrival of the rebels, to call in his men, who were scattered over the country recruiting, or from his unconquerable desire to fight the rebels at every opportunity, this command was not obeyed; and on the 9th of August he found himself attacked by this rebel cavalry from Knoxville. Many of his men were out recruiting at the time, his Lieutenant-Colonel, Alex. Hoagland, an Indianian, from Lafayette, being engaged on the day of the attack in delivering a speech to a crowd in the vicinity, endeavoring to persuade the young men to enlist; so that not more than one hundred and fifty or two hundred men were left with Clift in the fort at the time to resist eighteen hundred rebels.

Having an advantageous position, and his men protected by breast-works, with an obstinacy characteristic of the man, he defended himself for an hour and a half against eight or ten times his own numbers; and fortunately without having any of his men either killed or wounded. An attempt of the rebels to gain his rear compelled him finally to retire, which he did in time to escape with his entire immediate command to the adjacent mountain, overlooking the Sequatchee valley, a retreat inaccessible to the rebel cavalry. A moderate stock of supplies, with a box or two of army muskets, fell into the enemy's hands. Twelve of Clift's men—of those absent when the attack was made—were the next day picked up by the rebels, and were taken to Knoxville as prisoners.

Some time after the battle the rebels published their

loss in the Knoxville *Register*, stating that it was from fourteen to sixteen killed and wounded.

After this affair, Col. Clift personally adhered to his purpose of recruiting in that part of Tennessee; but it was thought best for his men to join the nearest Federal army. Accordingly, under the command of Lieut.-Col. Hoagland, all that could be collected started to join Gen. Morgan at Cumberland Gap, a distance of about seventy-five miles. After being out several days, and when within two miles of Barbersville, Ky., to their mortification they were informed that Gen. Kirby Smith with his army was then passing through Barbersville, on his way to invade that State. This rendered it impossible for them to proceed, while it was unsafe for them to remain where they were; consequently, the only alternative appeared to be to retrace their steps with a view to join Gen. Thomas at McMinnville, in Middle Tennessee, a point much further from their late battle-field than they had already traveled, and exactly in the opposite direction. It was nearly a hopeless task; but they undertook it as cheerfully as possible, and a few days brought them back to their old fort and battle-field in Scott county, which they passed, taking the crest of the mountain range, and after many more days of hardship and weary traveling they began to descend the western slope towards McMinnville. Gaining the foot of the mountain, and hopefully proceeding to within seven miles of that town, all at once their joy was turned into sorrow by the discovery that Gen. Bragg's army was then passing between them and McMinnville, also on its way to Kentucky, to act in conjunction with Kirby Smith, from whom they had just fled at Barbersville. So anxious were they, however, to join General Thomas, that, in their efforts to do so, Col. Hoagland was captured. After this loss, it was decided that before they could possibly cross Bragg's trail it would be too late to reach Gen. Thomas. They were now being left in the rear of both rebel armies, and of course would be exposed to the guerrillas and bushwhackers who would infest the country; and, as joining Gen. Thomas was impracticable if not impossible, they determined once more to retrace their steps and make another effort to join Gen. Morgan at Cumberland Gap. Accordingly, after ranging the Cumberland mountains the third time, having in all traveled a distance of three hundred and fifty miles, they finally reached the Gap in safety, but one day, however, before it was evacuated by Gen. Morgan. Though completely worn down and debilitated, they were compelled to accompany Gen. Morgan in his march to Ohio; where, as a regiment, they were left at Gallipolis. Here they were joined by Lieut.-Col. Hoagland, who had, in the meantime, been exchanged. Remaining at Gallipolis two months, they were ordered to Lebanon, Ky., where they were joined by Col. Clift himself, who, since his battle at Huntsville to this time, had been recruiting for his regiment in that vicinity.

Col. Clift's regiment was the 7th Tennessee Infantry. At this place, Lebanon, his was consolidated with the 8th Tennessee, commanded by Col. F. A. Reves; after which, the two thus merged were known as the 8th Tennessee. What position or rank in the Eighth after this change, was held by Col. Clift, or how long after this he remained in the service, we are not informed. This change was made December 13th, 1861.

Before bidding adieu entirely to the subject of this famous Clift War, a remark should be devoted to the character of Col. Clift himself. The worst thing that can be said of him as a military man is, that he was not a strategic general. Mathematical military strategy was altogether too slow a process for the enthusiasm of the Colonel's nature. He promptly reduced one of his officers for manifesting cowardice at the approach of the rebel cavalry at Huntsville. Fear, or cowardice, was a visitor whose disgusting form never crossed the threshhold of his patriotic spirit, or even crouched, so far as he was concerned, in the vicinity of his camp. To "*find the enemy*," or, "*let them come*" were his principle and most inspiring themes —subjects to which every thing else was only auxilliary. Long and tedious campaigns with no results but the wasting of an army his righteous soul abhorred. With him, fighting was the principle argument to be used against the rebellion; and as soon as an enemy could be reached his daring and fiery spirit cried for a hand to hand encounter, relying upon the justice of his cause, cold steel, grit and gunpowder, to give him the victory.

As a patriot, a soldier, a politician, or a public man in any sense, more moral principle reddened under his little finger nail than ever volunteered to aid the rebellion during the war. To some, this may appear like a sensational remark, but such is not the case. It is but the utterance of an incontrovertible truth. Doubtless many persons inately possessed of moral principle, but vitiated by education and contact with error, perhaps through life, espoused the rebellion; but not an individual upon the green earth naturally disposed to be just to all men, and uncorrupted by association, ever *volunteered* in its aid. Justice never dictated to any mind that the rebellion was right. When we, therefore, state, that Col. Clift was the embodiment of more moral principle than the whole rebellion could honestly claim, the assertion does not transcend the limits of historical truth.

CHAPTER VIII.

CAPTAIN WM. L. BROWN AND THE FIFTH DISTRICT ELECTION.

WE return now to the history of the rebellion as it progressed and subsequently existed in Bradley county.

After the rebel forces which had attempted to capture Col. Clift on Sails Creek, had returned to their respective vicinities, their organizations, generally, were not only preserved intact, but rebel military rule from that time, especially, was instituted in a manner plainly to indicate the fate of those who dared to oppose, as well as of those who failed to comply with rebel demands.

Two rebel regiments were raised in Bradley and adjoining counties, both, we believe, going into camp on Bradley county fair grounds, there to remain while recruiting and fitting out, grounds about a mile from the village of Cleveland. One of these regiments was the 4th Tennessee Cavalry, the other the 36th Tennessee Infantry. The infantry regiment, from the fact that it was armed principally with squirrel rifles and double barrel shotguns, many of which were forcibly taken from Union citizens, was by way of jest denominated the *squirrel brigade*. After its completion this regiment was ordered into the vicinity of Knoxville. The cavalry regiment, which was under the command of Col. Rogers of Bradley county, was finally ordered to Knoxville also.

The following from the Cleveland *Banner* of November 15th, 1861, shows about the time this cavalry regiment went into camp for recruiting.

"MILITARY CAMP—Cleveland has been made a military camp, and Wm. H. Tibbs has been appointed commissary. Captains McClary and Brown's cavalry companies have gone into camps."

We know not that these companies were the very first that occupied the fair grounds, but probably they were among the first. This cavalry regiment left for Knoxville toward the last of January, 1862, being in camp at Cleveland about three months: this being the period in which the reign of rebel terror in that section rose to its zenith.

In entering fully upon the history of the rebellion in Bradley, we propose to introduce and briefly sketch, the character of one of the most prominent actors in the drama, Capt. Wm. L. Brown, one of the officers mentioned in the above extract; but more commonly known as Capt. Bill Brown of Bradley.

Unquestionably, this Capt. Brown was one of the most notorious characters, in many respects, of all the rebel leaders that figured in East Tennessee. Being admirably fitted by nature to execute the dirty work planned by others, with this ability made constantly restive by a natural feeling of great self-importance, he was, of all others, the most blustering, insulting, and overbearing, the most reliable to be entrusted with the meanest and most disgraceful enterprizes. He was a natural liar, as well as a natural thief, and so far as moral forecast is concerned, the next thing to a natural fool; religiously as well as otherwise a practical hypocrite, a base tyrant and a vile deceiver. Altogether, his composition, as a human being, was such, that his greatest earthly happiness flowed from the privilege of being a dictatorial or governing spirit in the midst of just such a rebellion, as that in which he acted so conspicuous and disgraceful a part. Never was he so deliriously happy; never so emphatically in a world of ecstacy, as when in Bradley county, swaggering in all the license and riot of his commission, he displayed himself as Capt. Brown of the rebel army.

At the opening of the rebellion, Brown perhaps was forty years of age, had been a resident of the county from an early period, was a member of the Cumberland Presbyterian Church, by trade a tailor, having followed the business of this craft for a number of years in Cleveland, but never, it appears, relied upon it as the permanent business of his life. His first surplus funds, instead of being invested   the enlargement and permanency of of his business, were prostituted to the work of shaving notes, and being invested in loans at high rates of usury, and in otherwise taking advantage of the unfortunate, by which means, he soon won the name of being one of the most hard-hearted money dealers and swindling speculators in the country.

As a solitary instance among many that might be given of Browns innate villiany, we noted down from the recital of one of the most prominent citizens of Cleveland, the following case.

Mr. ———, a man well known in Bradley, and who by many readers in the county will be instantly called to mind as the person referred to, had failed, by the regular proceeds of his industry, to procure means for the liquidation of a debt, which was of the utmost importance to him to pay at the appointed time. Money matters were close, and being unsuccessful in his first efforts to borrow the amount, as a last resort he applied to Brown. Brown pretended to be out of money, whined about his own poverty, complained of the hard times, scolded about dilatory creditors, etc., but told him to call again in a short time, and he would give him an answer. Agreeably to appointment the man waited upon Brown the second time. Brown informed him that times were so hard that he had no money to loan, and that if he had obligations on the best of men, he could take them only at such and such discounts. The terms amounted to a swindle, but the man was compelled to have the money or suffer infinitely more, and consequently he submitted to Brown's proposals. Brown took the notes, counted out the man a part of the money, saying that was all he had with him at the time, but the rest should be forthcoming without fail before he would need it. Having not the least idea that Brown, by this maneuver, intended to swindle him, and knowing that he was able at any time to get the remainder, made no particular objections. The next day, however, or as soon as the time drew near, that the whole amount coming from Brown should be in his possession, the man called to procure it; but to his astonishment Brown was perfectly unapproachable on the subjet, coldly and indifferently pretending that he had been disappointed in collecting; and that he could do nothing more about it at present. The man enquired what he meant by such conduct, and if he considered the extent of the injury he was inflicting upon him by such a rascally forfeiture of his word. Notwithstanding these appeals, Brown gave his victim no satisfaction; but left him to extricate himself from the dilemma into which he had led him as best he could. This, however, was not the sequel of the transaction. The injured man, as a matter of course prosecuted Brown for the debt, and for aught we know for his villainy also: but one way and another Brown staved off the issue, evading the action of the law, and keeping Mr. ——— out of the residue of his money, till long after the notes he delivered to Brown had matured, and Brown had collected on them both principal and interest.

Taking this transaction as a basis of Brown's moral character as a private citizen before the war, none will be greatly surprised at the following developements in this chapter in regard to his conduct as a public man and a civil officer, nor at the future developments in this work of his character as a soldier and a rebel officer.

THE FIFTH DISTRICT ELECTION.

Although it will place us for the time in advance of some parts of our narrative, yet as we have been sketching Capt. Brown's private character, that the reader may without too much surprise meet the facts in the history of his military career; and as this election illustrates Brown as a public man, also as a civil officer, and as it reveals the animus of the rebellion in this section at the time, we shall introduce it here.

As already stated, Brown entered the rebel service in the fall of 1861. His military career was short. In June, 1862, he resigned his commission, becoming once more a private citizen, and residing upon his farm with his family in the fifth district, about three miles from Cleveland.

Early in the spring of 1863 an election was to take place in that district, at which, among other officers, a Justice of the Peace was to be chosen. Brown was the rebel candidate for this office against Mr. Hiram Smith of the Union party. The Union party in this district, as well perhaps as in others at this time, was considerably in the ascendancy; and a fair trial at this election could have resulted only in the success of the Union candidate. Being aware of this, in conformity with the general character of the rebellion, Brown and his friends must make preparations to counteract this Union advantage. At this time the whole of East Tennessee was writhing in the jaws of a rebel military despotism, by the aid of which power it was easy for rebel citizens to control elections as well as all other matters throughout the country.

Mr. James Donahoo, one of the most bitter and relentless rebels in the district, working in the interest of Brown, managed to get himself appointed by the Sheriff of the county as President or Conductor of this election. The duties of this officer are to open and close the polls at the proper hours, to see that the balloting is legal, and that the election throughout is held strictly in accordance with law and in a manner to preserve inviolate to all parties the right of the elective franchise. Utterly ignoring these obligations, however, Donahoo, after procuring his appointment, connived with the rebel military authorities at Cleveland, stealthily effecting an arrangement, perhaps the day before the election, that all under the age of forty-five who appeared at the polls must have permits from the Provost Marshal to do so. Then, as a clincher to this, news of this arrangement was to be immediately circulated among the rebels, that Brown's friends could have ample time to get their permits; but kept a profound secret from the Union men till the moment of the opening of the polls. The election was at the Blue Springs school house, just five miles from Cleveland.

Brown and Donahoo were old and crafty performers in the work of rebellion, and in this particular case engineered their scheme through with so much stealth and skill that it succeeded entirely to their own wishes, allowing them to have entirely their own way at the polls, whisky and all. Every rebel voter perhaps in the district having been secretly posted in regard to the treacherous game, was promptly at the polls with his permit concealed in his pocket, ready to fulfill the farcical obligation of being there by military authority. In regard to the Union voters, however, just the contrary was their condition. Not a Union voter in the district knew that it was his duty to obtain a permit to attend the election till the balloting commenced. To spring this villainous trap, however, with additional certainty, Donahoo, although sworn to open the polls at nine o'clock in the morning, delayed to do so, purposely dallying away time, till between eleven and twelve in the day. Some Union men present asserted that it was even after this time when the polls were opened. This put it beyond the power of the Union voters to comply with Mr. Donahoo's military regulation. Not one in ten, unprepared as they were with animals, at that late hour could reach Cleveland, a distance of five miles, obtain his permit, and return in time to vote.

By the success, therefore, of this infernal scheme, every Union man in the district under the age of forty-five was debarred from voting, for Mr. Donahoo refused to allow any of them even to approach the polls for the want of these permits, having in the meantime brought with him a guard of six rebel soldiers whom he had already stationed at the door to enforce these abominable regulations. As a matter of course the Union voters were indignant at such treatment, some of whom expostulated with Mr. Donahoo and Capt. Brown, asserting that this regulation should have been published to all the day before, that they as well as the rebels could have been prepared. These expostulations, however, were met by these men with all that insolence and positive abuse that one would expect from those endeavoring to carry an election by such measures.

A part of these Union voters, compelled to do so by the rebel authorities, were then at work, not as soldiers, but simply as employees of the Confederate government, on the railroads, getting timber, procuring wood, etc., all of them, we believe, within the District; and Mr. Donahoo in answer to their complaints replied, that having left their work to attend that election without permits, they were all deserters, rebel deserters, and ought to be reported and arrested as such.

Most of these Union employees were at work near the polls, a quarter and a half mile from them, and had they all been permitted to vote, as they had a right to do, could have done so with the loss of but very little time, without going out of the District. Many of them would have voted during the hour of recess at noon, without being absent from their work at all. Besides, doubtless, none of the men did leave their work without the consent of their gang boss, hence their absence was no injury to his business. Yet, notwithstanding these palliating circumstances, Mr. Donahoo calls these men deserters, simply because they were there without permits. Inasmuch then, as this was Mr. Donahoo's own position, voluntarily taken, he cannot object to having his own conduct brought forward and put to the test by it. No man can complain when he and his theories are tried by rules which he has made himself.

Now, if these men were deserters, because without permits they left their work to attend this election, then by the same rule, they would have been deserters, had they left their work and gone five miles to Cleveland to get the permits he required of them. And not only so, but the latter would have been a much stronger case of desertion than the former. In this case some of the men—those whose work was a mile or two south of the school house—would have been compelled to travel from five to seven miles to Cleveland, entirely out of the district, and back, being absent from their work perhaps the whole day, while, as we have seen, in the first instance, none of them had to go out of the district. Many of them had to walk but a short distance, necessarily being absent from their work but a few minutes. Some of these men were but a few yards from their work when Donahoo was accusing them of desertion. According to Mr. Donahoo's own interpretation of desertion, therefore, it was impossible for these Union voters to comply with his regulation, not only without being guilty of desertion simply, but without being guilty of it in a much more aggravated sense, than they were in coming to the election as they did. Even Mr. Hiram Smith himself, Brown's opponent, had he at the time been an employee of the Confederate government, could not have attended that election and cast a vote for himself without first being guilty of desertion, and laying himself liable to be arrested and tried for the crime. Had these Union voters by some accident discovered Mr. Donahoo's military clap-trap in time, and early on the morning of the election, left their work and hurried to Cleveland for their permits, very likely Donahoo or Brown, or both, would have met them at the Provost Marshal's and had them all arrested and punished for desertion. According to Donahoo's own theory, he could have done so. The management of this election, therefore, was such as to drive a portion of the Union voters of the district, effectually from the polls, or drive them into desertion, and consequently to subject them to arrest and punishment by the rebel authorities. There is no escape from this conclusion. All the rebels in Bradley county, with the sophistical editor of the *Banner* thrown in, can never extricate these men from this humiliating and disgraceful dilemma. Little did Donahoo, Brown and Shugart, think at the time, that their villainy was thus preparing a hook to be put into their own jaws, and by which they were to be historically drawn up and left exposed and helplessly dangling before the whole country, a disgrace to themselves and their posterity, while their names are known in Bradley county.

The above, however, is not the whole of the rebel history of this election. Major D. G. McCulley, a Union man of the district, and living near the polls, was, as a mere pretense to fairness, put on the bench as one of the judges, Dr. Shugart also of the district, and a Mr. Reed of Georgia, both relentless rebels, being the other two. At the discovery of Mr. Donahoo's military valve for shutting off Union votes, Major McCulley promptly entered his protest against it, and as other abuses and violations of law developed themselves through the day, raised his voice against them, also. At the closing of the polls, he told Mr. Donahoo and the other judges that Union men had been prevented from voting by intrigue and the presence of rebel bayonets; that as they had conducted the election, throughout, it was not only illegal but a positive fraud; that consequently, he should not sign the scrolls, but, as one of the judges, send up his protest against the whole affair. Donahoo and the other judges attempted to win him over but without effect; and after exhausting their powers of persuasion their patience gave way, and threats were employed instead. He was told that if he did not sign the scrolls he would be arrested by the military. One of Donahoo's guards, one that had indulged too freely in artificial stimulants to his patriotism, also was allowed to abuse the Major as a Lincolnite, a traitor, a tory, and so on. He swore that he would sooner run his bayonet through him than to do anything else. The Major, however, was not more easily frightened at their threats, than cajoled by their importunities, persisting in his refusal to append his name to the scrolls; and the returns went up under his protest as one of the judges of the election.

In justice it should be stated here, that two others of this guard, while this contest was going on, interfered in Major McCully's behalf, rebuking the drunken guard for the abuse he was heaping upon him, and saying that the Major had as good a right to his opinion as the other judges had to theirs; that he had a right to express his opinion, that as to the election, they believed the Major was right in holding that the election had not been fair, and that they were sorry it had been necessary for them to have anything to do with it.

Under the circumstances, only six Union votes were cast, and only sixteen rebel votes, notwithstanding an unusual effort was put forth by the rebels to get their friends to the polls. By actual count, at the time, of the Union voters in the district, it was demonstrated that had the election been legal, the Union majority would at least have been two to one.

Mr. Hiram Smith, Brown's opponent, discovering early in the day the intervention and proscription inaugurated, and so insolently enforced by Donahoo, considering himself insulted as well as disgraced by such company, immediately left the polls in disgust, advising his friends to do so also, and save themselves the shame of attending such a farce. In fact Mr. Smith objected in the beginning to having his name announced as a candidate in opposition to such a man as Wm. L. Brown.

One would suppose that the foregoing combination of disgraceful means would have been thought sufficient by these rebels, not only to carry this election, but as comprising all the corruption and wickedness that one occasion of the kind ought to bear. The fact, however, was otherwise. Even the exhilarating effects of whisky, as well as the temptings of bribery were added to complete the list of abominations with which these rebels were polluting the polls of the fifth district.

Early in the day, Brown procured of Mr. Joseph Henderson, then manufacturing liquor not far from the polls, a quantity of the needful article, which was slyly, though liberally distributed by Brown to all that would accept of it, at the election, to induce them to vote for him, and to prepare them to more effectively electioneer in his favor. The first supply being soon exhausted, Brown arranged with Mr. Henderson to furnish the article through the day as it was needed. The contract was faithfully kept by Mr. Henderson till the closing of the polls, Brown's money footing the bills. In addition to this contemptible business, Brown offered this same Mr. Henderson a bribe of five dollars for his ballot. Mr. Henderson was a Union man, and Brown's offer was indignantly refused. No ways abashed at this, Brown instantly raised his bid to twenty-five dollars, providing Mr. Henderson would, besides giving him his own vote, interest himself and secure him the votes of certain other parties. This proposal, however, was as quickly rejected as the other.

The polls being finally closed, Brown was declared elected; and although the returns went up under the protest of Major McCulley as heretofore given, yet this proved no impediment to Brown's claim, not even eliciting the least inquiry, or causing the least hesitation. His name was immediately forwarded to Governor Harris as the legally elected candidate, and forthwith his credentials were returned installing him as the lawfully elected and authoritative justice of the peace in the fifth district. He held and exercised his office until he fled before our army to Dixie in the winter 1864.

ARREST OF MR. SAMUEL WYRICK.

We will now follow Capt. Brown for a moment as a civil officer, and view the harmony that existed between the means by which he obtained his office and the manner in which he subsequently distributed its justice to the people. Having opened his office for business in Cleveland, soon after he obtained his commission from the supreme authority of the State, Brown ascertained through some of his rebel advisers, or through some of his rebel spies, that Mr. Samuel Wyrick of the ninth district, a Union man, had purchased for a sick woman, the wife of a Union soldier then in the Northern Army, a quart of spirits as a medicine. Brown kept the matter quiet, but watched his opportunity to ensnare Mr. Wyrick, remembering, perhaps, the amount of whisky fees it had cost him to obtain his *sacred* office. In a few days the opportunity presented itself, when Brown issued a process against Mr. Wyrick, and had him arrested and brought to trial for the offence of buying spirits for a sick woman. The process was founded upon some temporary regulation established by the rebel military authorities, either as a specific tax on sales and purchases, or as a prohibitory regulation in regard to the sale of spirits in the country. Mr. Wyrick acknowledged that he purchased the liquor, but explained that it was for another person who was actually in want of it as a medicine, and that he was ignorant at the time, that in such a case he was violating any law, or that any tax was imposed on such purchases, saying, that if he had violated any law, he was ready to make restitution to any proper extent. Brown, however, was in no mood for compromises, or for yielding a particle of the advantage in his hands, and at once fixed the penalty to the extreme end of the law, mulcting Mr. Wyrick in a fine with costs, amounting to $106, which had to be paid forthwith. Mr. Wyrick not having that amount in his pocket at the moment, Brown seized upon a quantity of goods in his possession, which he had just purchased in Cleveland, principally for other parties, and for which he had paid $140 in cash. In addition to this, Brown attempted to levy upon the horse which Mr. Wyrick rode into town, but Union friends smuggled the animal out of his reach until Mr. Wyrick finally escaped with him to his home, some eight miles from Cleveland, where he had to settle with his neighbors for his loss of their goods as best he could.

Thus was Mr. Wyrick robbed by this infernal brute, and that upon the hypocritical pretence only, that he had violated a law which the wretch, but a short time before, had so shamefully violated himself in order to obtain the office, by the authority of which he now prosecuted and fined Mr. Wyrick. The facts of this transaction were furnished by Mr. Wyrick himself, and may therefore be relied upon. They will not be doubted by those who know Mr. Wyrick. All the information in regard to the election narrated in this chapter, was furnished by the most reliable Union men in the fifth district, and although in some instances we may have used strong language—for none other is suitable in describing such abuses, yet it is believed, that as a general description the abuses of this case have not been exaggerated, and that Union men who were present, and saw for themselves all the facts, will testify to the general truthfulness of the statements here given.

In fact this account is not the aggregate of the villainy and demonstrations of treason connected with this affair. Dr. Shugart in particular, at this election, availed himself of the opportunity to falsify and berate the Government, stating in substance that the Government had become an engine of oppression, persecuting and grinding the Southern States generally; that in view of the prohibitory enactments of Congress in regard to the institution of slavery, the Union ought to have been overthrown and completely demolished twenty years before, etc.

Such delineations of the separate, distinct rebel crimes and abuses in the South are tedious and laborious. They require great patience and industry in the collection as well as in the arrangement of the facts, but we deem them of the utmost importance, for nothing else will save to history, or place before the country in its true light, the studied wickedness and unrelieved depravity of the rebellion.

CHAPTER IX.

UNION PEOPLE OF BRADLEY ROBBED OF THEIR PRIVATE ARMS.

INTRODUCTORY to this chapter we will give an extract from the Cleveland *Banner*, taken from an issue dated July 19, 1861. The extract closes with a sentence of editorial advice which we take the liberty to put in italics. Unquestionably this editorial was the first instance in which the idea of robbing the Union people of Bradley of their private arms, was thrown, broadcast, before the rebel masses of East Tennessee. The extract is as follows:

"A MOVE IN THE RIGHT DIRECTION.—Gov. Pettus, of Mississippi has issued a proclamation calling on the State and county officers to collect up all the arms, rifles and shot guns new or old, in or out of order, and send them to Jackson, the capital of the State, where they may be repaired and held in readiness for the use of the soldiers. He also notifies all citizens to arm themselves with double-barrel shot guns, and hold themselves in readiness at an hour's notice. By these means the State will be in possession of a large quantity of good arms that might otherwise be useless. *We hope the proper authorities will follow up the more of Gov. Pettus.*"

We are not in possession of the exact date at which this "move in the right direction" commenced in Bradley; but from other dates in our possession of the times at which individuals had their guns taken from them by Brown and his men, it appears that the movement was in progress in September, 1861. The work was continued through the following winter, or as long as rebel soldiers could find Union guns to confiscate.

In gathering in these guns, as in every other rebel enterprise within the county, Capt. Brown and his men were the most conspicuous. In many instances Brown issued orders for these arms to be brought into camp by their owners; and in some cases this was done, the owners hoping by a ready compliance to have their property returned, or to receive its value at some future day. Most of the Union guns, however, collected by the rebels in

Bradley were forcibly taken by Brown, or at his instance, his men being sent through the county in squads for this purpose. Everything in the shape of a fire-arm, from the finished rifle to the most insignificant revolver or pocket-pistol, was taken from Union men in this scheme of rebel plundering. Everything in the shape of weapons were taken — old sabres, bowie-knives, and even common butcher-knives were taken. Hundreds of these arms were no better than elder pop-guns for military purposes —were never used by the rebels as such—but were wasted and wantonly appropriated to the amusement and gratification of those whose reckless villainy had made this property an object of plunder.

From the most reliable information on this subject, it appears that at least one thousand arms, of all grades, were taken from the Union people in Bradley in this abominable raid upon personal rights. We make this statement, feeling confident that many Union men in the county, who were in a position to judge, will regard this estimate as below the actual figures. We are aware that rebels will argue that these guns were collected in obedience to an order issued by Gov. Harris. This excuse was made by the rebels when they were engaged in the robbery. It was made by Brown himself to Mrs. Harle, of Cleveland, just before his attempt to murder her husband, an account of which affair will be found in the latter part of this chapter.

Fortunately we are able to produce the order from Gov. Harris under the authority of which this master-piece of rebel iniquity was perpetrated upon the Union people of Bradley. It reads as follows :

" To the Clerks of the County Courts of the State of Tennessee :

" You are hereby requested to issue to each constable in your respective counties an order requiring them to make diligent inquiry at each house in his civil district for muskets, bayonets, rifles, swords, and pistols *belonging to the State of Tennessee,* to take them into possession and deliver them to you. A reward of one dollar will be paid to the constable for each musket and bayonet, or rifle, and fifty cents for each sword or pistol thus *reclaimed.* You will forward the arms thus obtained, at public expense to the military authorities at Knoxville, Nashville, or Memphis, as may be most convenient; and will inform the Military and Financial Boards by letter addressed to them at Nashville, of the result of your action and the expenses incurred. A check for the amount will be promptly forwarded. It is hoped that every officer will exert himself to have this order promptly executed. "ISHAM G. HARRIS,

"*Governor of Tennessee.*

"Nashville, Aug. 10, 1861."

Now, whatever might have been the concealed purpose of Gov. Harris in the premises, this order sufficiently explains itself. It instructs the clerks of the county courts, and the county constables, and these officers only, to execute its requirements. Besides, the "*muskets, bayonets, rifles, &c., belonging to the State of Tennessee*" were those to be taken, not those that were the private property of individuals. These constables were to be paid for all the arms "*belonging to the State*" that they could thus "*reclaim,*" not for all that they could *steal* and press from the Union people throughout Tennessee. It is incontrovertible that this order was no license whatever for these constables, or the rebel military, or any other class of men or officers to touch private property. Arms, for instance, that individuals, who were or had been members of independent companies, had drawn from the State, and had not been returned, were those, and those only, that this order, ostensibly, at least, contemplated procuring. How disgusting the predicament, therefore, in which the very face of this order places the rebel officials and rebel military, not only of Bradley, but of other parts of the State. The order not only had no reference to the military whatever, and conferred upon it no authority in the case, but particularly, in form at least, it did not dictate the favoritism and the cruelties practiced by the rebels under it in Bradley county. Capt. Brown and his men pretended that this order made it their duty to collect in all the surplus or useless arms in the county, both such as were "*in*" and such as were "*out of order,*" for the benefit of the rebel army. If so, why then did not they proceed to do it justly, civilly, and in a proper manner, as obeying an important order from the highest authority in the State? Why did they in tumultuous gangs, with

Capt. Brown in their lead, rave through the country like so many Devils, ruthlessly seizing upon all the Union arms, leaving unmolested at the same time every rebel family in the county? If this order made it the duty of the rebel military to collect up all the arms in the whole country, irrespective of parties, why did they utterly neglect it in respect to one party, and drive its fulfillment beyond all decency in regard to another? Not one in a hundred of that immense collection of guns thus brought and piled up in Cleveland, were forcibly taken from rebel owners. Some few rebels, possibly, volunteered to give some of their arms, always, however, reserving enough for themselves; while many, perhaps, put them into the hands of their sons when they sent them to the rebel ranks. But in every instance, rebel families, known to be such, and who thought they needed their guns to shoot Lincolnites, and to aid the rebel military in catching conscripts, were allowed to keep them. Not an instance occurred, perhaps, in the whole county, in which a rebel family donated all its arms, or was required by the rebel military to do so; while, on the other hand, Union families were completely stripped.

But more than this, we were credibly informed that, in some instances, arms were taken from Union families and given to rebel families, who in this respect were destitute. The pretext was to procure arms for rebel soldiers; but the *real* design in Bradley was to disarm and render helpless Union citizens, and arm the whole rebel element, citizen as well as soldier. This is precisely what was accomplished by this rebel raid upon Union people, or, as the rebel editor styles it, "A move in the right direction."

With the utmost propriety, as a rebel, could the Cleveland editor, in speaking of this as an enterprise in the interest of the rebellion, announce it as "A move in the right direction." This Slaveholders' Rebellion, in view of the great light and great blessings bestowed upon us as a people, was the greatest crime ever perpetrated on the earth. It was an aspiration of half the nation, fanned into a white heat of Satanic frenzy, to culminate in every abomination and wickedness for which God ever punished angels or men. The means it used and all the ends it proposed were degrees of wrong and human violence which in their collidings with the justice of Omnipotence, ultimately would have extinguished the race. Most emphatically this rebel plundering of Union arms in Bradley was a fit means to promote such an end. It was attended with all the violence, murder and reeking oppression requisite to make its completion no mean stride in the direction of such an end—an end installing these curses as laws of society and rules of human life. With great propriety, therefore, in this sense, but in this sense only, could this editor announce it as "A move in the right direction." Wrong was the rule of the rebellion, both as to its means and its end. Wrong permanently triumphant was the great end proposed. This rebel enterprise in Bradley was violence itself, and fraught with incalculable wrong —consistent with the end proposed—consequently, to the rebels was "A move in the right direction." Had this Cleveland editor rounded out his announcement to include the end as well as the means, it would have had more philosophic completeness, and might with its emphatic truthfulness in this case, have been enlarged as follows: This rebel raid upon Union families in Bradley was one of the moves in the right direction to ruin the American people, insult God, and curse the world throughout time.

This rebel editor might not have seen nor felt the subject exactly in this light, yet this is the exact philosophy of his remark above considered.

If any of the rebels in Bradley take the position, or in other words shift their position, and argue that, while this order purported the arms only belonging to the State, it nevertheless had a secret design through the military to reach the private arms of the Union people also; thus, with a view to strengthen the rebellion, proposing completely to disarm the loyal people of the State—just what it accomplished in Bradley,—yet this by no means relieves them from "guilt" and "shame" in the transaction. Although this position may be nearer the truth than the other—for we believe that this order was in reality designed by Gov. Harris as an instrument of cruelty against the Union people of East Tennessee—it does not at all relieve these Bradley rebels, but brings down Gov. Harris to a level with themselves, and equally criminates him with them in this infamous and hypocritical piece of business.

We will close our history of this affair with an account of Capt. Brown's assault upon the family of Mr. Baldwin Harle, of Cleveland, ostensibly to carry out the provisions of this order from Gov. Harris. The following statements of the case are from Mr. and Mrs. Harle and their two sons, the most of which are given in their own language.

About the 15th of October, 1861, Thomas Hawkins, who had, when a boy, lived with Mr. Harle, came to his house with nine other armed rebel soldiers. Hawkins was met at the door by Mrs. Harle, when he enquired if Mr. Harle or the boys had two guns in their possession. "Well, what if we have?" was Mrs. Harle's reply. "I must have them," he returned. "You shall not have them if I can help it," was her rejoinder. Hawkins then ordered his men to enter the house and take the guns, attempting at the same time to force his way by Mrs. Harle into the house, she, however, preventing him by maintaining her position at the door. At this juncture, Joseph Harle, a son, being in some part of the building, and attracted through a back door to the spot by the disturbance, standing near his mother, told Hawkins that if he came in he should shoot him. At this Hawkins and his men desisted, held a short parley among themselves, and left the premises.

In a short time Hawkins re-appeared, with about sixty men; the company was led this time by Capt. Brown himself. Brown and his men immediately forced their way into the house, he very abruptly demanding the two guns of Mrs. Harle, saying at the same time that Gov. Harris had ordered all the guns in the country to be taken, and that his men needed them as they were going to capture old Clift, then fortifying on the Tennessee river. Mrs. Harle replied, "Well, if it is right for you to have the guns, then I suppose you can take them." Mr. Harle, absent until then, approaching and hearing his wife's remark, continued by saying, "Well you shall not have the guns by *my* consent," emphasizing the pronoun my in a way to give Brown the idea, that although his wife had given her consent, and although he presumed that his force would enable him to take the guns, yet he would have to take them against his consent.

At this, Brown immediately raised and leveled his gun to shoot, or as though he would shoot Mr. Harle. Mr. Harle, however, quickly caught the muzzle of Brown's gun, and held it to one side. Brown soon got his gun at liberty, drew back, and taking deliberate aim at Mr. Harle's breast, pulled the trigger, but the cap bursted without discharging the piece. Seeing himself thus foiled, Brown instantly raised his gun, and with it struck Mr. Harle, apparently with all the force that anger could summons, dealing him a blow across the forehead which opened the flesh to the skull, knocking him against the side of the house, which together with being caught by Mrs. Harle, prevented him from sinking entirely to the floor. While he was in this position, if possible, with more fury than before, Brown raised his gun and the second time struck at the senseless and bleeding head of Mr. Harle. But Mrs. Harle throwing herself before her husband, received the blow upon her arm and shoulder, from the effects of which she will probably never entirely recover. Notwithstanding this injury, Mrs. Harle, with what remaining strength she had, continued to protect and defend her husband shrieking for help, and crying for Brown to desist.

By this time, Joseph Harle had come to his mother's assistance, and also plead with Brown to refrain, saying "You have already killed my father, and is not that enough?" At this remark from Joseph, Brown's rage was transferred to him, Brown asking him in a vociferous manner, if he "had come to take it up?" Joseph promptly replied that he had. Some of Brown's men then near, hearing this, leveled their guns at Joseph, threatening to shoot him for interfering with Brown. Mrs. Harle, yet holding her husband, covered with blood, implored them to put down their guns, saying, " You see that Brown has killed his father, don't take his life also.

At this moment, a younger son, compelled by Brown's men, or acting on his own judgment, thinking it best to deliver up the guns, as soon as possible, was bringing them through the door of a small out-house, a few steps to the rear of the main building, and handing them to the men. Brown seeing this said, " Well men, we've got the guns, let's go." And this murderous brute, with his equally murderous gang of rebel villains left the premises, gloating over their savage and bloody victory.

Mr. Harle's dwelling stands upon the west side of a north and south street, in the village of Cleveland, and of course fronts to the east. At the commencement of this outrage, while most of Brown's men were surrounding the house and ransacking the premises, Brown and a few of his body guards entered at the front or east door, into one of the front rooms, where he had his conversation with Mrs. Harle, and where, near a door of this room conducting into a porch attached to the rear of the main building, he met Mr. Harle. In Brown's assault upon the old gentleman, he forced him back through this door into this porch on the floor of which he was standing, when Brown knocked him against the side of the main building; and from which place he was taken up insensible, and apparently dying, by Mrs. Harle and her sons, after the rebels had disappeared. With careful watching and medical treatment, however, Mr. Harle revived, and finally recovered, at least so far as a man of his age can recover, from such an injury as he received.

Mr. and Mrs. Harle were perhaps, upwards of sixty years of age at the time, and were among the oldest and most respectable citizens of the place. Mr. Harle was a quiet, peaceable, inoffensive man, constitutionally the very reverse of that calculated to enrage or induce the assault of an enemy.

Notwithstanding this affair transpired in the very heart of Cleveland, and was known in less than an hour to the whole community, rebel and Union, yet no attention was paid to it by the rebel authorities. Nor was Brown called to an account for his conduct any more than if he had assaulted a lot of swine on the street. Mr. Harle and his family were "Lincolnites," and this was not only a bar to anything like an arrest or prosecution, but it was the reason that rebel praise, oftener than rebel censure was awarded to Brown for the brutality which he inflicted on them.

While this injured man was lingering upon his couch for weeks, in a critical condition, Brown was frequently seen galloping by his dwelling, not only at his case, but with greater self-complacency, more individual pomposity and insulting defiance, as he would look in the direction of his victims, than could have been put on, perhaps, by Jeff. Davis himself.

CHAPTER X.

MONEY EXTORTED FROM UNION PEOPLE, UNDER THE PRETENCE OF PROVIDING FOR THE FAMILIES OF REBEL SOLDIERS.

REBEL recruiting in Bradley and the adjoining counties had not progressed very far, before another subject of excitement arose, still better calculated, if possible, to enlist the activities of Capt. Brown, and call forth his peculiar talents, than the work of confiscating private Union arms. His avarice carried him beyond the seizure of mere property; and an excuse was soon found, connected with the subject of suffering rebel families, that enabled him to revel in the midst of huge piles of the people's money.

The rebel soldiers had left their homes, to meet the Northern invaders, and as a matter of course, some provision must be made for the support of their families during their absence. This necessity, whether real or apparent, was readily laid hold of by Capt. Brown, and made a pretence for inaugurating and carrying on, for weeks and months, one of the most audacious swindles, one of the most heartless systems of robbery that even the rebellion itself ever produced. This branch of business being added to Brown's general work of driving forward the rebel cause, he followed the promptings of his avarice, even at the expense of his Southern patriotism. He wanted rebel soldiers; he wanted obstinate Union men out of the country; but still more than either of these he wanted *money;* and these were the alternatives to which his victims were universally reduced—they must go into the rebel army, be sent to Tuscaloosa, or they must pay the price of exemption. Those who had the most money could generally settle with Brown, not only the easier for themselves, but the most satisfactory to him!

8

An instance that will illustrate the barbarous extreme to which Brown, in many cases, pushed this iniquitous business, was furnished by Mr. T. H. Calloway of Polk county, a gentleman well known in East Tennessee, and whose statements will not be questioned by those having the honor of his acquaintance.

The following letter is Mr. Calloway's account of the case referred to.

CLEVELAND, TENNESSEE. }
November 12th, 1865. }

J. S. Hurlbut, Esq., Michigan City, Ind.

DEAR SIR:—Your letter of the 1st inst., has just been received. The case you refer to was that of Jacob Hadrick, a man seventy-five years old. Capt. Wm. Brown had old Mr. Hadrick and his three sons arrested and taken to Cleveland under guard, in very cold weather, during the winter of 1861 and 1862. After keeping them under guard for several days, he released them, taking the old man's note or obligation for $50—to be paid in corn and pork. The old gentleman lived in my neighborhood, was a very poor but hard working Dutchman, who made his living by blacksmithing. I was from home when he was taken off. Just about the time he returned I came home, and going to his blacksmith shop, found him preparing to kill his hogs. They, however, were not fat enough to kill, and I asked him the meaning of his killing his hogs, when they were so poor, and he told me that he had bound himself to pay Capt. Brown $50 in pork and corn. I told the old man that he could not spare the hogs from his family, and must not send the meat to Brown. He persisted in saying that he must do so, as Brown had told him that if he did not, that he, Brown, would send him and his three sons to Tuscaloosa, during the war. I finally prevailed on the old man not to do so, promising to pay the money to Mr. Brown for him. But when I offered to pay Brown, I did it before a lot of rebel officers, publicly, and Brown refused to take the money, saying that his men had done wrong to exact such a thing from the old man.

I gave you a good many particulars in relation to Brown's acts when you were here, which I suppose you have. Old Mr. Hadrick died soon after.   Very Respectfully,

THOS. H. CALLOWAY.

Some months previous to writing the above letter, with other accounts of Brown's conduct, Mr. Calloway furnished more particular statements, verbally, of this case of Brown's brutality, and of the manner in which he played the hypocrite before his brother officers, in order to shield himself from their censure in regard to it. When approached by Mr. Calloway in the presence of these officers, on the subject of his treatment of Mr. Hadrick, Brown pretended ignorance, and consequently innocence in regard to the whole matter, charging the wrong entirely to his men. The letter itself, however, shows that Brown was the leading criminal in the case; and from Mr. Calloway's verbal statement, it appeared that Brown was perfectly acquainted with the destitute condition of Mr. Hadrick's family at the time; that he was present when, in obedience to his own personal order, Mr. Hadrick and his three sons were brought prisoners into the rebel camp. Mr. Calloway further stated that the old gentleman was also put into the guard house, and confined during these "several days" by Brown's personal supervision; and when he was released, the note of $50, which Brown exacted, was written with Brown's own hand, he threatening at the same time, as stated in the letter, that if the note was not paid the day it was due, he would send Mr. Hadrick and his three sons to Tuscaloosa during the war.

It was well known also, as confirmed by Mr. Calloway, that the guard-quarters in which the old gentleman was kept, (the same in which Union prisoners were placed,) was totally unfit for the most robust man in the vigor of life, much less for a man seventy-five years of age, especially considering the severity of the weather. Mr. Hadricks' death, which followed soon after his release, was unquestionably induced by the cruel treatment he received from Brown.

This was not the only aggravated case of this peculiar system of robbing, in which persons in a similar condition with him—persons almost entirely helpless and defenseless in regard to themselves — were shut up in Brown's rebel guard-house, fit only for brutes, till by their sufferings nature was broken into compliance with his tyrannical exactions.

This rebel military camp, it will be recollected, held carnival in Cleveland in the winter season of the year. A few days, or at most weeks in the miserable pens of this rebel camp, under a subjugating regimen, together with the every-day prospect of being sent to the still more loathsome, death-dealing dungeons of Tuscaloosa and Mobile, were sufficient to make men feel the difference—

especially those on the down-hill side of life—between this grinding oppression and personal liberty; between the value of money and the value of life; between Tuscaloosa prisons and their own homes, even if those homes were in the midst of the whirlpool of the infernal rebellion. As we will hereafter see, Brown's treatment of old Mr. Stonecypher was another aggravated case of cruelty, being part and parcel of this same system of iniquity.

It would be impossible, within the design of the present work, to give an account of all the acts of unusual brutality and wickedness inflicted by Brown upon Union people in and about Bradley, under the cover of pretending to collect supplies for destitute rebel families. The particulars in full of a single case as emphatically illustrate the general character of this piece of rebel iniquity, and, consequently, the general character of the rebellion in East Tennessee, as would numberless repetitions of similar scenes.

Upon this principle we have given a somewhat detailed account of the case of Mr. Hadrick; and the reader can draw his own conclusions as to the amount of crime committed, the personal abuse and injury inflicted by Brown in extorting money and property from, perhaps, three hundred Union people.

The following names of persons, among the many whom Brown compelled to pay tribute, was furnished by Jesse H. Gaut, Esq., of Cleveland. It was furnished in some degree from memory, nearly three years after the occurrences referred to, which accounts for the incompleteness of the list as indicated by Mr. Gaut's accompanying remarks.

"A few of the Names of Men in Bradley County from whom Capt. Wm. L. Brown extorted money, and the amounts taken from each:

William Blair, Esq.,	$100 00
George Munsey,	50 00
Wm. Morrison,	50 00
Wm. Francisco,	50 00
Rev. Noah Smith,	50 00
William Humburd, Esq.,	25 00
A. J. Collins,	25 00
—— Brown,	25 00
William Hawk,	20 00
James O. Dickinson,	15 00

Benj. Hambright.	50 00	Samuel Hyrick.	12 50
Robert Hambright.	50 00	John Stanfield.	10 00
George Cox, of Georgia.	100 00	John Gance.	10 00
J. H. Huff.	50 00	Little Berry Moore.	10 00
Wm. Lacey, Esq..	50 00	Thomas Prator.	10 00
Wm. Mahoney.	100 00	John Osment,	100 00
Jacob Hysinger.	50 00	William Stanfield.	5 00
Asa Fitzgerald.	25 00	William Wyrick,	5 00
John Francisco.	25 00	Dempsey Cooper.	15 00
Dr. J. M. Campbell.	25 00	Samuel D. Richmond,	25 00
Philip Mahony.	25 00	Hazard Bean.	10 00
James Gamble,	25 00	Edmund McKinny.	10 00
James Hinkle.	25 00	Wm. Smith,	25 00
Aaron Lee.	25 00		
Burrel Lee,	25 00		$1132 50
Gabriel Deford.	25 00		

These were only a few persons comparatively who were forced to pay money by Capt. Brown. They had only one election, and that was to pay or go to the rebel military prison at Tuscaloosa. Some only gave their obligations to pay their amounts. Greenbury Cate gave his obligation for $50.

It was said upon reliable authority that Brown got in notes and obligations about $4,000."

The above list contains forty names. From the verbal statement of Esq. Gaut, and from all other information, aside from this list, that could be obtained on the subject, it appears that Brown and his agents, in this particular enterprise, extorted money and property of one kind and another from not less than three hundred persons.

As to the amount actually collected, it was variously estimated, some putting it at one thousand dollars, others at fifteen hundred, and some as high as two thousand.

In regard to the disposition made of these levies, among Union people but one opinion prevailed. For the rebel opinion on the subject we never inquired. The universal opinion of the loyalists was, that not a fourth of these piratical levies ever reached the destitute rebel families of the county.

Similarly with the work of confiscating Union guns, this enterprise was conducted without system. It differed with the former, however, in that it had not even the semblance of valid rebel authority. It was impossible to trace it to a source higher than Brown,—in fact impossible to trace it to any other source. No authoritative enactment, civil or military, gave it shape and form, prescribing limits, holding parties responsible, bringing them to report to proper disbursing officers, or anything of this nature. But a kind of general reckless rebel consent prevailed, and all, or nearly all, encouraged this self-elected tiger, Brown, and his followers, in the pursuit of their prey. Upon this principle Brown imposed, confiscated, and collected to suit himself, keeping his own secrets, and naturally disbursing and appropriating in the same manner. As he doubtless looked upon himself as the most profitable servant in the good work, considered that he was deserving of the most prompt and liberal pay. The produce and other articles collected were more frequently carried off by the rebel officers and men, than systematically distributed to suffering mothers and children in the county.

As to the money collected, it was the universal opinion of Union men that the greater portion, if not the whole amount, was smuggled away for Brown's private uses, and otherwise expended upon his own personal and military aggrandizement. Only enough of money or goods was systematically given out to the needy families to blind those disposed to be honest, and to conceal the theft of Brown and those with him in the secret.

Brown was captain of a company in a cavalry regiment then in camp at Cleveland. Articles of general warfare were needed; but especially those suitable for cavalry. In connection with the above system of foraging, Brown extended his business till it was sufficiently general to cover even the demands of the extensive preparations of the whole rebel camp. Horses, mules, wagons, harnesses, saddles, blankets, blacksmith's tools, and all other property needed that could be found, was taken or ordered to be brought into camp and delivered at his headquarters.

Truth requires us to state that, in most instances at this time, and during the first year of the war, when valuable property, such as horses and mules, was taken for the benefit of the rebel army, it was either paid for in Confederate money, or vouchers were given by rebel officers.

Notwithstanding this, however, it was seldom if ever the case that Union owners received the full value of what was taken from them. Although this was ostensibly the rule with the rebel authorities in regard to valuable property taken for the Confederate Government, yet, under the leadership and through the rascality of Brown, the rule was frequently outraged even in important cases, and generally in all cases where his acts had not to pass under the supervision of the higher authorities.

Brown was too bad a man to serve even the Devil himself with prosperity to his cause. He was too dishonest to be honorable even among thieves; and had he been a public man in any other cause than this Southern Rebellion, he would have been hung as high as Haman by his own friends before he had more than half finished his career. Notwithstanding the opportunities his position gave him to gorge himself with the substance of his enemies, his reckless greed of gain goaded him to steal systematically from his friends also. This was usually performed in that base and cunning manner that left him the widest margin for escape, and, consequently, his victims the narrowest chance for obtaining redress. The weakest and most helpless—those having the least opportunity to defend themselves—were usually the persons of his own party whom he selected to wrong, rob and plunder. His cruelty was as ready and as venomous against his own men when they intercepted his wishes, as against the Lincolnites. On his return from the expedition against Col. Clift, he fell out with one of his men by the name of Swatford, and as punishment fastened one end of a log chain around his neck, compelling him to march dragging the length of it in the sand till he was exhausted and could go no further with his load.

It was too well known in Cleveland to need any caution in the statement, that a portion of the choicest articles solicited and voluntarily provided by rebel families for the rebel soldiers, and even rations of sugar that belonged to them, were not only freely used at his headquarters, ut secretly transferred to the private use of his own family.   When successful raids had been made by Brown and his men upon Union people, he would invariably smuggle some of the most valuable articles, such as counterpanes, choice quilts and blankets, pillows and pillow-cases, and other articles of the kind, and covertly pass them on to his own home.   This system of dastardly theft was persevered in till it became a proverb among the Union people that Brown's dwelling was the depot of stolen goods.

CHAPTER XI.

THE TUSCALOOSA PRISONERS.

MANY Union men in Bradley saved themselves from incarceration in Southern prisons—some by purchasing their freedom with money, others by instantaneous flight to the North, and still others who could neither pay nor flee, by connecting themselves with the rebel army until opportunities offered for their escape.

We purposed to obtain, from some one of the victimized party, a written statement of the particulars of these incidents, but failing to do so, we are enabled to record the tragedy of the "Tuscaloosa Prisoners," only in its general aspects.

Although many rebel citizens in the different parts of the county, such, for instance, as W. H. Tibbs, James Donahoo, Joseph Tucker, and others of the worst stamp, participated, acting as spies and informers. As usual, Brown was the principal actor in arresting these men, seventeen in number, and sending them to Southern prisons.

The following are the names of the victims.

Maj. James S. Bradford,	Allen Marler.
Dr. John G. Brown.	George V. Marler.
Capt. C. D. Champion.	Samuel Hunt.
Col. Stephen Beard.	John Beene, Esq.
Dr. Wm. Hunt.	Samuel Richmond.
Levi Trewhitt, Esq.	Thomas L. Cate, Esq.
Capt. John T. Kincheloe.	Jackson Spurgen.
Jesse Taylor.	S. B. Wise.
John Boon.	

Lawyer Trewhitt one of the above prisoners, was arrested at his own house, about four miles from Cleveland, on the 19th of November, 1861, by a posse of Capt. Brown's men; the posse being headed by John Dunn and Jo. Horton. Although Capt. Brown was the authoritative actor, Esq. Trewhitt's arrest was made at the instance of Cleveland rebels. Col. Wood, then in command at Knoxville, telegraphed to Brown to make the arrest. Wm. H. Tibbs, E. F. Johnson, and other Bradley rebels, either were then at Knoxville influencing Col. Wood to do this, or telegraphed to him from Cleveland to this effect.

Soon after his arrest, lawyer Trewhitt, with Doctors Brown and Hunt, and possibly some others, were sent to Knoxville, where they requested of the rebel authorities a trial. They were promised, or at least made to believe, that their request should be granted; but through the influence of Cleveland rebels, then at Knoxville, and through the representation of some who were not there, these prisoners instead of being granted a trial, were immediately dispatched for Tuscaloosa. Others, we believe, were sent to Knoxville before being doomed to Tuscaloosa. Be this as it may, however, not long after the arrest of Esq. Trewhitt, the whole were incarcerated in the Tuscaloosa prison.

Esq. Beene lived in the fifth district; James Donahoo the inveterate rebel lived in this district also. Mr. Beene was arrested at the instance of this Donahoo. Brown and his men, or his men alone, acting under his instructions, came to Mr. Beene's house in the night, arrested him in the presence of his family, and took him to Cleveland.

Of the particulars of the arrests of the others, we have no knowledge. *Reports* entitled to credit justify the statement that none of these men, had committed any overt or extravagant act of hostility against the rebellion, and that nothing of this kind was alleged against them as the cause of their arrest. They were, however, known to be uncompromising Union men—men of talent and influence, men whose presence and example were dreaded, and whom it was considered important to put out of the way as unceremoniously as possible. Thus, without regard to justice, with no specified charges against them, and denied the chance of trial, they were suddenly dispatched to the prisons of Tuscaloosa, intentionally for the term of the war.

They were sent in the month of December, 1861, in three

different parties, but all within the period of two weeks. All but two or three, and possibly all, were from Bradley county. The two Marlers might have been from Hamilton.

Being forced to engage in the drudgery of carrying heavy sacks of corn, Spurgen soon died at Tuscaloosa, with a naked billet of wood for his pillow. His death was induced by hard fare, the want of proper food, bad quarters, etc., as well as by being compelled under these circumstances to perform this hard labor. We have not the date of his death.

After being kept at Tuscaloosa for some time, a part, if not the whole of the rest, were sent to Mobile. While at Tuscaloosa their fare was, as a general thing, decidedly objectionable, and in some instances, perfectly shameful. At Mobile, their condition in this respect was somewhat improved. Some of the ladies of Mobile—whether Union or otherwise, we know not, to their credit be it recorded—interested themselves in behalf of the prisoners. The latter were supplied with food and other comforts, which made their transfer, at least in this respect, a matter of gratitude. These blessings, however, came too late for the recovery of lawyer Trewhitt. The mental sufferings occasioned by his arrest, the physical hardships of his trip from home, together with the privations and other effects of his imprisonment at Tuscaloosa, were too severe for a man of sixty-four years; and he died at Mobile on the 31st of January, 1862.

Judge John C. Gaut, D. C. McMillen, and other Union men in Bradley, as well as some in other parts of East Tennessee, especially Mr. T. H. Calloway of Polk county, knowing the injustice and cruelty, as well as the suffering and danger to their lives, of the imprisonment of these men, were exerting themselves for their release. An appeal was first made to Judge T. J. Campbell, one of the most influential and far reaching rebels in East Tennessee, but with no other effect than to rouse in him the most determined opposition to the application.

Mr. Birch, of Chattanooga, then serving on Gen. Pillow's

staff at Murfreesboro, happening in Cleveland shortly
after the appeal to Judge Campbell, was approached by
Judge Gaut on the subject, and the case fully explained
to him in its true light. Notwithstanding Mr. Birch was
engaged in the interest of the rebellion, he at once comprehended the injustice of such proceedings; and though
he then had to return to Murfreesboro, promised to give
his attention to the matter in a few days, when he would
render the Judge all the assistance in his power. The
Judge communicated these facts to Mr. Calloway; and
arrangements were made for a meeting at Loudon, a place
about fifty miles west of Knoxville. Mr. Birch was at
London agreeable to appointment, when the parties proceeded to Knoxville and made known their business to
the military authorities by whom these men were imprisoned. Here, however, they came in contact with the old
and inveterate influence which was at the bottom of the
rascality in the beginning. The notorious Wm. H. Tibbs,
then at Knoxville, opposed the proposition with all his
might, meeting the arguments of Mr. Birch as well as
those of Calloway and Judge Gaut, with his usual disregard of principle and justice. He succeeded in exciting
the opposition of Judge Campbell, and making it, if possible, more bitter than before. In view of this opposition,
precisely to what extent the applicants succeeded with
these authorities at Knoxville, is not known. Their efforts
here were either an entire failure, inducing them to agree
among themselves to lay the matter before the rebel Secretary of War at Richmond, or possibly their case was
referred to him by the Knoxville authorities themselves.
Mr. Galloway and Judge Gaut furnishing the requisite
funds, Mr. Birch hastened to Richmond, and the rebel
Secretary of War, J. P. Benjamin, without much delay
ordered the immediate release and transportation to their
homes, of the Tuscaloosa prisoners from Bradley county.

As soon as possible this order was forwarded from
Knoxville, and passed Cleveland the day Mr. Trewhitt
died at Mobile. Could these proceedings have been hastened a few days, or had they not been retarded at Knox-

ville by the Cleveland clique of Tibbs, Tucker and company, possibly news of his release might have been in time to save Mr. Trewhitt's life.

After an imprisonment of about four months, with the exception of Esq. Trewhitt and Mr. Spurgen, all reached their homes in comparative safety, only, however, at the expense of sufferings, risk to health and life, which, doubtless, they could not be induced to take the second time for the treasures of Tennessee.

Notwithstanding the release thus granted to these Union men amounted to an acquittal from all the charges which Bradley rebels informally alleged against them, yet, no sooner had they returned than they found themselves the persecuted objects of suspicion, the same as before. The most of them found it necessary secretly to leave the State in order to escape from their old enemies. Doctors Brown and Hunt, under the pretense of going on a fishing excursion, with hook and line in hand, left Cleveland soon after their return from Mobile, and reached Nashville in safety.

Both subsequently entered the Federal service as surgeons,—Dr. Hunt in the 9th Tennessee Cavalry, and Brown in the 4th East Tennessee Cavalry. Major Bradford was subsequently Major in the 5th East Tennessee Cavalry, while Beard was Lieutenant-Colonel of the same regiment. Kincheloe and Champion were Captains in the 4th East Tennessee Cavalry.

Thus, with two exceptions, this loyal and memorable seventeen of Bradley, after imprisonment and suffering, fleeing and fighting, resisting and hoping, lived to see the rebellion crushed, and their individual and political enemies subdued. They are now wearing the honors of victory and enjoying their homes in peace.

In 1864 and 1865, some three years after their imprisonment, a portion of these victorious Tuscaloosanites enforced the civil law, and mulcted their rebel persecutors in heavy damages.

This subject ought not to be dismissed without reference being made to the honorable conduct of Mr. Birch as to this affair. Mr. Birch was a professed rebel, and doubtless felt an anxiety for the success of the cause equally with that of the most vehement of its advocates. Yet he had too much Christianity to allow himself to ignore all justice in the defense of any cause. He had too much civilized and cultivated humanity, too much good breeding, to turn savage at once and incarcerate and murder by starvation and slow tortures his nearest neighbors and best friends, especially when among them were the venerable sires of three generations, who had stood the virtuous supports and leading ornaments of society for half a century—simply because of an honest difference of political opinion, a natural right of theirs as well as his.

Had such men as Mr. Birch controlled the South from the beginning, the rebellion never would have existed Had not such men as he, and those like him, from the be ginning been controlled by such men as Judge Campbell, Judge Rowls, Wm. H. Tibbs, and his company of leading Bradley rebels, they never would have been rebels at all.

The following *bull* from the Cleveland *Banner* of May 9th, 1862, was hurled at the backs of Doctors Brown and Hunt, who, as we have seen, were compelled to flee from Cleveland after their return from Mobile. It was also hurled at the back of Mr. M. Edwards, who left about the same time :

"DECAMPED.—Some three weeks ago Doct. John G. Brown. Doct. Wm. Hunt. and R. M. Edwards, Esq., all citizens of this place. very mysteriously left, and have not been heard of up to this present writing. But little anxiety or solicitude has been felt for them since they left. as it was supposed by their friends that they had gone to old Abe's bosom. Doct. Brown was considered a gentleman in all his social relations—stood high in his profession, but a man who was corrupt in his political opinions as we conceive. The two latter gentlemen were like small potatoes in Ireland, 'no damned big things.'— had neither money nor reputation to lose in the operation. and we think it is a perfect God-send to a country to get rid of such men. All the harm we wish them is that they may never get back."

It appears they did get *back* notwithstanding your *wish*, and that you finally *took back* your abuse of them by taking the *Lincolnite* oath which sanctioned their return.

CHAPTER XII.

CAPT. BROWN'S WHIPPING OF THE CAMP WOMEN.

THE tragedy which we have to relate here, is among the most revolting cases of rebel inhumanity, perpetrated in East Tennessee ; and will cause feelings of indignant horror, aggravated by a thought of the wretch who could, under the circumstances, inflict this scandalous punishment upon helpless females, perhaps in advance of those occasioned by any other act of Brown's unparalleled career. We regret that we are not in possession of all the particulars.

It appears that two women were either in, or lingering about the rebel camp at Cleveland, being induced to come there by some of the most abandoned of the soldiers, especially by Brown's own son, who was a member of the same regiment with himself, and we believe of his own company. It was also currently reported at the time that Brown himself, previous to inflicting on them this punishment, had visited these women, either at their own homes or somewhere in the vicinity of the camp, thus incurring himself, more than they, the guilt of their presence among the soldiers. Whether this report is true or false, it is one of the facts connected with the affair, and is given only as such, with the balance of probabilities, however, in its favor. That Brown's son was one of the principals in inducing these women to visit the rebel camp, is given upon the most reliable authority ; and this, his son's guilt, could not have been unknown to Brown.

Partly, perhaps, as an apt strategy by which he endeavored wickedly, to hide the truth, and make the public disbelieve the reports so justly rising against him and his son, and partly from a desire to revenge on the women for the public disgrace which he and his son were suffering from their secret guilt with them, Brown had them

CAPT. BROWN WHIPPING THE CAMP WOMEN.

arrested, tied them to trees in the vicinity of the camp, in the meantime procuring a supply of green whips, and after compelling them to remove their clothing down to the waist, with his own hands lashed their naked persons until their arms shoulders and breasts were completely disfigured with cuts and bruises, and their persons covered with blood.

No other act of Brown's abominable career was spoken of by the Union people of Bradley, with so much loathing and disgust, as his brutality to these women. One of the rebel soldiers, whom Brown compelled in some measure to be accessory to the foul deed, also asserted that it was one of the most shocking, heart-sickening, and heart-rending tragedies that a human being ever committed or witnessed.

It was reported that one of these pitiable creatures, was in a delicate condition at the time, and from the extent of her injuries, was brought to a premature confinement, resulting in her own death and that of her offspring. So far as the woman's own death was concerned, this report was found to be untrue, but with a pretty strong probability, that in other respects it was correct.

CAPTAIN BROWN'S ARREST.

At what particular period of Brown's military career, the event indicated above occurred, we are not informed; but probably it took place in the last of December 1861, or in the first of January 1862.

A Mr. Stewart, a rebel, but not yet entirely lost to all human propriety, in view of Brown's entire course, for the honor of the Confederacy, for the sake of humanity and Christianity, as well as a matter of policy, thought it high time to bring his career to a check, if not to a close. Consequently he reported him to the rebel authorities at Knoxville. The charges preferred against Brown by Mr. Stewart were so remarkable, and environed with so much apparent truthfulness, that these authorities at once arrested Brown, who was, we believe, then at Knoxville,

9

and preparations were **there** progressing to put him on trial.

No sooner, however, had a knowledge of these proceedings reached Cleveland, the immediate locality of Brown's vandalisms, than a movement was inaugurated by his friends, the Bradley rebels, those who had been eye-witnesses to his entire behavior, to have these proceedings intercepted, and Brown released from arrest. A petition was drawn up, endorsing his conduct, and after being signed, perhaps by every active rebel then in Cleveland and its vicinity, with one exception, was forwarded to Knoxville.

The petition, it appears, was a systematic and somewhat elaborate document, taking strong ground against the justice of Capt. Brown's arrest, fully endorsing his entire course in Bradley, hinting at his efficiency, and the value of his services to the common cause, and earnestly praying for his immediate release from arrest, with full permission to continue his work, and finish his career without further molestation.

The matter was pushed with great perseverance, and very strenuous efforts were made to procure a formidable array of signatures, especially to obtain the names of those who were wealthy and influential. From all the information that could be obtained, but one individual, rich or poor, to whom the petition was presented, refused to sign it. Mr. John Craigmiles objected to the honor of having anything to do with the transaction. Mr. Craigmiles was a gentleman of talents, wealth, and influence, which made it very important to the success of the enterprise, to have the petition go up to Knoxville with the weight of his signature upon it. Consequently, no means were left untried to obtain it. The petition was first presented to Mr. Craigmiles by Joseph R. Taylor, who, on its presentation, was informed by Mr. Craigmiles, that he never sanctioned the course of Capt. Brown, and that he could not endorse it now. Mr. Taylor pressed his suit, but was compelled to pass on with his petition in despair, so far as he was concerned, of obtaining the name of

Mr. Craigmiles. The name, however, was of too much importance to be given up, at least without one more effort to secure it. Mr. John H. Payne was the individual selected the second time, to bear down upon Mr. Craigmiles, on the subject. Mr Payne was a man of some considerable influence, was also related to Mr. Craigmiles by marriage, and it was thought would be as likely to win him over as any other person. The fact, however, was otherwise. Mr. Payne also uselessly exhausted his ingenuity to convince Mr. Craigmiles, that it was his duty and for his interest to sign the document. Though Mr. Craigmiles was a rebel, he could not be convinced that it was either his duty, or for his interest to endorse the abominable career of such a man as Wm. L. Brown. Feeling himself about to fail, Mr. Payne informed Mr. Craigmiles that he was already suspected of being wanting in devotion to the cause, and that if he persisted in his refusal to assist them to extricate their favorite leader from arrest, he need not be surprised if it worked to his pecuniary disadvantage, lessened his rebel popularity, and caused him to be closely watched by his particular friends in future. All considerations, however, failed of having the desired effect on Mr. Craigmiles; and the petition went to Knoxville without the benefit of his signature. What they lost, however, in this, was probobly counterbalanced in numbers; for as already stated, this was the only instance in which the friends of Brown were known to fail with the entire rebel community at Cleveland.

Others besides Mr. Payne and Mr. Taylor were active in Brown's favor. Mr. James Donahoo was one of the principal concoctors of the scheme—watched it and interested himself in its progress, and when the petition was completed volunteered his services to bear these important dispatches to the authorities at Knoxville, where with his personal presence and representations, the petition prevailed with these authorities, and Brown was immediately set at liberty.

It is very much to be regretted that this petition, without the alteration of a syllable, or the loss of a single name from its column of signatures, could not have been preserved and sent to Washington, and stored among the documentary archives of the rebellion, there to remain, though an infinitesimal, yet a memorable curiosity in its line. As the present, when it recedes into the past, becomes almost an entire blank to existing generations, on condition that we, or any one else succeeds in giving to posterity, a faithful portraiture of Wm. L. Brown, in a hundred years from now, this petition, if accessible, would throw more light upon the animus of the rebellion in East Tennessee, than fifty times the same amount of manuscript that will ever be written about it. As much as the historian has desired to recover it, and as much as the antiquarian may lament its loss, this singular scroll of a communities' infamy and crime, has doubtless, long since, been consigned, even by its own friends, to the common receptacle of unhallowed and condemned communications.

In view of certain possibilities, in which a knowledge of the persons connected with this transaction might be important, a few of the names attached to this document were preserved; and the parties were kind enough to place them at our disposal. We give them upon the authority of those who preserved them, which, however, we are enabled to state is perfectly reliable.

These few signatures are as follows:

J. F. Rogers.	D. C. Kenner.
Joseph Tucker.	Wm. Grant.
Wm. H. Tibbs.	Wm. H. Grant.
Joseph M. Horton,	Dr. P. J. R. Edwards.
David Kincannon.	Robert McNelly,
John H. Payne.	James Donahoo,
Wm. J. Hughes,	Isaac Guthman.
Joseph R. Taylor,	Louis Guthman.
Wm. Johnson.	James Johnson,
C. L. Hardwick,	Dr. Pepper.

These names can be but a small number of the whole that went to Knoxville in behalf of Brown. Those acquainted in Bradley at the time are aware that rebel numbers were not wanting to justify the conclusion, that, perhaps, three or four times this number were on the petition. With the single exception already given, with the rebels in and about Cleveland, it was a complete success, as it was with the authorities at Knoxville. As we know all who did not or would not sign the petition, allowing for accidents, we know all who did sign it. As all acted one way or the other, having the negative, upon general principles, we are in possession of the affirmative also. If Mr. Craigmiles was the only one who refused to sign the petition, then, of course, all the rest consented; and as this petition must have been from one to three days in circulation, it is reasonable to conclude, that all or very nearly all the rebels in and about Cleveland had an opportunity to sign it, and consequently must have done so. Thus, not only those whose names are here presented, stand committed, but the entire rebel community of Cleveland and the immediate vicinity, are seen to have endorsed the course of Capt. Brown, as emphatically as those whose names are here given.

The sudden effect of this petition upon the authorities at Knoxville is also evidence that, so far as signatures were concerned, it was a triumphant success. The effect was Brown's immediate release. This shows that the petition embodied the strength of the rebel element of Cleveland. Had it represented an insignificant clique, or few, it could not have had this effect.

It is perfectly unavoidable, therefore, that not only the twenty persons, whose names are here given were guilty, and are held responsible for endorsing Brown's conduct and for turning him loose to continue his depredations, but we might with propriety add to the above list, and publish the names of every other rebel then in, and around Cleveland, for the names of all such were as surely upon the petition, as were those we have given.

When this petition was gotten up Brown was under arrest for grave, serious offences and cruelties — complained of, and charged with these by one of his own party before his superiors; and had it not been for this petition he would have been tried and doubtless convicted, and his career of cruelty and shame brought to a close. This petition, however, turned him loose with encouragement to rob, steal, and murder with less fear of being brought to justice than before. Bradley rebels, therefore, were the perpetrators, equally with Brown himself, of all his subsequent villainies.

It is not remarkable to find in any community, however civilized and moral, a few unprincipled men, or even some who are notoriously wicked, whose lives are a continued scene of rascality and dire oppression; but it is remarkable, that the ruling portion of a civilized and Christian community, should voluntarily indorse the conduct, and publicly justify the career of one of the worst men in existence. Indeed this fact is so remarkable, that it is not to be accounted for upon any of the ordinary principles governing civilized and Christian society. A solution of the problem, that such a case contains, can be reached only upon the supposition that the cause by which the parties were driven forward, was nearer a personification of satan, than a scheme originating with a society of rational and dispossessed human intelligences.

The parties whose names are here given, as well as the entire rebel element of Cleveland and vicinity, are reminded that this rebellion is the subject of history; and that history is for the benefit of present and coming generations; consequently must include the errors and vices that corrupt as well as the virtues that bless and redeem the times narrated. Individuals, as much as communities, who engaged in this rebellion, thereby made themselves the property of history. This was the contract voluntarily entered into by them at the time; and he who faithfully details the conduct of the bad as well as that of the good, individually and collectively, is only holding both parties to their own proposals thus voluntarily made at the beginning. Those who were in the wrong have no more right to complain that a record is made of their errors followed with legitimate deductions, than those in the right that the same course is taken with their virtues. Those who had the misfortune to fall into wrong, and especially those who embraced it from preferences of disposition, must be held to their position and compelled to meet the consequences. There is no other alternative, the vital interests of history are at stake, truth is required. Consequently all parties must be historically classed among the followers of him whom they delighted to serve as their acknowledged master.

In our conversation with Union people in East Tennessee upon the malignancy of the rebellion in that part of the country, it was very frequently their remark that they never even imagined the actual depravity of mankind till it was taught them by the conduct of the rebels towards themselves. That the human heart could reduce itself to such outrageous beastliness, that it could be guilty of conduct so fiendish as was the case with the rebels in some instances, had escaped all their former observations upon the character and actions of mankind.

Among many Union people in Tennessee whom we heard speak of the same thing, relating instances of the same fact, namely, that the rebellion, in many cases, actually developed the spirit of the devil, one of the most intelligent and influential ladies in Cleveland, one whose talents, position and refinement entitle her statements to unlimited credit, in relating her sore experience among the rebels,—especially among the lady rebels—declared it as her honest and religious conviction, that in many cases she had to fight the Devil face to face in the persons of her rebel enemies. That not only the men manifestly displayed the tyranny and wickedness of attending and prompting demons, but many of the women, from "*the loss of their rights*," passed from one degree of individual rebellion to another, till they were no longer themselves, no longer the same women—till the malignant excitement had transformed them into the very embodiment of furies, and left them a prey, she believed, to actual demoniac possession.

This lady stated that in some of the worst specimens the diabolical spirit seemed to take possession of the physical as well as the mental constitution, that it was unmistakably present in every look, word and action: that it pushed itself out upon every lineament of the features, where it couched a visible *demon*, changing the whole countenance from that of a human being to that of a rankling and malignant fiend.

The above is but the statement of a historical fact—a fact for which the historian is no more responsible than he is for other facts, and from the statement or recording of which he has no more right to shrink than he has to shrink from the recording of other facts.

This rebellion presents us with a moral as well as a political problem; and before the former can be solved we shall doubtless find it necessary, especially in view of the character of the rebellion in East Tennessee, at Andersonville, Belle Island, and other particular places, to deal with such facts as the above.

As a subject of special attention, with the following summary remarks, we shall now take our leave of Capt. Brown, although his name will occasionally appear in the remainder of this work.

As already seen, Brown was Captain in the 4th East Tennessee Rebel Cavalry, commanded by Col. J. F. Rogers. Many of Brown's company, as well as many of the whole regiment, were Union men forced into the rebel service. The regiment was first ordered to Knoxville, then to the vicinity of Cumberland Gap, where it remained a few months, during which many of the men deserted to the Federal lines. On account of its Unionism, in the spring of 1862, this regiment, we believe, and certainly the 36th Tennessee Infantry, otherwise *the squirrel brigade*, because of the Union spirit which it betrayed, and the number that daily deserted from it to the Federals, were ordered to report to Savannah, Georgia. In June, 1862, what were left of these troops were recalled from Savannah to Cleveland, and there disbanded. Thus released, those of these men who were rebels at heart enlisted in other rebel commands, some, however, from their love of plunder, connecting themselves with different guerrilla bands, in which they served not only to the end of the war, but as long as the mountains of northern

Georgia and of North Carolina could afford them protection.

As a soldier, as it naturally would be, Brown's career was short. He commenced recruiting his company early in the fall of 1861, and resigned when his regiment was disbanded at Cleveland, making his term of service only about seven months. After this his patriotism did not prompt him to fight for the Southern Confederacy. He remained in Bradley from his resignation, exercising his office of Justice of the Peace, collecting specific taxes for the Rebel Government, and robbing both parties, till he was compelled to leave his family and flee to Dixie before our army in the winter of 1863–64. After an absence of some months he had the audacity to write to his former minister, Rev. Hiram Douglas, enquiring if it would be safe for him to return to his family in Bradley on condition that he would take the oath of allegiance to the Government of the United States. What advice he received from his spiritual adviser is not known. Mrs. Brown counselled with lawyer J. H. Gaut, of Cleveland, to the same effect, who frankly informed her, that if her husband valued his life, the farther he could keep from the Union people of Bradley the safer he would be. Shortly after this, Mrs. Brown stealthily left Cleveland, assisted by the Rev. Mr. McNutt, another implacable rebel Christian, and it is supposed joined her wretched husband in some part of Georgia, where, unless he is detected and brought to justice, both may linger out the remainder of their miserable earthly existence.

As we are about to take formal leave of Capt. Brown as a distinct subject in this history, it may be appropriate in this connection to sketch the character and take leave also at the same time of his son, already introduced in this chapter.

The name of this precocious scoundrel was Samuel, who at the opening of the rebellion was but sixteen years of age. Serving as a rebel soldier in the same regiment with his father till the latter resigned, the son, from this time, floated loosely away upon the inland sea of the rebellion in northern Georgia and southern East Tennessee, assuming the character of rebel soldier, guerrilla, bushwhacker, horse-thief, robber, murderer, or whatever guise was best suited to perfect his crimmal course and render him a finished specimen of the illustrious stock from which he descended, and by which he had been effectually schooled in iniquity. Some time after his father resigned, he went South and pretended to be a member, for some months, of a Tennessee regiment of rebel cavalry.

His most noted career, however, after he became detached from his first regiment, was perpetrated in the summer and fall of 1864 as a guerrilla in the rear of Sherman's army. He was with Gatewood, a leading guerrilla chief, an account of whom will be given hereafter, and at one time when on an excursion of plundering, boasted in the presence of a Union family, or in the presence of Union people, of having cut the throat of a Union Tennessean—whose name we have unfortunately lost—after his victim had been shot down and rendered helpless by himself and his guerrilla companions. He displayed and flourished the knife with which he performed the deed, and swore to the satisfaction it gave him to "cut the throat of the d——d Lincolnite."

On the 17th of August, 1864, Gen. Wheeler appeared in the vicinity of Cleveland from the direction of Dalton, and tore up the railroad connecting the two places, seven miles south of Cleveland, near the residence of Mr. Hiram Smith. Young Brown and another young guerrilla followed in Wheeler's wake near enough to keep under his protection, robbing and plundering all the Union families they could reach.

In Bradley, Brown, with pistol in hand, first robbed Mr. Benjamin Hambright, taking ten dollars in greenbacks from his person, after which he demanded his hat; but Mr. Hambright immediately turned from him and passed on, the stripling thief cursing and threatening to shoot him, but Mr. Hambright disregarding, was soon out of his sight and saw him no more.

Brown and his companion next assaulted the premises of Mr. Hiram Smith, which they plundered while Wheeler's men were tearing up the railroad track within sight and but a few yards from Mr. Smith's door. Mr. Smith was not at home. He, his father and brothers, were strong Union men, and had done good service against the rebellion. Young Brown cursed and abused Mrs. Smith, alleging that her husband and brothers-in-law had been the principal cause of the troubles that came upon his father and mother—that the Unionism of her husband and brothers-in-law drove his father and mother out of the country, &c. He made a sentinel of his companion to watch for Mr. Smith or other persons who might approach the house, while he, vandal like, tore through the house opening chests, ransacking bureau drawers, and insultingly invading, in Mrs. Smith's presence, every other private apartment in the dwelling that he could discover, in quest of money, watches, revolvers and other valuables. In prospect of visitors of his stripe, Mr. and Mrs. Smith, long before that time, had deposited in a place of safety all the valuables in their possession of the kind he so much desired, consequently his search was fruitless. Enraged at his failure, Brown levied upon an army oil-cloth and a half worn out hat, swearing that Mrs. Smith's father was rich, and must have by him a plenty of money; that he knew him to be the owner of a gold watch and valuable black mare, and he'd be d——d if he did not pay him a visit.

Mr. B. F. Jones, Mrs. Smith's father, sixty-seven years of age, lived a half-mile to the west over a ridge in another valley. The two thieves then mounted their animals and dashed up the ridge at a furious rate, Brown, to be ready for any emergency, swinging his revolver over his own head and over the head of his animal in a menacing manner, in which plight they disappeared over the hill in quest of more valuable booty. They found Mr. Jones, his wife, and Mrs. Martin V. Jones, a daughter-in-law, at home. As in the previous case young Gregory was made sentinel, while Brown, with revolver in hand, took possession of the premises. He first, with curses and threats, thumping his revolver against him, searched the person of Mr. Jones for money and the gold watch. He examined his person closely for a money-belt, which he hoped to find, and hoped to find it containing a large amount. Money and watch, as well as the black mare, however, had been placed beyond his reach. Through with Mr. Jones personally, bureau and stand drawers, cupboards, pantries, trunks and private rooms of the whole house hurriedly passed under his fiendish and greedy supervision. He demanded of Mrs. M. V. Jones, the daughter-in-law, the keys to her private room, which he entered, tore to pieces and plundered, more like a savage hyena or youthful devil incarnate than a natural born human being. In this room he discovered and captured an empty pocket-book, a five dollar powder-flask and a lot of gun caps, property of the husband of the young lady from whom he extorted the keys. He also captured three dollars in Confederate money, which he found in a glass tumbler in one of the cupboards. These were the sum total of his burglarious gatherings from the family of Mr. Jones. Money, gold and silver watches, and similar valuables, had been placed where his robbing propensities were taxed in vain to find them. Three valuable watches belonging to different members of the family were not far from him, yet beyond his reach during the whole of his wicked onslaught upon them.

If possible, more chagrined and enraged at his much unexpected failure to raise a pile from Mr. Jones than he was at his failure at Mr. Smith's, he cursed and terribly threatened the old gentleman as a last resort to make him disgorge; but all being of no avail he and his companion rode off, Brown at the same time striking up a vulgar song as an insult to the women.

Returning in a gallop to Mr. Smith's, the thieves found that their protecting companions, Wheeler's cavalry, had left some time before. Brown, in particular, appearing alarmed at his isolated condition, eagerly inquired of Mrs. Smith the direction his friends had taken, which being pointed out, the two suddenly disappeared, following the trail of the rebel cavalry.

A few days previous to committing the foregoing depredations, young Brown robbed a Dr. Leach, a Union man, a short distance south in Georgia. Dr. Leach had formerly lived in Cleveland, Bradley county, and for many years was Capt. Brown's family physician. He sustained this relation to the family when young Samuel was born, and was his mother's physician on that occasion; consequently Samuel was regarded in after years by the doctor with more than ordinary interest among the rising generation in and around Cleveland. These semi-paternal feelings, however, were very suddenly cooled when the stripling presented the deadly revolver to the doctor's breast, and with the hardened face of a three-score pirate demanded and took his money (forty dollars,) and a time-keeper that cost him seventy-five dollars. Little did the doctor think eighteen years before, that he was *catching* a viper that would one day, not only *leach* him in this manner, but strip the hat from his head, leaving his person uncovered and unprotected in the open air. The doctor moved from Cleveland, perhaps sometime previous to the war, consequently, he and young Brown, had not, since that time, been very conversant. Brown while he was perpetrating the villainy, assumed a fictitious personality that the doctor might not suspect that it was the identical Samuel Brown of Cleveland, who was robbing him. The doctor informed him, however, that he could not be deceived, that he had not only known him from a child, but was with him when he was born, assisting his mother to bring him into the world, and now to be robbed or murdered by him, was a poor return for such favor. All appeals, however, made to Brown glanced off as though they had fallen upon the head of a young alligator. The vandalism was completed, and the doctor left moneyless, watchless and bareheaded, a pitiful object under the circumstances, especially considering the unclean brute to whose manipulation he had been subjected.

Young Brown continued his depredations in Tennessee and northern Georgia, upon principles similar to the foregoing, under one guerrilla leader and another, yet as often being leader himself, until sometime, perhaps in the spring of 1865, when he either drifted toward Mexico with Gatewood, or fled south to join his justly execrated and exiled parents.

Young Brown's career is by no means an isolated case in the country where he thus operated.

PAYNE PRESENTING HIS PETITION TO CRAIGMILES—page 123.

CHAPTER XIII.

THE CLEVELAND BANNER.

THE history of the Rebellion in Bradley would be very incomplete without a few paragraphs devoted to the Cleveland *Banner*.

The *Banner* had been published in Cleveland, the county seat of Bradley, for a number of years previous to the breaking out of the rebellion. Its editorial department was under the control of its present editor, Mr. Robert McNelly, we believe, from the commencement of its publication, until it was suppressed by the Federal military authorities, shortly after the battle of Missionary Ridge.

Judge Rowls, a resident perhaps of Polk County, a man of some talent and influence, but an unprincipled rebel leader, was said to have an interest in the concern ; and it was known that his articles contributed to the columns of the *Banner*, as well as the influence he exerted as a partner, tended very much to make it the bitter, relentless, dishonest and disgraceful rebel sheet it proved itself to be. Previous to the war, the *Banner* was a faithful exponent of Southern principles and Southern dogmas. Consequently, when the rebellion came, it is not singular that it so readily espoused a cause, the crime of which its previous labors contributed to induce.

A faithful portrayal in book form of the Southern press as it existed during, and for some time previous to the rebellion, would constitute a most useful lesson to history. The extremes of good and bad among men are of more importance and are more instructive as subjects of history, than the medium of these qualities. The medium of good and the medium of bad in this life, live together in comparative peace, both comparatively indifferent as to ascendancy, while their extremes only are at open war, coming occasionally into fierce and terrible conflict. Consequently, a knowledge of how the distant struggle goes, tells us which way the world is drifting, whether towards good or evil. It is the victory of the active few at these extremes that sets the general tide, in fact, that controls the many, moulding the form and shaping the destiny of the massive elements between.

This truth is strikingly illustrated in the instance of the Northern and the Southern press, far many years past. Southern slaveholders, politicians and statesmen, the controling element in the South, were the active extreme of the evil power on that side. The Adamses, Lovejoys, Sumners, Beechers, and Colfaxes in the North, were the active extreme of the good opposing the evil of these Southern leaders. The masses both North and South were comparatively idle, and indifferent about the important struggle between the two sections, kept up by these extremes for the past forty years.

As an instance of the extreme evil, on the part of the Southern press, of which we have been speaking—an instance of low flung falsehood, published with a view to fan the passions of the ignorant and create a thirst for blood, we give the following extract from the Cleveland *Banner*. It is taken from a number dated April 9th, 1863.

"HANDCUFFS FOR THE SOUTH.—The Southern papers, says the Richmond *Dispatch*, should keep before the people of the South and of the world, the astounding and unparalleled fact, that the army which invaded Virginia, brought with them thirty thousand handcuffs, which were taken with other spoils from the enemy! This surpasses all that we have ever heard of Russian or Austrian despotism. It is almost impossible to realize, that in the United States, a country boasting itself as the freest—the most deliberate, inhuman and atrocious plan should have been formed to degrade and enslave a free people, of which there is any record of in this or any other age. Who ever heard, even in despotic Europe, of an invading army traveling with thirty thousand handcuffs as a part of its outfit."

The Army of the Potomac, like all other armies, doubtless, provided itself with a suitable supply of army handcuffs, in view of the necessity of their use in extreme cases, and that of course, without especial reference to rebel prisoners ; and it is possible that some few of these were captured by the rebels. The idea, however, that this army prepared itself with thirty thousand of these articles, a burden sufficient, in all kinds of weather, and on all kinds of army roads, to load down at least twelve or fifteen six-mule teams, with an intention to send to Washington, thirty thousand rebel prisoners in irons, is so perfectly senseless that the report could not for a moment gain the attention of any respectable journalist. No journalist, even under the corrupting influence of the rebellion, unless he was a natural fool, could give publicity to a thing of this kind, honestly thinking it to be true; and certainly, none but a natural and ingrained knave, would do so, knowing it to be false.

Treating this subject in this positive manner, the manner in which all subjects of the kind should be treated, there is no escape from this conclusion; and the editor of the *Banner* can hang himself upon whichever horn of the dilemma he pleases. In all probability, there was not a rebel sheet in the whole South, whose columns were not disgraced, sooner or later, with this ridiculous and heathenish lie.

From the few copies of the *Banner* that fell into our hands, it would be easy to fill pages of this work with extracts equally false and equally low-bred, with the foregoing. The *Banner*, like all other rebel sheets, appeared to take a fiendish delight in venting its rebel spleen, and in pouring out its treasonable venom upon the head of President Lincoln.

The following extract, among hundreds of others of the same revolting nature, that might be given, will not only illustrate this point, but will afford a clue to the moral and intellectual character of the *Banner*:

We have taken the liberty to italicise a few of the most ominous passages in these extracts.

"The news from the old Government is of rather an unimportant character. The administration at Washington appears to be in a quandary—one day it concludes to evacuate the Southern forts—the next day it reconsiders and talks about re-enforcing them, but does neither. The fact is the Black Republican administration of Lincoln, Seward & Co., to use a common phrase, is "*is in a hell of a fix*" *and don't know what to do.* While *they are pursuing a hawk and buzzard policy, crying out good God, good Devil,* the Southern Congress is perfecting *a government that will stand the test of human scrutiny, and challenge the admiration and wisdom of the world for a superior*—a government not susceptible of two constructions, but a plain direct democratic government—such an one as our fathers contemplated—a government about which there will be no differences of opinion as to its spirit and meaning. There is a marked difference between the conduct of the Black Republican administration at Washington and the Democratic administration at Montgomery. The former conducts its affairs stealthily, cunningly and secretly—keeps its policy to itself—wont tell the people what it is going to do with their government—the latter comes out and tells them in plain language what it intends to do—tells it with no forked tongue, to deceive them—no double construction can be placed upon its policy—it is emphatically the white man's government. Can as much be said for the present government at Washington?" [April 5th, 1861.]

"THE REIGN OF TERROR.—One by one, the bulwarks of liberty, under the old Union are being ruthlessly destroyed. A reign of terror prevails in the Northern States in as violent a form as swept over France in the days of Robespierre. As one of the New York peace journals remarks, it requires but one more step to inaugurate the scenes of the French revolution, when the guillotine was a perennial fountain of blood. Men and woman are daily arrested in Washington, New York and Philadelphia, and thrown into loathsome dungeons, without warrant of law, and without being confronted with their accusers or advised of the charges against them   Journals are suppressed for denouncing the action of the Government. Editors are lynched and their printing offices destroyed by the mob. Forced loans are demanded of the banks. A system of detectives is organized at Washington to dog the steps of peaceable citizens, report to tyrants and arrest persons suspected of opposing the usurpers will. No Russian despotism or Spanish Inquisition ever exceeded, in the measure of its cruelty, the present dictatorship at Washington. *The Doge's dungeon in Venice, near which the Bridge of Sighs yet stands a monument of tyranny, is reproduced in Forts Lafayette and Hamilton,* names that are worthier of a more honorable fate. The Government of the United States is prostituted to the vilest purposes of the most infamous men that ever walked the earth. There is no such thing as public or individual liberty in the United States. *Men, to be free, must sing psalms to a Baboon,* and worship the Government of usurpers. They must sanction the most unholy war ever waged against a free people. They must approve of the destruction of their own liberties. They must become slaves, in order to enjoy exemption from molestation. There is more in these arrests than meets the eye. It indicates a deep and determined opposition to the acts of the Government, among the wiser and more virtuous men of the North. It evinces that the tyrants are trembling on their thrones and fear the day of reckoning, which will sweep them violently from their seats of power. They fear not only the armies of the Confederate States which, in the language of a member of the Cabinet, are already "thundering at the gates of the capitol." They stand in awe, not merely of those gallant legions, which have driven them, like dogs, howling back to their kennels at Manassas and Oak Hill. But they fear the as yet unorganized masses of their own section, *who are preparing for them the doom of Belshazzar,* and who will hold them to a just and stern accountability for their crimes. They fear the rising indignation of an outraged and down-trodden people, who have been betrayed by passion and excitement into an acquiescence in the usurpers acts, but who have not been educated in the short space of five months, to support the yoke of an absolute despotism, after having received the blood-bought heritage of freedom from their fathers, and enjoyed its blessings from their birth." [August 30th, 1861.]

"Several of the bridge burners in Greene county, have been arrested and brought to Knoxville and lodged in jail. Their names are Loomy McDaniel, three Harman brothers and —— Haun. We hope the last one of them may be found out and punished."

"One of the bridge burners was to be hung at Knoxville on Wednesday last—sentenced by the court-martial now sitting there."

"LINCOLN'S USURPATIONS.—A cotemporary says the usurpations of Lincoln far exceed the wildest prophecies and the most excited apprehensions of those Southern men who were prepared for acts contrary to the Constitution and oppressive to the South. Had even the most ultra secessionist in South Carolina ventured to predict of the Lincoln Administration what has actually occurred, he would have been regarded as a madman. Had his most determined enemy in Tennessee asserted that he would not be in power four months before *he would strike down the habeas corpus, suppress the freedom of the press, as in St. Louis, call into the field 300,000 troops, increase the regular army and navy without authority from the Legislature, shoot down unarmed citizens in the streets by his mercenaries, invade the Southern States, harbor fugitive slaves in his military lines, supercede the civil power in Baltimore,* countenance the partition of Virginia, and seize the railroads, he would have been laughed at as a man without candor or reason. And yet Lincoln has done all these things in open day, and attempts to justify them in his message on that plea of tyrants—necessity."— [July 19th, 1861.]

"WE sympathise with our brave boys who are so impatient at delay and chafing under the curb like a blooded steed. We hope they may soon have an opportunity of trying their metal in some manner worthy of them. In the meantime, while they are nursing their wrath, let them whet their knives, pick their flints, and be fully ready for the frolic." [December 13th, 1861.]

"OLD ABE has decreed that every man who loses his gun on the field of battle, shall have twelve dollars deducted from his pay. The poor Yankee devils who are fighting to enslave themselves, have a hard master to deal with—one who resorts to the most contemptible tricks to cheat them of their pay."

"The struggle which has been forced upon the people of Tennessee involves the entire issue between freedom and slavery. It is the second war for independence. If there is any difference, *the exactions of King George III. and his Parliament were more tolerant than those of Mr. Lincoln and his supporters.*"

"PROTECTING PUBLIC PROPERTY. — *The ourang-outang President,* who in his inaugural and proclamations, has dwelt with marked emphasis on the duty which devolves upon him of 'protecting the public property,' seems to be possessed of strange ideas on this subject. He commanded the destruction of the works and arms at Harper's Ferry. He instructed the naval commandant at Norfolk to burn the navy yard and its vast stores at Norfolk. The noble Merrimac was scuttled, and other war vessels in the harbor of Norfolk, by order of the august protector of public property. The magnificent capitol.

with its decorations, its frescoe work, and polished marble halls, is converted into a barracks for filthy Hessians, and is said to be mined with a view to its total destruction at no distant day. *Lincoln will retire from Washington lighted by the flames which consume the sacred edifice that contains the archives of the once glorious nationality of the United States. He may be pardoned for reducing the former to ashes, but the unpardonable sin from which his soul can never be cleansed, is the destruction of the peace of the American continent.*"

"BILL ARP TO ABE LINKHORN.—*Mr. Abe Linkhorn*—Sir: I suppose my letter were taken by you as an insult, tho it want intended. I have hearn that you sent it to the Dead Letter offis. Well, I don't know, of course; but its my opinion you had better not put any more trash in that Semetary, for you'll need all the burying ground you've got about Washington for other purposes soon. I've been doin all I could to keep things quiet and consilliate you, but I see you are bent on scrowgin our boys into a fight, so I can jest tell you, I'm again you, and you can git as feroshus a fight as you desire. Your konduct has riz my pisen—you've trod on my rattlesnake sir, and everything I handle at these presents is infectious, so look out, and if you don't want to swell up from handlin this letter, you had better take another drink.

"We sent a few thousand of our boys to see you, and present arms, and fix up this difficulty. But I suppose you thought they were obeyin your 20 days notis, and was carryin their guns to you, and so you come out with more proclama-shuns, and Marshall law, and a blockade, and other nonsense, and now I don't know what our boys will do. I will notify you they never give no bonds to keep the Peace before they left home—the fact is, they couldn't give security; so Mr. Linkhorn, you can look for 'em."—*Rome Southerner.* [July 12, 1861.]

The last extract is a small portion of one of a series of long letters of the same caste found in the *Banner*, and may be taken as an illustration of its journalistic culture and the tone of its moral sentiment. Any number of pages of the same obscene ribaldry and billingsgate, utterly beneath the dignity of any public print, might be extracted from the few issues of the *Banner* in our possession.

The following extracts are important as giving information in regard to the rebel war spirit that not only actuated the editor of the *Banner*, but that prevailed among the rebels in the country, at the commencement of the rebellion:

"POLK COUNTY.—We spent a portion of this week in Polk. We found the war spirit considerably in the ascendant, and great unanimity of feeling among the people of that county. Capt. J. F. Hannah is now in camp at Knoxville with a company of 90 men, from that gallant and patriotic county, and Capt. E. P. Douglass will march, in a few days, with a company of 100 men—this will give noble little Polk 190 men in the field. In addition to this, Maj. Bob. McClary is making up a cavalry company, which he will be able to report in a week or two. The war feeling in Polk is aroused, and it knows no ebbing. Her boys are made out of the right kind of material, and we venture that if they ever have a conflict with the enemy they will give a good account of themselves." [May 24th, 1861.]

"VOLUNTEERS!—All who have joined and wish to join a cavalry company, are requested to meet at Cleveland on Saturday next.

"Capt. Harris will drill the members as infantry on that day.

"Speeches will be made, and the ladies are invited to be present.

"John H. Kuhn, George Tucker and others, are getting up the company.

"Come on—now is the time to join the armies for Southern Independence. The company is already nearly made up, with choice men, and if you wish to go with a good crowd now is your time."— [July 12th, 1861.]

"A company of volunteers, for immediate service, was raised at Chickamauga, on Monday last. The following are the officers of said company:

GEORGE S. GILLESPIE, Capt.	J. D. Ellis, 3d Lieut.
J. S. SPRINGFIELD, 1st Lieut.	D. D. WILKINS, O. S."
ROBT. WATKINS, 2d Lieut.	[May 10th, 1861.]

"John N. Dunn, Esq., of this place (Cleveland), is making up an infantry company for the Confederate service. He desires all who wish to volunteer to give him a call. He is authorized and empowered to muster them into service as they enroll their names."

"LEFT.—On Tuesday last Capt. Dill and his company left Calhoun, McMinn county, for Knoxville. Capt. Dill served two campaigns in Mexico, and a more gallant man never led a charge than he. Success attend him and his company." [May 10th, 1861.]

"A company of volunteers is being formed at this place (Cleveland). It now numbers about 40 members. Men wanting to join can report themselves either to Col. C. H. Mills, S. A. R. Swan or Capt. John D. Traynor." [May 10th, 1861.]

"We learn that the Legislature has passed an Ordinance of Secession, to be submitted to a vote of the people on the 8th day of June; also authorizing the Governor to call out 25,000 troops for immediate service, and 30,000 as a reserve to protect the border of the State, and appropriating $5,000,000 for arming and equipping the State." [May 10th, 1861.]

"THE SPIRIT OF TENNESSEE.—It has been scarcely ten days since the law calling 55,000 volunteers in this State was published, and we are informed that about 25,000 have already been reported to the Governor as ready to defend the liberty and honor of the State."— [May 24th, 1861.]

"It is estimated by competent judges that Middle and West Tennessee will give a majority of from 60 to 75,000 in favor of the State declaring her independence. Our news from there says the people are almost a unit for 'Separation and Representation.' We are honestly of the opinion, that if we all live, that we will get up members of the Southern Confederacy, on Sunday morning, by at least a majority of 40,000 votes." [June 7th, 1861.]

"VOLUNTEERS.—By reference to their card, it will be seen that J. M. Horton and J. G. M. Montgomery are making up a volunteer company for the Confederate service. We are personally acquainted with both the gentlemen, and can say that we know of no two men that are better adapted for the enterprise they propose than they are. They will make first-rate fellows to go to war with. Pitch in, boys, and make up the company instanter." [December 13th, 1861.]

" Within the last ten days some 8 or 10,000 troops have passed over the East Tennessee & Georgia Railroad for Virginia. At our depot, as at all others we have heard from, the citizens, and especially the ladies, turn out and cheer, applaud and bid them God-speed in their patriotic devotion to their country. It is said that their passage through East Tennessee is a perfect ovation."

" MR. VALLANDIGHAM'S SPEECH.—To the exclusion of our usual variety of news, we publish the speech of this gentleman, in the House of Representatives, on the 10th instant. We want everybody to read it—it is a bold and fearless expose of Lincoln and his policy. It should be recollected that Mr. Vallandigham is a Northwestern man, representing a congressional district in Ohio."

As stated in another place, the *Banner* was suppressed in the winter of 1863 and 1864 by the Federal authorities. Mr. Robt. McNelly, its editor, notwithstanding his loud protestations of Southern courage, and his own personal determinations of final resistance, when the trying hour came, found his rebel ardor chilled by the first blast from the Northern blue coats.

Mr. McNelly could follow Union men, fleeing for their lives from the wickedness of rebel persecution with his wishes that they might never return. He could see Union men by the thousand hunted like so many wolves over the country, and hung by the necks like dogs, their families dashed to pieces as with bolts of lightning, their wives made widows, their helpless children orphaned, scattered, impoverished, with sighs and tears for their only solace by night and by day. All this he could see and encourage, and could heap upon the most worthy men in Bradley epithets that would disgrace a savage, not only with the *nonchalance* of one apparently destitute of humanity, but with approval of the general work, sent broadcast through the land in the columns of his contemptible *Banner*. When, however, it came Mr. McNelly's turn to choose between the endearments of home and his love of the Jeff. Davis Government, his chivalrous Southern patriotism would not allow him to move a step to aid the latter in its extremeties. To leave home and family, wife and children, was not so pleasant a pastime, nor so trifling a matter, when his own fireside and threshhold were to be tried by it. The Confederacy kept him alive while he was in it, but when the Confederacy had to leave Bradley, so far as he was concerned, it must fight its own battles.

The same nature that did not care for the guilt, nor count the consequences of the first crime, could now resort to meanness and submit to every humiliation to be permitted to still live among those whom he had so deeply injured. He could take the oath more with a view to

EDITOR OF THE BANNER TAKING THE OATH.

escape punishment than as a confession that he had done wrong, with a mental reservation to remain the same as he always had been to the farthest possible verge of safety to himself and family. He could submit like a spaniel to be ridden on a rail through the streets of Cleveland by the Union boys whom he had injured, and when the performance was finished could implore them to give him a chew of tobacco to excite physical relief from the pain of the operation.

This was the editor of the Cleveland *Banner*, who, perhaps, did more than any other one man of his intellectual calibre to keep alive the rebellion and fan the fires of rebel persecution in Bradley county. Though his treason while the rebels were in power saved him and his family from the sufferings and devastation which they usually visited upon the Union people, and though his pardon from the Federals remitted the punishment justly due for his sins, yet the part he acted was too conspicuous, cost too many lives, caused too many hearts to bleed, caused the shedding of too many tears, for him to be allowed to escape entirely the just severity of the historical pen.

In September, 1865, the *Banner* was resuscitated by Mr. McNelly, and is now being published again by him in Cleveland. The real character of the *Banner*, as well as the proportion of suffering in Bradley actually traceable to this source, can be measurably inferred from the numerous extracts from its columns given in this work.

ILLUMINATION.

On receipt of the news in Cleveland of the rebel victory at Manassas, great joy was felt by the rebels, so much so that a perfect tumult of excitement prevailed among them, and in the evening, expressive of that joy, and in honor of the great event, the town was brilliantly illuminated. The following is the editorial of the Cleveland *Banner* upon the subject:

"ILLUMINATION.—The Southern people of our town, in honor of the victory won by Southern troops, at Manassas, illuminated their houses on Wednesday night, which was quite a creditable affair. The people were addressed by T. J. Campbell, S. A. Smith, G. W. Rowles, and W. H. Tibbs. Everything passed off finely." [July 26th, 1861.]

The following are the names of some of the rebels in Cleveland who participated in the illumination:

Alexander Davis, dwelling.
Ocoee Hotel, kept by Thomas Johnson.
Frank Johnson, store.
Hardwick & Tucker, store.
Robt. McNelly, editor, dwelling.
Joseph Horton, store.
Rev. Elder Worley, dwelling.
D. C. Kennor, store.
James Hoyl, store.
Widow Traynor, dwelling.
Wm. H. Tibbs, store.
Dr. Edwards, store and dwelling. A bonfire was also built before Mr. Edwards' store.
—— Edwards, store.
Patrick O'Conner, store.
James Craigmiles, dwelling.
Guthman & Brothers, store.
G. W. Cook, store.
J. G. M. Montgomery, store.
John F. Rogers, store.

SLAVERY A BIBLE INSTITUTION.

"REV. WM. McNUTT:—*Dear Sir:* The undersigned respectfully solicit you for a copy of your sermon on 'Slavery,' delivered at the Baptist Church in Cleveland, on the 27th January, 1861. We think you established the right of slavery by Divine authority, beyond all cavil, and we want it in print for the people to read. Will you comply with our request and very much oblige,

"Yours most respectfully,

ANDERSON CAMPBELL,
W. P. LEA,
S. D. BRIDGEMAN,
JOHN H. PAYNE,
G. W. COOK,
G. L. TUCKER,
S. P. GAUT,
J. L. M. BRITTAIN,
JAS. M. CRAIGMILES,
JOHN N. COWAN,
TIMOTHY HANEY,
R. E. JOHNSTON,
W. W. GIDDENS.

"GENTLEMEN:—In compliance with your request I present you a copy of my Sermon on Slavery, preached at the Baptist Church in this place, on the 27th of January, 1861. When I delivered the Sermon it was not written out, but by the aid of the notes I used on that occasion I have very hastily drawn up the whole sermon, in the same form and order in which it was delivered, and humbly hope that under the blessing of God it may accomplish good.

"I remain yours, most respectfully,

W. McNUTT."

[From the Cleveland *Banner*, Feb. 22d, 1861.]

Mr. McNutt was a Baptist Clergyman resident in Cleveland, and among the most rampant Reverend gentlemen in the county.

CHAPTER XIV.

THE STONECYPHER FAMILY.

ONE of the early settlers in Bradley county was Mr. Absalom Stonecypher. He lived in the third district, and but a short distance north of the Tennessee and Georgia line. His family consisted of his wife, two sons, one about eighteen at the opening of the rebellion, and the other some years younger, and two or three daughters still younger than the boys.

Mr. Stonecypher, with his family, lived upon a small farm of his own—was an honest and hard working man, quiet, peaceable and unpretending, of feeble constitution, and toward the close of his life, a perfect invalid. The rest of the family, characteristically, were the counterpart of the husband and father, the whole living in peace and harmony; were home abiding, meddling with no one; and by their joint industry and economy procured an humble livelihood, with which, being contented, they were proportionately happy.

Mr. Stonecypher never owned any slaves, nor any of his family, nor ever hired any, consequently never bouhgt, sold nor whipped any; yet they paid their honest debts, government taxes and all. In regard to virtue and good morals, the family was above reproach, all its members loved their country, venerated the old flag, hated secession, resisted rebellion, never lost their rights under the old Government, but felt the obligations of loyalty for the protection which this Government had afforded them and their humble home for so many years.

Though not the *poor*, yet it will be seen that this description places this family among those whom the fastidiousness of society prefers to denominate the *poorer class*.

Though this family will serve as the ground of our narrative in this case, yet a neighboring family had so much to do with the shading of the picture, that it may be a help to the view to describe the two in juxta-position as our field premises.

This neighbor was Mr. John Bryant, who, though living but a short distance south of Mr. Stonecypher, was a resident of Georgia, and also among the earliest settlers of the country. Mr. Bryant was the owner of a somewhat extensive and rich plantation, proportionally well-stocked with slaves, by the aid of whom his fields were systematically cultivated with a view not only to a competence for himself and family, but with a distinct aim to enlarge his possessions and be counted among the wealthy and influential of the land. For many years this family had lived not only entirely above want, but independent of systematic and severe labor, all its members moving at their ease in society, with a fair prospect, under the existing state of things, of the continuance of these blessings.

As a citizen or neighbor, nothing positively objectionable was known against Mr. Bryant. Nor was anything known particularly disparaging to the character of his family. He, however, was known as one of that intellectual stamp, one whose moral philosophy allowed the mere preferences of human nature, instead of original and independent moral convictions of right and wrong, to frame rules for society, and to dictate governmental policy. He was also known as one whose practice persistently agreed with his theory — as one who lived, bought and sold, moved in community, politically electioneered, and publicly and privately instructed his family upon this principle. In all worldly points of view, and before this narrative closes, the reader, perhaps, will think in some other points also, the two families thus described, presented exactly opposite phases of social life.

Having thus lived in these respective positions, both locally and socially, for many years, with no other differences than these, without any animosity arising between them, the great rebellion came howling around both of these families, and was before each for its suffrage or to administer its own punishment if that suffrage was withheld. As might have been foreseen in both cases, Mr. Bryant and his family welcomed to their bosoms the crimson crowned monster and bid him God speed in his work of blood, while Mr. Stonecypher and his family in the simplicity of their convictions of duty, grappled with him as a personal and national enemy.

We shall now drop the family of Mr. Bryant, until the history of the other brings the two again in contact, when we shall elucidate them in connection or separately, as the case may be, to the end of the chapter.

Mr. Stonecypher at the breaking out of the rebellion, was not far from sixty years of age. Though never forward as a public man, and though he was now unable, from ill health, to influence any, for or against the rebellion beyond the circle of his own family, was nevertheless, soon known to both parties as an unwavering Union man. This fact, surrounded as Mr. Stonecypher was with hundreds of rebel citizen informers, could not long remain a secret from the notable Capt. Brown, then encamped with his men at Cleveland.

Some time in December, 1861, Capt. Brown ordered the arrest of old Mr. Stonecypher, sending about twenty men to execute the command and bring him a prisoner to Cleveland. Among these were James Miller, Wm. Brittain, Berry Gillian, and others, dressed in citizens garb, neighbors of Mr. Stonecypher, living some of them not more than a mile from his house.

These and many other rebels in the third district acted in the double capacity of informers and soldiers, first informing, then as rebel soldiers under Brown's instructions, arresting those whom they had reported.

Mr. Stonecypher was taken to the rebel camp at Cleveland, and by Brown confined in the guard-house. After enduring for a short time, the hardships common to that as a place of disciplinary punishment concocted by Brown, he succeeded in obtaining a hearing before his majesty, the only result of which was, that he was insultingly told that he was marked for Tuscaloosa. After being under guard four days, and becoming fully satisfied that Tuscaloosa was his intended doom, he obtained the privilege of addressing a letter to his family. In this letter he stated to his wife, that every time a Southern train stopped at the depot he expected to be put on board for Tuscaloosa. Receiving the letter, Mrs. Stonecypher and John her eldest boy, a lad perhaps between sixteen and eighteen, hastened to Cleveland, a distance of eleven miles, where the old lady appealed to Brown and others in behalf of her husband. She proposed to have him put on trial, and his case investigated. Failing in this, Brown in particular, refusing to give her husband a trial, she appealed to their honor and sense of justice, informing them that on account of his age and feebleness her husband could do them nor the rebellion any harm, that he had not been off the farm for weeks before they brought him to Cleveland, and though he was a Union man, he had conspired with no one, nor influenced any against their cause.

She told Brown that if he sent her husband to Tuscaloosa it would be the means of his death, and that immediately; and that it looked to her like great cruelty to send a man of his age, and one in his condition, to a Southern prison, when it was evident that it would cost him his life, and all for no crime, only that he did not think as they did about the rebellion. This effort however, was as fruitless as the other, and as she could avail nothing, Mrs. Stonecypher returned to her home, if not in utter despair, yet with less hope than ever before, that her husband could be saved. The boy, however, in view of some further effort or something of the kind, did not return with his mother, but remained with the intention of following her the next morning. The next morning came, but when the hour drew near that he was to part with his father, all appeals thus far having proved in vain, the intensity of his feelings suggested one more method, as yet untried, by which his father possibly might be saved. The boy went to Brown and offered to take his father's place and as a prisoner submit to his father's fate, whatever it might be, if on these conditions his father could be released, or as the boy's mother expressed it, "offered to yield up his own life to save the life of his father." Brown told the boy that if he would enlist as a rebel soldier, and obligate himself to fight like the other rebel soldiers for the rebellion, he would release his father. To promise faithfully from his heart to do all this, is what, perhaps, the boy never did; but his father's life was at stake, there was no other salvation, he immediately enlisted, his father was released and went home instead of himself.

On releasing the old gentleman, Brown put a guard over him, with instructions to the guard to take him immediately out of camp and out of Cleveland, and to go with him toward his home until he was three miles away. Mr. Stonecypher had walked but a short distance after the guard left him, before a gang of rebels from camp overtook him and insisted that he should guide them to his nephews, a Union man, whom they were in pursuit of. The old gentleman objected to this, saying that it would take him three miles out of his way, and if he was compelled to act he could direct them, so that it would be the same to them as for him to go with them. They cursed him, and told him that they would trust to none of his directions, and if he made any further objections they would take him back to Cleveland. He went with them, and was not released until he had revealed to them the residence of his nephew.

The old gentleman finally reached home in comparative safety, but not without manifest injury to his already sinking constitution from the mental vexation and rough physical treatment occasioned by his arrest and imprisonment.

Young Stonecypher having thus enlisted, was put into Capt. Dunn's company, serving in the same regiment with Brown. Not long after this regiment was ordered to the field at Knoxville. The boy was in fact unfit for a soldier, not only being too young, but constitutionally incapable, especially in the cold of winter, of bearing up under the effects of a sudden change from the quiet and comforts of home, to the hardships and privations of camp life. It was evident to many of his friends at the time, that his enlistment was the forfeiture of his life. He enlisted some time in December, and although in camp at Cleveland but a short time, his health began to fail before his regiment was ordered to the field, and he died on the 6th of January, 1862, at Knoxville, serving in the rebel ranks, perhaps scarcely one month.

Though young Stonecypher was serving the rebels against his will, he was an obedient and submissive soldier, easily imposed upon, a proper subject for the abuse of indolent and tyrannical rebel officers. The same day he died, he was made to perform double duty as camp or picket guard, being compelled to stand not only his own hours, but in addition as one tour, those of another, when it was known to every reasonable man in his company, that he was not nor had been for days, fit to perform any duty whatever. His double duty being ended he went into his tent, laid himself down in his blanket and never woke again.

The mournful fate of this virtuous and loyal youth, whose filial affection, saved the life of his father, for the time, only at the sacrifice of his own, is one of that long catalogue of crimes that will confront the spirit of his brutal murderer in the day of final reckoning, if it does not before.

Brown's object in hurrying old Mr. Stonecypher immediately out of camp and out of sight, as soon as released, is not altogether clear. The only plausible explanation seems to be the following:

Conscious of his own abominable villainy in arresting and imprisoning such a man, also in compelling his son to enlist to save his father from Tuscaloosa, and knowing that the Union people, as far as they had a knowledge of the transaction, looked upon the whole as in keeping with his usual course, Brown, perhaps felt it for his interest to close the matter up as much in the dark as possible. Had Mr. Stonecypher been permitted to communicate freely among his friends in Cleveland for a day, or even for a few hours after his release, immediately revealing the fact that his son was sacrificed to effect it, the general indignation would have been more deep and wide-spread at the time, and the atrocity more likely to reach the ears of some of Brown's own party not altogether imbruted like himself. As a bar to these possible contingences Mr. Stonecypher was slipped away, which, together with being captured by the gang of guerrillas, prevented him from communicating with any person till six or seven miles from Cleveland.

From the death of this boy at Knoxville till the summer of 1863, the family of Mr. Stonecypher escaped, perhaps, with as little injury from the rebels as the generality of Union people in the third district. In fact, the condition of the family after and in consequence of the death of this boy, and in consequence of the feeble health of the old gentleman, enhanced by the treatment he received from Brown, was such that none but the most abandoned even among the rebels, would have entertained a thought of offering any of its members further molestation.

A younger son was still left, who in the summer of 1863 passed his sixteenth birthday. He must be eighteen, however, before he could be reached by the rebel conscript law. But few fears, therefore, were entertained by his parents that he would be taken from them, as it was easily presumed that before two years longer Tennessee would be wrested from the hands of the rebels. Past experience, however, might have suggested that neither these nor any other considerations were perfect security to any one under the reign of the Southern Rebellion.

The war had now lasted nearly two years and a half. Its novelty had worn off, and its pressure began to be severely felt among all classes at the South. The sons of many rebel families who enlisted in the spring of 1861 had grown tired of the service, and were anxious to return to their homes. Among other things, as a method of relief, a system of substitution began to be resorted to, which, from the abominable wickednes of the rebels, was soon brought into general use.

Among the rebel families in Northern Georgia, who in the summer of 1863, attempted to avail themselves of the benefit of this system of substitution, was that of Mr. John Bryant, the family contrasted with that of Mr. Stonecypher's at the commencement of this narrative.

A son of Mr. Bryant enlisted in the rebel army in 1861, and had served on the Potomac till June, 1863. This son now felt that he had passed through his share of bloody battles to liberate the South, an opinion in which his father and the rest of his family coincided, and as his father was rich he felt that the rest of his term might be substituted by wealth in the person of some other soldier. Accordingly, Mr. Bryant offered $2,500 for a substitute to take the place of his son in the rebel army on the Potomac. This bid, however, was not altogether a public one, a bid that should become a contract with the person who should first offer himself as the desired substitute, himself to receive the bounty; but the bid was made to rebel substitute brokers, who were making it a regular business to arrest or kidnap Union boys and Union men, and sell them to rich rebel parents and those who were in need of substitutes for their sons and relations in the rebel army.

This proposal was made by Mr. Byrant sometime in May or in the first of June, 1863. Before the tenth of the latter month four men came in the night, about ten o'clock, to the house of Mr. Stonecypher, rapped at the door, and, though the family had retired, were soon admitted by Mrs. Stonecypher, the old gentleman being confined to his bed and unable to rise. Mrs. Stonecypher was well acquainted with two of the men—Wm. P. Tracy, and Samuel Kincannon, the others, who subsequently proved to be Richard Acock and Charles Davis, she had recollections of seeing but did not know their names. They informed Mrs. Stonecypher that they came to conscript her remaining son into the rebel army, and pretended to have papers from the rebel authorities for so doing. She replied that this could not be, that her son was clear of the conscript, being only sixteen years of age.

11

Appearing to doubt her word she showed them in her Bible the record of her son's birth. This appeared to unsettle them for a moment, and they pretended to be on the point of leaving, requesting of Mrs. Stonecypher to take her Bible with them. Being asked what they proposed to do with her Bible, they replied, evasively, that they wished to show the record of her son's birth to some persons. The Bible being refused, instead of leaving, three of the party went out, and a few steps from the door held a consultation, while the other remained inside talking with Mrs. Stonecypher. At the expiration of ten or fifteen minutes the three came in, when all joined in an attempt to persuade Mrs. and Mr. Stonecypher to allow their son to volunteer in the rebel army. Meeting with no success with the parents, they went to the bed where the boy lay and persuaded, or rather compelled, him to get up and go out with them, stating that they had something to tell him. Getting the boy out, they proposed to him to enlist in the rebel army. He objecting and they being unable to persuade him, they commenced to threaten him, using also different strategies to frighten him. The night was very dark. They told him if he did not go with them that night to join his regiment, that there were persons not far away who would certainly shoot him. Some of the party standing not far from the boy bursted the caps on their revolvers to help on the work of frightening him into submission. Demonstrations and threats of this kind not having the desired effect, they invented a scheme which in proportion as it was more depraved and diabolical was more successful.

They told the boy that he could take his choice of two things, he could go with them and enlist as they desired, or he could go with them and be sent to the Penitentiary. On being asked by the boy what he had done for which they could send him to the Penitentiary, they told him that he knew well enough what he had done, that he knew that he, not long before, had been guilty of rape on the person of a little girl in the neighborhood, that they could prove it on him, and if he did not confess it and go into the rebel army they would arrest him then and there, have him immediately tried and convicted of this crime and sent to the Penitentiary.

After being tortured in this manner by these four men, or rather Devils, some of them perhaps over fifty years of age, for half an hour, the nerves of the boy gave way, and bursting into tears, he consented to enlist in the rebel army. The men then went into the house, told his parents that Absalom had volunteered, that it was his own choice, in which case their objections could be of no avail, that the rebel authorities would take him, and after making Mrs. Stonecypher promise to meet them some time the next day at the house of Mr. Harrison Taft, about two miles from her own home, notwithstanding all the parents could do or say, they hurried the boy off, taking him that night about four miles to the house of a Mr. Tucker, a rebel, on Cooahulla Creek, reaching there about two o'clock in the morning. The agony that wrung the hearts of those parents, as well as the hearts of the other members of the family, the rest of that night we will not attempt to describe. Soon after reaching Tucker's two of the four men left on some other business, and did not return until after the family had breakfasted. The two having charge of Absalom, also went about a mile from Tucker's, taking him with them, to get another Union boy, who, however, eluded their grasp, and the three returned to Tucker's, being absent about two hours. Shortly after breakfast the four men started with Absalom for Varnal's Station, distant but a few miles, from which point Kincannon alone took him to Dalton, distant but a few miles further, the other three remaining behind, two of whom, it appears, repaired to the house of Mr. Taft to meet Mrs. Stonecypher according to arrangements, which she was compelled to consent to the night before as just related. Anxious about her boy, and hoping to obtain some information in regard to his fate, Mrs. Stonecypher was promptly at Mr. Taft's agreeably to her promise, where she found these two men in company with a Esquire Dean, who to some extent, no doubt, had also been connected with Absalom's arrest. These two men compelled Mrs. Stonecypher before Esq. Dean to testify, or make some statement in regard to her son's age. Being in deep trouble, and withal confused at the time, she was afterwards unable to recall the exact nature of the statement drawn from her. All the information she could get from them in regard to her son, was that he had enlisted in the rebel army as a substitute.

From Taft's she returned to her home sad enough, a sadness that grew heavier and heavier as the darkness of night drew on, and as she reflected upon the melancholy fate of her two boys. One was already murdered, and the other was now torn from her in a manner that left her but the faintest ray of hope that she would ever see his face again. The information she received from the two men at Tafts, namely, that Absalom had already left Varnal's Station, on his way to his regiment in the rebel army, apparently revealing the fact that to serve in the rebel ranks until his death, or until the end of the war, was now his certain doom—was a bolt that shivered her heart to atoms, and weighed her down with a load of sorrow, such as none but a mother can feel. The other members of the family also, the father stretched upon his bed of sickness, the daughters and sisters, all, with the mother deeply felt the severity of this additional affliction and sore bereavement. The last hope of the mother, and last strong support of the other members of the family also, the rebellion had now taken from them, leaving a vacancy around that hearth which, with their reflections upon the mournful fate, at best, that awaited the boy in the hated rebel army, far from home, exposed to a thousand evils, sent them to their couches that night with a pungency of grief and bitterness of life, which, perhaps, scarcely ever smote their hearts before.

Kincannon and Absalom reaching Dalton about the middle of the day, Kincannon presented the boy to the Provost Marshal, who took his name, designating the regiment to which he was afterwards to be sent. It was a Georgia regiment.

Bryant, that same afternoon, unquestionably, according to previous arrangement, met the kidnapper with his victim at Dalton and Absalom was turned to him as the substitute for which he, Bryant, was to pay $2,500. Bryant took possession of the boy, and the two immediately set out for the rich man's plantation, preparatory to a start for Richmond, Virginia, the next day.

Seeing himself alone with Bryant, and smarting under a sense of the injustice of his fate, though but sixteen, Absalom began to calculate the possibilities of his escape. Notwithstanding in his judgement the chances in his favor would allow, if necessary, a sudden and bold attempt to free himself, yet he also thought that the nature of the case justified any advantage that deception and working upon Bryant's credulity might give him; and, therefore, determined on the latter course before resorting to more desperate measures. He requested of Mr. Bryant, inasmuch as he was going so far **away, with so** many probabilities that he would never return, to be permitted, instead of stopping with him, to spend the night at his own home, promising to return to Bryant the next morning. Bryant objected to this, alleging that his arrangements were all perfected for both to take the cars at Varnal's Station early the next morning for Richmond, Virginia. Absalom pressed his suit, and while discussing the subject they came to the house of the rebel Justice of the Peace, Esq. Dean, the veritable magistrate who has already been introduced to the reader. Dean here joined Bryant in dissuading the boy from visiting his mother, stating particularly that it was some distance to walk that night, that the night was dark, and he would be in danger of being bushwhacked, especially at a certain point, by George Klick and old man Cook. It is true that these were two notorious rebel bushwhackers then desolating that part of the country, but neither this nor the arguments of Dean and Bryant abated the boy's desire to see his friends once more before going to Virginia; and after leaving Dean's he renewed his appeals to Bryant more urgently than before, and pressed him so vigorously that he yielded the point on condition that Absalom would promise upon his honor to return to him the next morning. To this Absalom consented and the thing was considered settled. In a short time, however, Bryant reflecting perhaps, on the influences that might be brought to bear upon the boy to make him break his promise, and the risk he was taking, everything considered, re-called his words and insisted that Absalom should not leave him. This served not only to renew the former struggle but to increase its former intensity, and Bryant was soon brought back to his contract, based upon the same conditions as before, and on these conditions Bryant and Absalom parted, each directing his steps to towards his respective home.

It is a little remarkable that Bryant consented under any circumstances short of those actually compulsory, to let the boy visit his home. Although Bryant must have known before the boy was captured that he was to be the victim, being perhaps also informed by the two absent so long from Tucker's, or by some one of the three left behind at Varnal's Station, that he was taken and was on his way to Dalton, in consequence of which he went there to receive him; yet it is possible, that he did not know the whole of the wickedness by which he was secured. It is possible also, that Bryant was deceived in regard to the boy's willingness to go, by the leisurely manner in which he entered into conversation with him upon the nature of the trip, inquiring how much money he was to have for going as his son's substitute, &c. But whatever might have been the principal cause that induced Bryant to give the boy this advantage of him, the advantage was gained the boy reaching his home in safety; and we can imagine the relief felt by his mother after the sad forebodings the visit to Taft's had occasioned her, and the joy she experienced, when about twelve o'clock that night, or a little less than twenty-four hours from the time he was taken away, she unexpectedly heard his voice at the door, he having escaped from Bryant as just related. We can also imagine the degree of conscientiousness she as well as the other members of the family felt about his keeping his promise to return to the tyrant the next morning. Such were their joy and fear together at this moment, that he remained in the house but a few minutes, taking quarters for the rest of the night, if less comfortable yet of more supposable safety than the couch **he had been** forced to leave the night before.

Having a knowledge of all the facts, the **reader** can judge whether the boy was morally bound to keep his promise, and can judge whether he was encouraged to do so by his parents and his friends on his return; and accordingly can calculate the amount of joy experienced the next morning by Bryant, at meeting young Stonecypher preparatory to taking him to Virginia, as a substitute for his son in the rebel army.

Instead of meeting Bryant the next day **at ten o'clock**, and giving himself up to fight the battles of the rebellion for him and his son, before night he had selected a **hiding** place in some ravine or thicket, and for the present was secure against the kidnapping rebel **substitute brokers.** No sooner, **however, were these** brokers informed by Bryant that Absalom had turned traitor, than a combined effort was put forth to retake him, especially by the Gregories, who it was known had much to do with **his arrest** before.

Absalom remained in the **woods, occasionally slying** his way in the night to some Union **house,** where he would be secreted a few days, from this time, the first of **June, until the following October, during which** period his mother and her **Union** neighbors exhausted every strategy to supply him with food, without revealing the places of his concealment. Being at one time more hotly pursued than usual he fled in the night to Polk county, where a Union widow woman named Pitts, secreted him in her house three weeks.

The efforts of these rebel kidnappers to recapture Stonecypher being prosecuted without success, and the prospect on the whole becoming **rather** gloomy: it was planned by them that the Gregories, the family whose child it was pretended the boy had injured, should swear out a State warrant, on which he was to be hunted out and taken by the civil officers and punished for his alleged crime upon the child. The warrant was put into the hands of an officer by the name of Lemuel Jones, a notorious rebel; and the besieging parties waited with anxiety for results. Notwithstanding Mr. Jones was a rebel, in this case, to his credit it must be stated, that he acted with some principle. Knowing that the boy was as innocent of this crime as himself, or the most distant person in the world, and knowing that the warrant in his hands was the fruits of perjury, and malice, created by the boy's escape from Bryant, and their inability to recapture him, purposely allowed a knowledge of the proceedings to reach the boy's friends as an advance warning to escape, or as a hint for him to leave the country entirely. Profiting by this advice, as well perhaps, as by the advice of his own friends, the boy fled from Bradley, going North or Northeast, and finally enlisted in the Federal army, joining the 111th Ohio infantry. He served in this regiment faithfully, nearly three years with honor and credit to himself, securing the esteem of his officers, and was discharged after the war at Columbus, Ohio, on the first day of August 1865, and is now at home, the support of his widowed mother, as well as the guide and defender of his sisters, and a worthy, honored, and proud victor, to look with scorn upon his old enemies, and to laugh at the confusion and shame that have overtaken them.

It appears that when Bryant went to Dalton to receive Absalom from Kincannon, the plan was to take the cars immediately with him for Virginia, for he came to Dalton with a full supply of cooked and well prepared rations, sufficient for himself and the boy on the trip. What occurred to frustrate this plan and determine Bryany to take him to his own home until the next day is not known, whatever it was, it was this, perhaps, that saved the boy's life.

At the time Absalom was kidnapped his father was

lying upon his death-bed. His chronic difficulties having been increased by the abuse he received from Brown a year and a half previous, and being then aggravated by the troubles and sufferings through which he was still passing, he died a few days after this event and was buried while his son was hiding in the woods, the boy as well as his mother feeling it unsafe for him to visit his father in his last moments, or come out to attend his father's funeral.

When Bryant and the boy started from Dalton for Bryant's house, the boy asked him how much money he paid the men for getting him as his son's substitute, and how much of it he was to have himself. Bryant replied that he was to give old man Gregory five hundred dollars, and the other four each five hundred also, and whether they would give him any of the money he did not know.

What became of Bryant's rebel son, whether his father succeeded in procuring a Union substitute to fight his battles for him; or whether the five villains received each his five hundred dollars from Bryant, as a reward for stealing for him his neighbor's boy, is unknown to the writer.

That Bryant was deeply implicated, and guilty almost equally with the others in this crime, is beyond question. He probably knew as well as they before they went to Stonecypher's, that they intended to procure Absalom as the substitute, for which they were to receive the $2,500. The fact that Bryant met Kincannon at Dalton, with rations, which had required some time to prepare, for the boy's trip to Virginia, is evidence that he and his family knew beforehand the day on which this identical boy was to be delivered.

Jathan Gregory, one of the most vicious men in Bradley although a loud professor in the Methodist Church, and having one of the most wretched families in the county, the boys of which committed, perhaps, as great an amount of robbery, murder and incendiarism as those of any other family in the country, as already seen, was near neighbor to Mr. Stonecypher. It was supposed by Union friends that some of the Gregories were present, though not discovering themselves, the night Absalom was taken. It was supposed also that they first indicated to the others, that this boy could be seized and made the victim by which they could comply with Bryant's offer and secure the $2,500.

Although the pretended object of the Gregories and the other kidnapping villains in swearing out the civil warrant against Absalom was punishment for his alleged crime, yet the real object was to get the aid of the civil officer in bringing him to light and getting possession of him. These rebels all knew that it was patent to the whole community that the charge was a malicious fabrication; and they knew that no justice dare convict the boy and send him to the penitentiary on these charges. The real object, therefore, was, through the aid of the civil officer, once more to get possession of Absalom, when proposals of compromise would have been made as to the crime, the civil prosecution dropped, and he, through strategy, bribery, threats or kidnapping as before, retained and returned to Bryant as his runaway substitute.

We are now prepared briefly to remark upon the different parties concerned in this transaction.

The Gregories, Esq. Dean, Bryant, and the four scoundrels, Kincannon, Tracy, Davis and Acock, were all nearly equal in guilt as the perpetrators of this infamous business. Dean and Bryant might not have been privy to all the minutiae of its meanness, its consecutive and unmitigated shame, but their complicity in the matter criminates them equally with the rest, all having outraged in the affair every principle of humanity, Christianity and civilization. Almost every crime that humanity can commit was embodied in this transaction. All knew equally well the distressed condition of Mr. Stonecypher's family when the boy was taken. All knew that the old gentleman had been nearly helpless for months, and that he must soon die, leaving none, in the absence of the boy, but females in the family; and all knew what the family had already suffered from the rebellion. All comprehended perfectly the finishing blow of suffering and ruin it would be to the family to have the boy dragged off in the manner they proposed, and sent to the rebel army on the Potomac.

Dean was an old citizen, a man of family, and an acting Justice of the Peace. Bryant was an old citizen and an independent planter; and before the war was considered a respectable man. Gregory was also the head of a family, and a member of a Christian Church. The other four probably were all heads of families—Davis and Kincannon certainly were—and some of them men of some property and influence. The whole, before the war, pretended to be, and probably were considered, passably respectable citizens.

This case stamps all the parties concerned in it with infamy for life. Considering the innocence and helplessness of the victims, the extent of the injury contemplated, the abominable means employed to gain the proposed end, the number and social position of the perpetrators, the foregoing is a case of the most unrelieved blackness of human shame, beastly depravity, and uncompounded wickedness of any on the records of crime; and tells with unmistakable significance the moral character of the rebellion in East Tennessee.

The writer saw this same Esq. Dean in the Federal guard-house at Blue Springs, Bradley county, in the spring of 1864. He and another rebel prisoner were sent south through our lines in exchange for two Union men who had been captured by the rebels. Bryant is probably yet living upon his plantation in northern Georgia, south of Bradley. Gregory with his family is somewhere in Dixie. The last that was known of Davis he was in Loudon, a place some fifty miles west of Knoxville, engaged on the railroad. This Davis, with revolver in hand, was at one time in search of a Union man named Wm. B. Cowan, who was hidden but a few feet from Davis, in his own cellar. Being unable to find his victim, Davis presented his pistol at Mrs. Cowan, and threatened to shoot her dead if she did not tell where her husband was concealed. She, however, remained firm, and her husband was saved. Kincannon, Tracy and Acock, it was supposed by Union people, drifted south before the Federal army under Sherman

Should these pages ever meet the eye of any of these rebel subjects, they must remember that the rebellion is a matter of history; and though they have escaped the punishment due to their crimes, yet such cannot always escape that which, however displeasing to them, may nevertheless be a benefit to others, namely, the unmerciful pen of the vigilant historian.

It has been stated that the capturers of young Stonecypher were professedly rebel substitute brokers. It was known to be a fact that the Gregories and these four men who captured Stonecypher, with others, operated extensively through northern Georgia and southern Tennessee in this iniquitous business, and God and their own souls only know the deeds of blood they committed during the long years of 1862–63, in prosecuting this infernal work; and the number of helpless and innocent Union boys who finally lost their lives as the result of being captured and sold by these men into the rebel armies.

It is very probable that the whole of these blood-stained villains, unless justice has already demanded their lives, have taken the Federal oath, and are now not only pleading exemption from all prosecution in the matter of these crimes, but under the reconstruction policy of President Johnson are claiming restoration of all losses of property occasioned by the rebellion, and are also claiming equal political rights with those patriots whose friends they stole or murdered, and with those who fought and bled to save the country from being ruined by their treason.

CHAPTER XV.

CASE OF MR. WILLIAM HUMBERT.

MR. HUMBERT was born in Green county, East Tennessee, on the 27th of March, 1802, consequently at the outbreak of the rebellion, was about sixty years of age. He came to Bradley with his family in 1839, settling in the third district, where he lives at the present time.

Mr. Humbert's ancestors were true to the cause of the Revolution, a fact in the history of his family of which he felt an honorable pride, and which had always endeared to him the flag of his country, and the government which it represented. It was not singular, therefore, that when a choice was to be made between this flag and the flag of treason—the flag of the Southern rebellion — that the heart of Mr. Humbert clung to the flag as well as to the government of his fathers. He received both from their hands, had enjoyed their blessings as an heir-loom in the family for sixty years, never feeling them to be oppressive and could not now, as a man, as a Christian, and as a patriot, be persuaded to rebel against either.

This was Mr. Humbert's crime, the crime of adherance to the government of his country and of his fathers, a government that his conscience dictated had never wronged him, nor those who were seeking to destroy it. Mr. Humbert had lived a useful citizen in the third district for nearly twenty-five years, this being the first crime of which he was ever accused, even in his life, or for which he or any of the members of his family were assaulted, either by the civil or the military power of his country. He had been Justice of the Peace in the third district for eighteen years in succession, and all had felt, that in his hands the law had been honored, and that without respect to persons, justice had been awarded equally to his fellow citizens.

In the fall of 1861, Mr. Humbert, with other Union men of his district, for their sympathy with the Union cause, began to suffer persecution from their rebel neighbors, particularly from the Gregories, the Julians, and their most intimate associates, all of whom were the most brutal and bloodthirsty of any in the country. About the middle of October, to avoid being arrested and sent to Tuscaloosa, Mr. Humbert took up his abode in the woods, being supplied with food secretly by his two daughters, and occasionally stealing his way in the night to some Union house, until the last of December, a period of over two months. Toward the close of December, the noted Capt. Bill Brown of Cleveland, then in the height of his rebel glory, having Mr. Humbert among others in the third district marked for Tuscaloosa, with his plans preconcerted and a full posse of men, made a dash upon the Union people of the district. One Union man who at this time fell into Brown's power, was Mr. S. D. Richmond. Shortly after capturing Richmond, Brown and his party boarded the premises of Mr. Humbert. The family of Mr. Humbert at the time, consisted only of himself and two daughters, Rebecca and Sarah, the oldest in her seventeenth year, having buried his wife the year before, also his only son, the son in April and the mother on the 17th of May. Mr. Humbert, whom to arrest was the principal object for which Brown visited his plantation, of course was not in the vicinity of his home, but was in the woods as already stated. Brown and his men, however, made a thorough search for Mr. Humbert in doors and out, barn and out-houses included, threatening and abusing the two daughters, to make them tell where their father was concealed. Knowing where their father was, and having some fears that he would be captured, and knowing that he was marked for Tuscaloosa, the daughters managed, while the search was going on, secretly to convey to Mr. Richmond, their Union neighbor, just mentioned as Brown's prisoner, a small bundle of clothing and $21.45 in money for him to give to their father in case Brown should capture him. Before the search was finished, however, or soon after, Brown's men commenced to rob Richmond, and with his own money got that just given to him by Mr. Humbert's daughters. Richmond appealed to Brown in his own behalf, but the robbing was confirmed. Richmond then informed Brown that $21.45 of the money his men had pilfered from him, belonged to Mr. Humbert's daughters, that they had just given it to him to give to their father in case he too should be caught, and had to go to Tuscaloosa. Richmond also told Brown that he ought to give the money that belonged to Mr. Humbert's daughters, back to them, that if he would rob him he ought not to rob these defenseless and helpless children. Brown swore that Humbert was a traitor, and if the money taken belonged to his girls, it was the money of a traitor and he should keep it, and he would have Humbert also if he could find him, and joined in this strain of abuse by his men, they together berrated Richmond, Mr. Humbert and his family, in the use of other and similar language. This, however, inspired Richmond and Mr. Humbert's girls, though one was sick with the scarlet fever at the time, with a spirit to defend themselves. They appealed to Brown's sense of honor as well as to his sympathies, urging that he ought to have some regard to justice as well as some feeling for those whom he was kidnapping and robbing. Mr. Humbert's girls argued that their father, though he was a Union man, had never taken any part against the rebels, and never could on account of his age; and as to their condition, they had just lost their mother and only brother, and if their father should be sent to Tuscaloosa, it would probably be the means of his death, when as a family they would be completely desolated and ruined. Brown finally told them that as he already had $21.45 of their money, if they or their father's friends would pay him $3.55 more, or in other words, would raise the sum to $25.00, he would give up the search for Mr. Humbert entirely, and leave him a certificate of citizenship, or to use Brown's own words, he would "citizenize him and let him stay at home." Notwithstanding this attempt at strategy, Brown got no more money, but kept his $21.45, and after he and his men had robbed Mr. Humbert's premises of what they could find that suited them, gathered up their plunder and left, greatly chagrined that the old gentleman had eluded their grasp.

It is out of the power of language to describe the diabolical character of this man Brown. He comes to the third district to rob and kidnap Union men, and after exhausting his skill to get possession of the person of Mr. Humbert without success, a man sixty years of age, under the pretence that his liberty endangered the Southern Confederacy, stung with his failure to perpetrate this cruelty, he robs Mr. Humbert's children of their last penny, then to get more he turns traitor to his own cause, and actually tries to sell Jeff. Davis and his whole Confederacy for $3.55.

The miserly and unfeeling wretch is probably yet alive somewhere in this world, and should he accidentally keep with him in this life enough of the human to allow him, like other men, to die a natural death, or in other words, if his diabolical career and companionship on earth do not rob him of all humanity and leave his nature a stark devil, so that upon the principle of Satanic ubiquity, without dying he can pass in and out of this world at pleasure, whoever will dare, when death strikes him, to perform on his frightful remains a post mortem examination, instead of a human heart will doubtless find in his bosom a clump of hissing serpents.

It ought to be stated here that a Union man named A. Morton, one whom Brown had previously pressed into the rebel army, and who was compelled to be one of Brown's squad on that day, did all he could consistently with his own safety to defend and protect Mr. Humbert's family.

The next night after this visit from Brown, Mr. Humbert, influenced by his friends, notwithstanding the precarious and unprotected condition of his children, under the cover of night fled to the mountains of North Carolina. The point he wished to reach in that State was Haywood county, distant a hundred and seventy miles.

In performing this journey Mr. Humbert was compelled to avoid the settlements and public roads, keeping the unfrequented thickets, but more particularly following the ranges of mountains, traveling by night and concealing himself during the day. Sixty miles of his journey was performed on the crest of the highest mountains in the country. After thirteen days of toil in this way, being exposed to hunger, cold and fatigue, wading the streams and climbing the mountains, sleeping in the woods and swamps, or among the negroes, not daring to show his face at the door of a white man, unless previously advised by the negroes that it would be safe; and living in constant fear of being captured or shot down by the guerrillas, or the rebel cavalry, Mr. Humbert, with the exception of considerable injury to his health, reached Haywood county in safety.

In this county, and in Cox and Sevier counties joining it across the line in Tennessee, protected by relatives, old acquaintances, and newly made Union friends, Mr. Humbert remained a refugee four months. Part of this period he spent with a nephew, Mr. Wm. Humbert, and a Union family by the name of A. Duggan. Many other families extended their friendship to Mr. Humbert during his stay as Union refugee in these counties. Among these, in particular, was the family of Mr. Abraham Hopkins. Mr. and Mrs. Hopkins were people whose Unionism and love of country enabled them quickly to perceive the condition and anticipate the sufferings of refugees fleeing in the dead of winter, and burying themselves in the caves, or living in the forests to escape the merciless fury of their rebel enemies. On the head of Crosbys' Creek, Cox county, Mr. Humbert found a Union community that received him, as well as all other Union refugees, with open arms.

In April 1862, hoping that changes in Bradley had transpired which would permit him to remain at home, Mr. Humbert threaded his way back to the county, nearly in the same manner and nearly by the same route that he made the outward trip; and owing to the season, returned

12

with less suffering and less injury to his health than his outward trip occasioned him. The January nights on his outward trip were severe, during one of which in particular, one that he spent on the top of a high mountain, it was with the utmost mental and bodily exertion that he kept himself from perishing.

Though absent five months, the hatred of Mr. Humbert's old enemies had not abated. No sooner was it known by rebels in the third district that he had returned, than steps were taken to have him arrested. He fled the second time, and for six months longer was compelled to absent himself from home, concealing himself in the different parts of the country. Toward the last of October, or late in the fall of 1862, the face of things in the county having somewhat changed in regard to arresting and imprisoning men of Mr. Humbert's age, he ventured to make another effort to live with his family. Although no further attempts were made to arrest and imprison him, yet after this, in common with other Union people in his district, his premises were robbed, plundered, and torn to pieces, his plantation swept clean of everything in the shape of stock, his household goods, furniture, bedding, cooking utensils, and even knives and forks were carried off by the guerrilla gangs that frequently desolated the country.

Mr. Humbert and his two daughters had the good fortune to live to see the end of the war, though it may be truthfully said, everything considered, that it is remarkable that all of them escaped with their lives. After having suffered in common with others, with an exposure of life equally with others, but in this respect more fortunate than many, they are now living upon their extensive plantation of six hundred acres, in the third district of Bradley county, in the full enjoyment of the fruits of the great victory.

In presenting a history of the case of Mr. Humbert's family with the rebels, we have not done so from the fact that its remarkableness formed any exception to the general rule of cases in the third district, or in the south part of the county. Had any one case been selected as an average of what each family in the district suffered, this perhaps would have been as near an average as any other. The sufferings of every other unswerving Union family in the third district, other things being equal, were doubtless as great as those of the family of Mr. Humbert.

THE HOLLOW LOG.

The following incident occurred in Bradley county in the twelfth district, in the fall of 1862, an account of which was furnished by Mr. A. K. Potts.

"Wiley Willhoit was a good Southern man. He talked long and loud about his rights in the Southern Confederacy. His family was too large for him to leave altogether and enter the rebel army during the war, but when his country should be invaded, he would shoulder his gun and defend his rights. One Southern man could whip five Yankees, etc. Shortly after the rebel conscript law passed, which included all under thirty-five, Wiley just escaped it, his age being between thirty-five and forty, something entirely new to his acquaintance. Then came Wiley's time to show his patriotism. The enrolling officer came round ordering him to report at rebel headquarters immediately. Wiley, however, was not quite ready, but would report the next day. The next day came, Wiley put three days' rations in his haversack and starts from the midst of tears and sobs, of a beloved wife and children. Wiley walked slowly toward rebel headquarters with his gun upon his shoulder, and finally began to reason with himself thus : ' If I go into the army, and get into a fight I shall stand seven chances to be killed to one of escape. Those Yankees can shoot seven times to my one, and they are no respectors of persons. If I go to Kentucky, so many Union boys have already gone there, who are acquainted with me, that I fear they will kill me there. I am resolved what to do. I know these woods like a checker-board, peradventure, I can hide in the forest and dodge the war altogether.' Wiley now steps aside and takes up his abode in the bushes. The enrolling officer returned in a day or two but Wiley was gone. Weeks rolled on—no news of Wiley. At last the rainy season set in and there came a very wet night. It rained hard and was very dark. Wiley knew of a large hollow log, but how to find it in that dark night was the point. It appears, however, that somebody else knew of the log also. A Union conscript fleeing from the rebels, had crept into the log early in the evening. Wiley groped his way through the darkness, the rain pouring down in torrents and at last found his log. He stooped down and when in the act of crawling in, wet and shivering and boiling with rage, he was muttering to himself, 'ain't this h—l?' 'Yes,' cried a voice in the log, 'come in.' 'Whose there?' asked Wiley, '*Enrolling officer*,' responded the voice. Wiley skedaddled among the trees, cutting both rain and darkness as he went. But that night and that hollow log cured Wiley of his rebelism, and after that he lay many a day and night in a cave with Union men, hiding from the rebels.

A. K. POTTS.

Bradley Co., East Tenn., April 20th."

CHAPTER XVI.

CASE OF LAWYER A. J. TREWHITT.

THE following is a communication furnished by A. J. Trewhitt, Esq., of Cleveland, East Tennessee, giving his views of the Rebellion generally, and setting forth his experience as a Union man at the hands of the rebels. Mr. Trewhitt is a young man who is destined to succeed and rise in his profession; one who is already deservedly known as a successful lawyer in East Tennessee; and his communication will be read by his acquaintances of the profession as well as by the Union people of the State without the least suspicion as to the truth and candor of its statements:

" At the commencement of the rebellion I was following the profession of law, and as I thought getting a liberal share of patronage in the fourth judicial circuit of the State of Tennessee. I was satisfied with my success, and considered it my duty as a citizen of the United States to espouse the cause of the Union of all the States under the Constitution; never having seen where the government of the United States had become oppressive to any State or parts of a State, or any individual member of a State, no matter where located.

" In the month of February, 1861, an election was ordered by the Executive of Tennessee, Isham G. Harris, and his Legislature, by which the people were to decide whether a State Convention should be called for the purpose of taking steps as to what the State should do in regard to the secession movement. At that election I voted against a convention, and the popular vote of the State was largely againsst a convention. Shortly thereafter, the notorious Isham G. Harris called his Legislature together again, and with Washington Barrow and others as commissioners of some sort, to meet H.W. Hilliard from the

Confederate States, went into a secret session and made a kind of bargain and sold out the State, calling on the people to vote on the 8th of June, 1861, upon the question of representation or no representation, and protection or no protection. At that election I voted for no representation and no protection.

"The next step was to elect a President of the Confederacy and members from Tennessee to the Rebel Congress. At that election I refused to vote, and from this on refused to act for the rebel government in any respect or to treat it as a government, until the rebel conscript law was passed putting all into the rebel army between the ages of eighteen and forty-five. I was then guilty of the most disloyal act of my life. A friend of mine, a Union man, had taken a large contract of the rebel government, and I, having a sickly family—a good reason why I should desire to escape the draft—procured a detail from my friend as one of his employees.

"Thus affairs rested between me and the rebels, with the exception that I occasionally heard that they cursed and threatened me, swearing that I ought to be shot, hung, &c., until the 26th of April, 1863. Early in the morning of this day I went to my business, leaving my wife very sick and confined to her bed. That same morning, with a view to procure some tobacco, I started to go about three-fourths of a mile with my gun on my shoulder, hoping to shoot a turkey or some other wild game for my wife, in the woods by the way. On the trip I happened to fall in with a brother-in-law, two of his brothers, and three other neighbors, all good Union men, and all rebel conscripts. Soon after meeting these men, on a sudden I heard some one cry 'halt!' All but myself fled to the bushes. On looking around I saw five or six armed and mounted men about fifty yards from me. I immediately went to them, three of whom I knew, to wit, Capt. May, Jathan Gregory and Springfield May. Capt. May ordered me into the custody of Gregory, and after cursing me a few times, he and the others started after the other boys, leaving me to be guarded by Gregory.

"As I was going up to the rebels after hearing the word halt, when within about twenty yards of them I heard the report of a gun or pistol, fired by some one of their party either at me or some of those fleeing from me; but the shot was harmless. Very soon after the rebels left me and Gregory, I heard twelve or fifteen shots, mostly in the direction they went. In about ten minutes after these shots were fired they all returned, having captured none of my friends, but stating that they had shot one of them through the shoulder; and Springfield May stating that he was shot by one of them. Both statements, however, were false. They shot none of the men who were with me, nor was Springfield May shot by any of them; for I subsequently saw the entire company and got the facts in the case. Capt. May, in the chase, got within sight of two of the conscripts, who turned and leveled their pieces to fire upon him, when in a cowardly manner he wheeled and ordered his men to retrace their steps, which effected their return to me and Gregory, as just stated.

"Thus returned, Capt. May and his son Springfield, expended a few minutes in again cursing and abusing me in a manner that would have shamed the imps of Satan themselves. They took me to a house where a man lived by the name of Griffith. Here they had about fifteen infantry rebels belonging to Capt. Foster's company of the 3d Georgia regiment. Here, also, Capt. May, feeling himself re-enforced, his cub Springfield joining his father in the game, showed themselves brave and patriotic men. Armed as they were, and backed as they were, they could curse me as a tory, a bushwhacker, a d——d liar, and using towards me every other epithet of abuse, could also coolly inform me that I would never get to Cleveland alive. Brave men, they could not only curse a solitary prisoner, but could take the last morsel of bread from a lone woman and three children; curse and whip a granny woman not under one hundred years of age; and rather than be particular, if necessary could rob the old lady of her shroud after she was dead.

"After they were satisfied with cursing and abusing

me, Capt. May took my gun, gave it to Gregory, and with all the pomp of a rebel General turned me over to Capt. Foster's men, with a statement as false as secession itself. . He informed Capt. Foster that the crowd I was with fired on his men after he had halted them, and that I came to him with my gun in a shooting position, both of which was entirely false. The fact is Capt. May never halted us at all, for he told me himself that the word halt which we heard was given to his own men to get them together, he not having seen us at the time. Brave and truthful Captain, he will have his rights after he quits this world if he does not get them before.

"The next day I was taken to Knoxville and taken before John H. Tool, then Provost Marshal of Knoxville, who seemed more like a human being. He looked over Capt. May's charges, and asked me if I had been in the camp of instruction. I answered I had not. He said he reckoned I would have to go there. I told him that at home I was at work on a detail, and would prefer to return to that. He enquired who detailed me. I replied Col. Blake. He then looked at my detail and said he would send me to Col. Blake. I was guarded to Col. E. D. Blake, who looked at Capt. May's charges, after which he had a guard of two rebels with fixed bayonets placed over me, and then showed his bravery and good breeding by cursing me for a d——d liar, a d——d Lincolnite, a d——d tory, &c., till I was fully convinced of his qualifications to abuse an unarmed citizen, who was in his power and unable to help himself. He then notified me that I might write to my friends to come and do something for me if they could, for I was in great danger of being hung or shot. I answered him that I should not write them such news as that, but if I was permitted to write I would write what I pleased. He then in a pompous and vindictive manner sent me to jail, there to be kept in close confinement. I was thrust into a jail which already contained about three hundred prisoners, among whom I became acquainted with Dr. Samuel Snapp from Sullivan county, Capt. Harris from Jefferson county, Capt.

Deatow from Kent county, and Lieut. Rogers, all from Tennessee, and all of whom were Federal officers, and the benefit of exchange denied them. These officers were accused of being Federal spies. They were simply found within the rebel lines in full Federal uniform. Not a shadow of reasonable proof existed that they were spies. I have since learned to my sorrow that Capt. Deatow was executed, which, however, is nothing strange, considering that his captors were, in fact, a set of murderers. I remained in jail eight days, the gates being broken open from without, twice or three times, and the building set on fire once during the time. On the fifth of May, ten days from the time I was captured, I was released, Col. Blake resanctioning my detail, and allowing me to go home for two months, which of course gratified me very much, although it was at a *cost of several hundred dollars.* I reached home on the 6th, the next day after my release, and found that my rebel friends in Cleveland, contrary to their better information, had conveyed news to my family that I was to be executed on the 7th, the day after I reached home.

On the 7th and 8th I was secretly making arrangements to cross the rebel lines and find a free country. About nine o'clock on the evening of the 8th, I and my family having retired to bed, I heard a rap at the door. I opened the door and Capt. Foster, the same officer to whom I was before consigned by May, entered with an armed force and arrested me again, and sent me again to Knoxville to be tried. I then ascertained that one William H. Tibbs, Wm. A. Camp, and John G. Carter, had from the time I reached home, until I was arrested the second time, been cursing about my release, and swearing that I should be arrested again. During this time also, but keeping it a secret from me, these three men, aided by George W. Carter and his son-in-law, David Demot, who made lies and falsehoods for them, and for one McFee to swear to, were telegraphing to Knoxville, thus procuring my arrest. After being arrested by Foster, I was warned by the rebels of Cleveland that I would be shot as soon as I reached Knoxville.

Arriving at Knoxville, I was again taken before Col. Tool, who, as before, treated me kindly, and examined the home-made witness prepared against me, who made out his written statement as well as he could, as manufactured by Tibbs, Camp, Carter, Carder and Demot. When the examination was through Col. Tool informed me that I needed no witness, that their tale amounted to nothing; but that he would have to send me again to Col. Blake. Once more before Col. Blake, he gave me another lesson instructing me how a Federal prisoner could be cursed and abused by rebel officers of his importance, after which he sent me under guard to what he called their camp of instruction. This camp of instruction was a pole house about eighteen feet by twenty-six, with rebel soldiers about five feet from it and all around it as guards. From fifty to sixty conscript prisoners were inside of it, with lice as thick as they could well crawl; nothing in the world to cover us at night, and nothing but the naked ground to lie upon. Great God! such instruction as we received here, as well as in jail, with about one-fourth as much as we needed to eat, and that not fit to swallow, I pray that I may never have to receive again. I remained in this camp of instruction about six days, or until the 15th, when I, with about thirty others, was marched out like so many sheep to the slaughter, and placed in one box car, marked for the South—one door shut, the other filled with rebel guards. We knocked off one or two strips of plank so that we could see out and have a little circulation of air.

Arriving at Cleveland, I was permitted to look through one of these improvised breathing holes, and send word to my wife that I was marked for Vicksburg, and to send er a little bank money. The first day we arrived at Dalton, Georgia, where we were confined in the car until the next morning. Reaching Atlanta that evening we were guarded for about an hour, waiting for a train, during which I saw apparently more men, conscripts, between the ages of eighteen and forty-five, than could be found in the whole of East Tennessee. From Atlanta we reached Montgomery, Alabama, the next morning, where we stayed until evening. While there we were guarded in the shade of an oak tree, on which the rebels, a short time before, had hung a citizen because he was a Union man.

While under the shade of this oak tree the company fell to sleep, and I having slept about fifteen minutes, awoke, and found that some rebel rascal had taken my pocket-book with every cent of money it contained.

While at Montgomery we saw some Federals who were taken prisoners at Brandon, Mississippi, from whom I learned that they would never get us to Vicksburg. From Montgomery we were taken to Selma. While at Selma a day and a night, four of our company left, two of whom I afterwards heard were captured and conscripted in Alabama, the names of the other two were Hooker, from Polk county, East Tennessee—what fate they met with I have never heard. From Selma we were taken to Meridian, where the Jackson Railroad crosses the Mobile and Ohio Railroad. Here the rebel Lieut. E. G. Lea, who had gotten us assigned to his battery at Vicksburg, ascertained that Vicksburg was beseiged, and he sent us down to Enterprise and had us placed in the Mississippi conscript camp, where we arrived on the 20th of May, 1863. This camp was the first place where the guards were taken from immediately around us. Being put into this camp, we were left with the rest under none but the camp guards.

"Here I commenced to play my hand to convince the rebels that I would do to trust, and I was soon put on duty as other soldiers. While in this camp, within every few days from two to six of our company would leave, none of whom, as I heard, were ever captured.

"On the 2d day of June, myself, David M. Gilbraith, of Greene county, Tennessee, and Stephen Chemeo, from Lee county, Virginia, made our arrangements to start that night for the Federal lines. We were one hundred miles from the nearest Federal soldiers, those being around

Vicksburg, and Johnson's whole army between us and them. The next nearest Federals were at Corinth, a distance of two hundred and eighty miles. We chose to strike for the latter point. That day I was detailed as provost guard of the camp, and about nine o'clock at night I was called on to go to a certain post and change the guard, whom, it appears, the officers had some suspicions of. I removed the guard as directed, but replaced him with such a man as I preferred, gave him an empty gun with no cartridges or caps, but with very strict orders as to his duties. I then went to the tent of the two friends already named, when we gathered up our things, and walked immediately past the guard whom I had just posted and given the empty gun, out of the camp, and made our escape.

"With only the north star to guide us, we traveled all night through thickets and swamps till daylight, finding ourselves but about six miles from camp, being so near at least that we could hear the provost guards discharge their pieces. We concealed ourselves in the swamps till sunset, then traveled till dark in the woods, after which we took the Ohio and Mobile Railroad till daylight, which brought us in sight of Meridian, seventeen miles from Enterprise. Three thousand rebel soldiers were then stationed at Meridian, and we concealed ourselves in a deep gully about a mile from their camps. After dusk we attempted to resume our journey, but the night became so very dark that we had to desist till the moon arose, when we wound our way from among the houses and away from the rebel camps, took the Meridian and Ohio Railroad, traveling again till morning, and coming within sight of Marion, twenty-seven miles from Enterprise.

"We continued our journey during the day in the woods, keeping within sight of the railroad, at night attempting again to travel on the railroad. The night again, however, was so very dark, and the bridges and trestlework on the road so dangerous, that we bivouacked from the track about twenty yards to camp for the night. Just as we were laying down we heard the blast of a cavalry bugle followed by the tramping of horses, and soon discovered a horseman coming exactly towards us. I watched him and thought in my soul he would ride over us, but joy be with him, when within about fifteen feet of us he turned his course and passed about five feet to the right of us. We slept for awhile, awaking just as the moon, our great comforter, arose, when we took the railroad again, reaching Gainsville a little before day-dawn. Here we passed among two or three trains of cars standing upon the track, some of them with persons in them, talking and moving about. We flanked off to the west about a mile and lay in the creek bottom till in the evening, or till about one o'clock.

"Up to this time we had spoken to no person, nor been seen by any as we knew. We were out of rations, and, fortunately, while in this creek bottom, met with a negro man, of whom we procured a small quantity of bread and meat. Here, also, we heard of one Union man who lived near by. Fortunately again for us, we here met with another negro who was on his way to Scoba, a place that lay in our path, who also had a pass to travel. We all started together, and keeping the negro in advance he would cross the bridges before us and look for guards, but luckily we found none.

"We arrived at Scoba that night, and concealed ourselves for the day without food or drink. Here we learned that rebel companies were being made up, also packs of bloodhounds, with which to hunt Union conscripts. At dusk we started out, traveling that night and the next day in the woods. The next night we again took the railroad and kept it till morning, which brought us, a little before day, to Macon. The railroad here passes through the edge of the town, and we thought we could slip through, but all at once, we saw about twenty yards from us a rebel tent and something like a commissary establishment standing together. We left the track, bore round the tents, passing through a lot of cattle, thinking ourselves safe, when to our confusion, not far from the cattle we discovered a sentinel. We crouched as quick as possible, and by making another flank movement avoided him also. We struck into the woods, avoiding the railroad altogether; and by keeping the ridges avoided the principal streams.

"We continued a north course, passing within five miles of Starksville. Near this place we procured some provisions of a negro, who said his master was a Union man and a physician living at Starksville, and the owner of about forty slaves.

"Pushing forward we arrived opposite Artesia, and ascertained that about ten thousand rebel soldiers were there, and that the country was full of scouts. We, however, proceeded cautiously, and for two or three days after we left Artesia saw rebel scouts ranging the country; providentially, however, we escaped them. The chances looked critical enough, but trusting in God and the justice of our cause, we kept our course about the same distance from the railroad till we arrived opposite Oakland. We found that about ten thousand soldiers also were at Oakland, and three thousand at Houston, with rebel scouts passing thickly from one place to the other. We considered this our last great struggle, but by close watching and the aid of powerful thickets we passed their pickets unobserved.

"As yet we had heard of but two Union men, but we could still hear of guerrilla companies and bloodhounds. Negroes we found were becoming more scarce, yet after leaving Oakland we procured of them a side of bacon and a quantity of bread.

"Late one evening, our stock of bread having failed, I ventured to a lone house where I succeeded in getting a small quantity, and ascertained that we were within thirty miles of Corinth. The woman also informed me that the citizens were making up a horse thief company.

"About nine o'clock one morning we saw a house, apparently on a main road. Being out of provisions I ventured to it and found no persons but an old lady and her daughter. She had five sons and one son-in-law in the rebel army. I passed for a rebel soldier that had been taken prisoner, telling the old lady and her daughter a fine story about my sufferings. Astonishing how it took with them. The old lady and her daughter flew to baking, and hurried everything as fast as possible to give me my breakfast. Directly up rode a rebel soldier, but the same charm worked on him. So I got a good breakfast and bread to supply us on our way for some distance, and learned that we were within eighteen miles of Corinth.

"Some distance from this point we met with a man who said his name was Barnet. As we then feared, we afterwards learned that he tried to get the rebels in pursuit of us. We fooled him by changing our course for Tuscumbia, where we arrived in safety on the twenty-third day after we left Enterprise.

"Col. Miller, of the 11th Missouri Infantry, was then in command at that place. He received us with great caution but with great kindness. I shall never forget him nor his men for the hearty welcome they gave us. Col. Miller directed us to Corinth, stating that we needed no one to go with us, that there was not the least danger.

"At Corinth we became acquainted with Gen. Dodge, then in command at that place. We found him to be of the same true spirit with Col. Miller. He gave us transportation and passports to Nashville, where we arrived in just one month and one day from the time we left Enterprise. Here I found my East Tennessee friends by the hundred.

"On the 7th of September I left Nashville for home; and on the 18th arrived within five miles of Cleveland, almost within sight of home, where I heard that our forces had fallen back that morning, and that two thousand rebels occupied Cleveland. After hiding myself two days in the White Oak Mountains, I learned that the Tennessee River was lined with rebels, and I literally surrounded. Being acquainted with the country, and knowing of a place of perfect concealment within six miles of where I was, I went to it, where I remained till the 8th of

October, without as yet hearing from my family. Meeting with an opportunity I sent word to my wife when she immediately made her way through the rebel camps of two thousand soldiers to my place of self imprisonment, reaching me in just six months to a day from the time we parted. A happy, happy moment it was in the midst of our troubles.

"My wife returned in a few days, and found that in her absence everything inside and outside of her house had been destroyed by the rebels. I remained in my concealment till the 20th of October, when I made my way through the rebels to my family. I prepared me a place of concealment where i watched the rebels daily and saw them pass and repass, foraging in the country.

"On the first of January, 1864, I moved my family out of their lines. At one time, while I was concealed near home, I saw a command of rebels pass up the road towards Charleston. It proved to be the command of the notorious Wm. H. Tibbs, aided by Gen. Wheeler, who came out to charge on my house and family—my family consisting at that time of my wife, mother-in-law and one little girl. They took from them the only remaining horse we possessed, the few sweet potatoes my wife had raised during the summer in my absence, with other things as they liked. A great and honorable victory indeed! for Col. Tibbs and Gen. Wheeler, a thing which brave and high-minded men like themselves at all times are capable of doing.

"In conclusion I will say to the rebels, that for my wading the streams and swamps of Mississippi, ploughing my way through thickets and cane-brakes, climbing knobs and bluffs, lying exposed in the wet and cold, with all my other sufferings, and especially for their abominable abuse of my family, as well as for their cruel and outrageous treatment of my father—they having banished him from his family, imprisoned and so cruelly tortured him as to murder him, far from his home and friends, in a rebel hospital worse than a Federal prison,—referring particularly to Wm. H. Tibbs, John G. Carter, Wm. A. Camp, George

W. Carder, David Demot, and the scoundrel McFee, I can only ask God to forgive them, for I know that I never can.   ANDREW J. TREWHITT.

"CLEVELAND, TENN., March 25th, 1864."

THE GREGORY RAID.

The party who captured lawyer Trewhitt, as related by him in the preceding communication, was, on that day, perpetrating what may very properly be called the Gregory raid.

Jathan Gregory, spoken of by Mr. Trewhitt as the man to whom he was consigned by May, boasted after this affair that he was the instigator of the proceedings of this rebel party on that day. To organize for this raid, the day before, two parties of rebel soldiers, one from Cleveland, Bradley county, the other from Georgia, met at Red Clay station, on the Tenn. & Ga. R. R., twelve miles south of Cleveland, and that night repaired to Gregory's neighborhood, where they camped for the night. The next morning, the Gregories and a number of other rebel citizens, joined these rebel soldiers, all constituting a party of about forty. When ready to move they separated into three parties, so as to sweep as wide a scope of country as possible, Capt. May, Judge Mastin and Gregory, each heading a party. They struck north into Bradley, making a circuit through the country, returning towards Georgia. After plundering Union families to their satisfaction, and loading themselves down with as much or more than they could carry, the party broke up, its fragments repairing to their several localities.

The Union men the whole party captured that day, besides Mr. Trewhitt, were G. Humbert, Wm. Parks, Robt. Huffman, and one named Kelly.

The citizens who assisted the rebel soldiers in this raid were Jathan Gregory, Seth Gregory, W. H. Taft, J. B. Britton, Geo. Klick, Elber Dean, Esq., John H. Davis, Edward Fitzgerald, Marion Gillian, W. Tracy, F. T. Fullerton, Capt. May, Judge Mastin.

CHAPTER XVII.

TRIALS AND DEATH OF S. D. RICHMOND.

THE subject of this narrative is the Mr. Richmond spoken of in the preceding chapter, as the prisoner in possession of Capt. Brown and his men, when they were searching for Mr. Humbert and were robbing his family. It will be remembered also that this same Mr. Richmond was one of the Tuscaloosa prisoners, an account of whom has been already given.

Mr. Richmond was taken to Cleveland by Capt. Brown the evening of the day he made the search for Mr. Humbert; and as soon as possible was dispatched to Tuscaloosa. It is evident from this fact, that Mr. Humbert, with Mr. Richmond, would have suffered the same fate had Brown on that day been successful in finding him. Mr. Richmond had four sons who had reached manhood, Isaac, William C. John and Samuel, all of whom became soldiers in the Federal army. Isaac at the very commencement of the rebellion fled to Kentucky, and joined Wolford's cavalry. William C. was arrested by Capt. Brown and forced into Capt. Dunn's company in the 36th Tennessee rebel infantry, but deserted and joined the 1st Tennessee Federal cavalry. John also fled to Kentucky, and joined the Federal army. Samuel was arrested and forced into the rebel army, but deserted and joined the Federals.

Mr. Richmond reached home from Tuscaloosa in July 1862, after which, like many others, he concealed and protected himself from the rebels as best he could, until he was murdered by them, some time before our armies took possession of the country. Late in the fall of 1862, Mr. Richmond, among other losses by the rebels, was robbed by them of twelve or fifteen valuable swine. About a

13

mile from his house lived the family of Gregorys, already frequently spoken of in this work. Mr. Richmond being satisfied that Gregory was at least concerned in stealing his property, although surrounded with rebels, plainly and boldly told Gregory that he was the thief who robbed him. Gregory denied the charge, and though he and his boys were the principals in the crime, as finally discovered, yet supposing that rebel influence and rebel false swearing would clear him in a public investigation of the case, told Richmond that he would submit the matter to an arbitration.

The fact, however, of Gregory's guilt, on trial, was so perfectly manifest, that it was impossible for his rebel friends to clear him, and the arbitrators decided that he should pay Richmond sixty-six dollars for the part of the villainy perpetrated by him and his boys. This decision together with the fact, perhaps, that it was getting rather dark times in Tennessee for the Confederacy, caused Gregory to leave immediately, under the cover of night, with his family for Dixie.

A month, perhaps, after Gregory disappeared, three rebel soldiers, one evening came to the house of Mr. Richmond, pretending to be rebel deserters, threading their way to the Federal lines. It was quite late, and they requested entertainment for the night. They were taken in, given a good supper and comfortable lodgings. After breakfast next morning, having had their accommodations free, they desired Mr. Richmond to accompany them a short distance, particularly to guide them across a creek in the vicinity. Unsuspectingly, he went with them, and shortly after the report of a gun was heard by his family in the direction the party went. Mr. Richmond never returned, and for the time the three rebel deserters were no more heard from in Bradley, nor were they ever known to reach the Federal lines as such. Mr. Richmond's family, of course was alarmed, and thorough search was immediately made, but without discovering any traces either of Mr. Richmond or of the rebel deserters. It was evident that he had been either murdered or conveyed away as a prisoner.

The affair created considerable excitement in the community, and whatever had been the fate of Mr. Richmond it was at once suspicioned by the Union people, that Gregory, whom it was known was yet but a short distance south of the line in Georgia, was the instigator of the foul deed. A report was immediately put in circulation by rebel citizens, that Mr. Richmond had gone to Nashville. This was understood at the time by Union citizens as a rebel strategy, to weaken the evidence and counteract the public impression that Mr. Richmond had been murdered by the pretending rebel deserters. The Britton boys—malignant rebels—shortly after Mr. Richmond's disappearance, were overheard conversing upon the subject, to the effect that Mr. Richmond was put out of the way, and had met with his just deserts. The Brittons, Julians, and Gregorys in the third district were a rebel clan that hung together, and no matter what local changes took place among them, a crime committed by any one of the party was immediately known to the whole fraternity. Although the fate of Mr. Richmond appeared to be shrouded in mystery, yet his friends were deeply impressed that he had been murdered, and that the crime originated with the Gregorys, and was perhaps participated in by their general accomplices just named.

When East Tennessee fell into our hands, many of the Tennessee boys who had fled North and joined the Federal army were permitted to visit their homes. Among these were the four sons of Mr. Richmond. Once more at home, they immediately determined, if possible, to solve the mystery of their father's sudden disappearance, the fall before, and also, if possible, bring some of the guilty parties to punishment. As the result of their efforts, the remains of their father were found concealed in the boughs of a fallen tree, in the vicinity where the report of the gun was heard by his family the morning he disappeared. This confirmed his murder by the three men, who, as stated, decoyed him from his dwelling.

About the time Gen. Sherman started on his Atlanta campaign, May 1864, among other rebels who fell into the hands, either of the Richmond boys themselves or of other Tennessee Federals, was a rebel soldier suspected of being connected with the murder of Mr. Richmond. Being put to the test, he was recognized by Mrs. Richmond and other members of the family, as one of the three who decoyed Mr. Richmond into the woods the fall before. The fact of his guilt appearing beyond all question, it was decided that, under the circumstances, our army being under motion, the possibility of his escape if his case was delayed, with the unprovoked wickedness of his crime, he should die in the same summary manner as that in which he put his innocent victim out of the world. Accordingly, he was left in the hands of those who captured him, by whom he was drawn aside and dispatched, the fatal bullet sending his spirit into the presence of his Maker to be judged as a murderer.

Mr. Richmond's family is yet living in the third district, consisting of the widow, two daughters, three youthful sons, besides the four who served in the Federal army.

The other two of Mr. Richmond's murderers have probably never been brought to justice. The Gregorys, at whose instigation doubtless, the three rebels visited and murdered Mr. Richmond, the Julians and Brittons also, unless pursued and punished by Mr. Richmond's sons, will probably go unwhipped of justice in this world, for the part they performed in this crime.

Mr. Richmond was the owner of a tannery, and when murdered had a quantity of leather, the pieces of which were in different stages of finish. Shortly after his death his premises were robbed, after which the identical pieces of unfinished leather were seen in the possession of Hiram Julian, father of the boys who were overheard talking upon the subject of Mr. Richmond's disappearance.

The sons of Mr. Richmond, who enlisted in the Federal army and aided in putting down the rebellion, all lived to enter upon the enjoyment of the inestimable blessings of the final Union triumph; and are now honored and respected, while their rebel enemies and the murderers of their father are branded in history as the vilest of their race, and shunned and detested by the good as criminal vagabonds, unfit to live among men.

ISAAC RICHMOND AND WM. E. FISHER.

Wm. E. Fisher was a Union boy whose parents lived not far from Mr. Richmond's. Young Fisher and Isaac Richmond were driven out of the country by the rebels, perhaps about the same time. Both were members of Wolford's cavalry. Wolford's was the first Kentucky cavalry. After these two boys, with many others, had been driven away, those the most conspicuous in hunting them out of the country, particularly two named James Miller and Lewis Caygle, embraced every opportunity to abuse and insult the parents of these two boys, as well as other Union parents whose boys had been driven away, calling them d——d tories, traitors, etc., telling them that they themselves were the individuals who drove their sons out of the country; that they would see their sons no more, for they would never be permitted to return.

At an election in the third district, this James Miller was particularly vicious, and among many other things, told the father of Wm. E. Fisher, and other Union men, that Union parents who had encouraged their sons to leave the country and join the Federal army, ought themselves to be made to leave the country with ropes around their necks.

This was near the commencement of the rebellion. After this both Miller and Caygle joined the rebel army; and as chance or fate ordered future events, it so happened that all four of these neighboring boys, each party from its respective army, were at the same time home on furloughs. At this time the south part of Bradley, in which the third district is situated, was, perhaps, something like middle ground — ground between the two armies, occasionally reconnoitered by both, but really occupied by neither. Richmond and Fisher stole their way by night to their homes, and by remaining secluded their presence was not known to their rebel neighbors. Miller and Caygle—the third district being a rebel neighborhood—were less cautious, and the fact that they also were at home reached the ears of Richmond and young Fisher, who instantly reflected that possibly they could not only make some general capital out of the singular coincidence, but that then might be their time to revenge on their old enemies for the wrongs which they had inflicted upon them and their parents. Accordingly the two prepared themselves, and going in the night to the home or homes of Miller and Caygle, they passed as rebel soldiers till they drew their victims from their beds and got an advantage of them, after which they revealed themselves, at the same time presenting their revolvers, informing the rebels that they were prisoners. They also captured another rebel by the name of Berry Gillihan. Gillihan, however, not being a soldier, but having remained at home, and perhaps not having behaved himself very viciously as a rebel, he was released. But Miller and Caygle they marched straight out of the district that night, conducting them north till they reached the Federal lines, where they were delivered to our authorities as prisoners of war. They were retained by our authorities, and probably never again had the privilege of fighting in the rebel ranks against their country. Certain it is they never after enjoyed the opportunity of hunting Richmond and Fisher, or any other Union men, out of the third district.

CHAPTER XVIII.

REV. ELI H. SOUTHERLAND.

MR. SOUTHERLAND was born in South Carolina, October 10th, 1798. His grandfather was a Revolutionary soldier, serving under General Marion, drew a pension for many years, and died as he had lived, a patriot and a Christian, at the ripe age of ninety-five.

The subject of this sketch emigrated to Tennessee, Bradley county, in 1821, settling in the third district. In 1865 he had been a member of the Baptist denomination forty-five years, forty-four of which he had been a minister of the Gospel. For many years after he became a resident of Tennessee, Mr. Southerland labored successfully as a teacher of youth as well as a teacher of the Cross.

At the commencement of the rebellion he had lived in Bradley forty years, having been known during this period among the people of East Tennessee in the three fold capacity of citizen, Christian and Christian minister, without a blot or stain appearing upon his character. No sooner, however, was it known that Mr. Southerland was unfriendly to the rebellion, than the majority of his brethren, lay and clerical, manifested towards him a corresponding want of friendship, many of both classes making strenuous efforts to convince him of his error. Failing to throw upon the subject sufficient light to enable him to see that it was his duty to turn traitor against the government which his own father and Gen. Marion fought side by side to establish, he was denounced by these brethren as an enemy to his country; and finally, by an Association of his Baptist brethren in the ministry, was proscribed for his disloyalty and declared to be unworthy longer to be a co-laborer among them unless he would renounce his adherence to the Lincoln Government, and espouse the cause of the rebellion.

Thus proscribed by his brethren, together with malignant opposition from rebels generally, Mr. Southerland was compelled to suspend his ministrations during the war. One of his last attempts, near the commencement of the rebellion, to speak to the people as a Gospel minister, although it was at a place where he had successfully instructed his congregation for many years, was opposed by the majority of the people, including his brethren, and he forbidden to preach, unless he would publicly, at the commencement of his exercises, announce himself a friend to the rebellion. This Mr. Southerland could not do, and he and this portion of his people separated, not only as citizens, but as pastor and flock.

On another occasion, and in another place, after Mr. Southerland had entered the pulpit, twelve men, armed with revolvers and shot guns, entered the congregation and seated themselves in one corner of the Church. They soon unreservedly informed the minister that no more religious services could be held in that section unless they were performed by ministers loyal to the Southern Confederacy; and they desired him not to attempt it at that time. He replied that "he did not feel it his duty to invite a quarrel with them on the Lord's day, by an attempt to preach under circumstances which would insure such a result. If they persisted, and would not allow him to preach the Word without disturbance, he should consider himself forcibly ejected from the pulpit, and the responsibility of discontinuing the worship of God in that place would rest upon themselves." Notwithstanding this logical and forcible explanation of the responsibility they were taking, this band of ruffians stubbornly maintained their position and insisted that he, nor any other Lincolnite minister, would be allowed to speak to the people in that vicinity. Thus reassured that they were in earnest, Mr. Southerland replied that he would offer prayer, sing a hymn, after which he would dismiss the congregation, and for the future leave them and the peo-

ple of that section to their wishes. He then knelt before
his congregation and prayed, with words and in a manner
that appeared to have a good effect upon the audience
generally as well as upon the rioters themselves. After
prayer he commenced the singing of a devotional hymn,
one which he and that congregation had before sung together many times in joyful praise and happy worship of
their Redeemer. Before the hymn was finished two of
the ruffians broke down under the influence the singing
exerted, came near Mr. Southerland and begged his forgiveness. The two then told him that if he still desired
to speak to the people he should not be disturbed. He,
however, thought it best to dismiss the congregation,
which he did, and this place, like others, ceased to be a
point of his ministerial labors.

The natural temperament and disposition of Mr. Southerland were the very opposite of that lion-like combat-
iveness which enable some Christian ministers, mounted
upon the pedestal of their rights, to stand like war-horses
of resistance against all assailants, physically as well as
intellectually dealing out heavy blows upon the heads of
their unjust invaders. His power as a worker in the vine-
yard of the Lord lay in entrenching himself behind the
moral breastwork of sympathetic truth. In the absence
of physical strength, with a moral inaptitude for entering
the hubbub and invoking the danger of the clashing of
antagonistic forces, the personal contour—unwarlike face
—disarming tones of voice, and generally pacific mien, of
Mr. Southerland, formed a power more difficult for most
men to attack than to attack an equal antagonist standing ready and perhaps inviting a hand-to-hand contest.

Mr. Southerland, however, was no passive and truckling
coward. He was no skulking, non-committal, trembling
ghost upon the skirts of the crowd, when truth was
invaded, or rights infringed upon. On one occasion the
notorious Wm. H. Tibbs of rebel congress and negro driving fame, near the commencement of the rebellion, was
harranguing a company in the country, urging the people to secede, enlarging upon the glories of a separate

Southern Confederacy, the honor and praise of those who should stand by the South, and pointing out the disgrace and punishment that would be visited upon Union traitors. Mr. Southerland listened quietly until Tibbs had finished, after which, he mounted the stump and called upon the audience to listen to him. However prejudiced the audience was in favor of rebellion, Mr. Southerland's manner was such that it was difficult to refuse him a hearing. He had not finished his remarks before it was evident that many in the audience began to doubt the soundness of Tibbs' positions. The sophistry of his arguments, the untruthfulness of his statements, the great wrong and national injustice of the Southern movement, were explained by Mr. Southerland and lain before the people, with a clearness and earnestness, which if they did not entirely reclaim the secessionists, at least left the impression on the minds of many, that secession and rebellion were very hazardous enterprises. Like Mr. Humbert and Mr. Richmond, whose histories have been given, Mr. Southerland lived in the heart of a rebel neighborhood. His age clearing him from conscription, he managed to ride out the storm and remain at his home until our armies took the country. He then flattered himself that he had passed the crisis, and that his troubles occasioned by the rebellion were nearly terminated, the fact, however, was otherwise.

An account has already been given of the flag raising in Cleveland, in the Spring of 1864. Like hundreds of others, desirous to see the flag of their country once more triumphantly wave over the soil of Bradley, Mr. Southerland was present on that occasion. Highly elated with the prospects of participating in the patriotic ceremonies of the day, he remarked to some of his friends that he thanked Heaven that he was about to witness in Bradley, the triumphant waving of the stars and stripes—*the light of the world* once more! News of this remark reached his rebel neighbors in the third district, whereupon they managed to convey news back to him that he would soon see greater lights in his own neighborhood, than he saw that day in Cleveland. The threat was promptly fulfilled. In three or four days after the flag raising, Mr. Southerland's flouring mill and cotton gin, standing near each other, were burned to the ground. The loss, including the property in the buildings, farming implements, grain, etc., was between three and four thousand dollars. This satanic rebel deed was committed while our forces, were encamped at Cleveland and Blue Springs, eight or ten miles, perhaps, from Mr. Southerland's plantation. Suspicion fell particularly upon two rebels—John Woodall and Calvin Loftice. They were arrested by our authorities, tried at Cleveland, and found guilty. After their conviction they confessed the crime. They stated that twelve other rebels, all we believe, residents of the third district, were implicated in the act, and that they were paid by the twelve for executing the plot. The destruction of Mr. Southerland's property was traceable to the same head center of rebellion and crime in the third district, the Julians and others, that have been heretofore mentioned as so active in that part of the country in all iniquity. What sentence was pronounced upon these two villains, or whether they were ever, sentenced at all, is unknown to the writer. Some days after their trial, both were started for Chattanooga, either to have sentence pronounced upon them there, or to have punishment there executed, or for some other foolish thing; and on the way Woodall jumped from the cars and escaped. Soon after Loftice escaped from Chatanooga, and neither, perhaps, has been heard from since.

This case illustrates the very considerable, not to say insufferable looseness with which our military authorities transacted business of this kind in Bradley. If it was actually necessary to send these criminals away from Cleveland to be sentenced or punished, it was at the same time the easiest thing in nature to confine and guard them, beyond the possibility of escape, a duty for the neglect of which any officer should have been immediately called to an account by his superiors. These men never would have escaped, had the officers having them in custody, and superintending their transportation, been in the least impressed with the necessity, and importance of justice being done in the case. That the escape of both these guilty rebels thus, within a few days of each other, was purely accidental is problematical, to say the least. In fact no other sensible conclusion can be arrived at in regard to the matter, than that their liberation was designed by some of the parties having them in charge. Had energy, **prompted by a stern determination to bring the guilty to justice, been exerted,** not only these two might have been secured, but more of **the conspiritors in** this affair might **have been arrested and brought to punishment.**

Some time after the destruction of his property, Mr. **Southerland, with his family, abandoned his** plantation and took **refuge in Cleveland.** Unless the Government shall reimburse his loss, Mr. Southerland, in all probability, will not live **to see it repaired. His property was the** accumulation of many **years of laborious industry and** honest toil, borne by himself and family, but the fiendishness of the wickedest scheme **that ever cursed mankind, reduced it to ruins in a single hour.**

THE SHOOTING OF DR. GRIFFIN.

In the Spring of 1864 a small command of Federal cavalry camped in the ninth district, near Dr. Griffin's dwelling. What regiment this cavalry belonged to we were not informed. It appears, that many of the men were wild characters. Inasmuch as Mr. Griffin was a physician, these cavalry were under the **impression** that he kept liquor, and a number of them applied to him to **obtain the** article. The Dr. informed them that he had none, and did not keep it, therefore, could not give them any. **The soldiers left,** apparently dissatisfied, intimating that **he was not telling them the** truth. Shortly after this, procuring **a quantity of the article from some other** source, strongly under the influence of its use, two **of the soldiers** rode up to the doctor's gate, he standing in his door. The doctor walked toward them, at the same time inviting them to dismount and come in, and when within about **twelve** feet of them, both raised their navies and fired upon him, after **which** they wheeled and left, with demonstrations usual to men debauched by intoxication. One shot took effect, inflicting two severe wounds in the arm, from which, however, the doctor finally recovered. The names of the murderers, murderers at heart, were unknown to the doctor, and nothing was done about the matter by our authorities, to bring the villains **to justice.** The doctor was a **strong** and active Union man, a gentleman who had given these soldiers no cause to mistreat him.

CHAPTER XIX

In Tennessee, the Justices of the Peace in counties, form what is there called a County Court, answering, perhaps, to the courts of county supervisors in Northern States. In April, 1863, this court in Bradley was solicited and even compelled, by the rebel authorities, to pass an act taxing the property of the county to support its destitute rebel families, the male portion of which was then in the rebel army. The rebellion had then progressed two years, and had driven nearly a thousand Union men out of the county. The absence of these Union men caused destitution and suffering in their families also; the same cause producing the same effect in both classes of families.

The majority of these Justices in Bradley at this time, were Union men; and finding themselves obliged to act in behalf of the rebel families, made an effort to have their action cover the wants of Union families also. They felt justified in doing this from two or three considerations. In the first place, they knew that the rebellion was wrong, and that this wrong had occasioned the suffering of these innocent Union families, therefore felt that they were as deserving of help as those whose sufferings resulted from their own wrongs. Again, two-thirds, perhaps, of the taxable property in Bradley belonged to Union men, and therefore, inasmuch as two-thirds of the fund raised would be Union money, the destitute Union families had a right to their share of it. But more than this, these Justices saw the wrong that would arise in individual cases from this system of general taxation for the benefit exclusively of rebel families. They saw, for instance, the cruelty it would be, and the suffering it would occasion, to make a lone Union woman and her children raise money for the support of a neighboring

rebel woman, when, perhaps, the husband of the rebel
woman was the very person who hunted the Union
woman's husband out of the country. It is well known
that the rebel women of Bradley encouraged and urged
on their husbands and sons to persecute and drive the
Union men from their homes. This system of taxation,
therefore, proposed to make these Union women pay the
rebel women a premium for the suffering and destitution
the rebel women had malignantly occasioned them.
Every reasonable person will see that such were to be
the practical results of this rebel enterprise for the relief
exclusively of rebel families in Bradley.

The Bradley court taking this view of the case, exercised their privilege, and framed their enactment in the
following manner:

> "It fully appearing to the satisfaction of this Court, that there are
> in our county, and likely will be, persons in a suffering condition,
> and will need the aid of the county of Bradley; it is ordered by the
> Court, a majority voting in the affirmative, that an appropriation be
> made of twenty-five cents on every hundred dollars worth of taxable
> property in said county, alone to be used and appropriated for the
> women and children, or for all *suffering humanity*, in the county of
> Bradley."

A knowledge of this disloyal action of the Bradley
court threw the whole rebel element of the county into
commotion. The fact that the court had placed the
Southern soldier's family on a level with the families of
the "Lincoln renegades," and that they as well as the
destitute rebel families were to be provided for, was an
outrage not to be tolerated.

The following is the editorial fulmination of the Cleveland *Banner* on the subject—taken from an issue of
April 9th, 1863:

> "THE COUNTY COURT—A PREMIUM TO TREASON.—We learn, from
> what we consider to be reliable authority, that the Worshipful County
> Court, for the county of Bradley, on Monday last rejected or refused
> to act upon a proposition to levy a tax of twenty-five cents upon the
> hundred dollars worth of property, for the support of the indigent
> and unprovided for soldiers' families in the county. A proposition
> was introduced and passed, providing a tax of twenty-five cents on
> the hundred dollars, for the benefit of '*Suffering Humanity*' in Brad-
> ley county. Here, we have it, that the County Court is unwilling to
> vote relief to the family of the Southern soldier, who is periling his

life to keep off the invader, but willing when a proposition is introduced which includes families of the renegades that have left the country and joined Lincoln's army, to give it their cordial support. The welfare of the renegades' family is first with them—that of the Southern soldier secondary, or not at all. This is the conclusion we arrive at, after the proceedings on Monday. The 'suffering humanity' of Bradley county includes every class in want—no matter from what cause. The family of the renegade who is in Lincoln's army fighting against us is just as much included as the family of the Southern soldier who is fighting for us. Is such conduct as this by a County Court to be tolerated? Will the tax-payers suffer this imposition to be imposed upon them? Are they willing to support the families of men who are fighting Lincoln's battles? Are they willing to see the Southern soldier's family brought down to the level of that of the renegade? The County Court has made no distinction—they have placed both upon the same footing. Is this right and proper in a Court that is holding its sessions in one of the Confederate States? Taxing Southern people to keep men in Lincoln's army, who are on our border, threatening us with fire and sword! Great God! do we dream or is it a reality? Not a dream, but a reality. Southern officials giving aid and comfort to the enemy, by taking care of the men's families while they are doing everything they can to bring an army here to devastate and destroy our homes. If the minions of Lincoln are a part of the 'suffering humanity' of Bradley county, let Mr. Lincoln provide for them, or if it is too inconvenient to do so, he has plenty of sympathizers here, who can draw on their private purses for their support. Let it be done by private contributions, but for our children's sake, do not let it be a matter of record—they, would rise up and curse the duplicity of their ancestors. To the members of the Court we would say, to convene your Court again and expunge your action on Monday last. Do not let it remain on the Records of your county, 'lest it might damn you to everlasting infamy.' Had the same proceedings taken place in Lincoln's dominions, the last member of the Court would have been in a Bastile in less than twenty hours. The Court has said in effect, and put it upon record, to every malcontent, 'go and join Lincoln's army and we will take care of your family as a part of the 'suffering humanity' of Bradley county.' Is this not offering a premium to treason? According to our version of the matter it is most assuredly so. The Court may not have intended it so, but it inevitably leads to that."

Remarks upon the foregoing editorial are unnecessary. The editor of the *Banner* was pleased with the position in which this article placed him before the country at that time, and he will now have the satisfaction of looking at himself in the light in which it places him before the country at this time and will place him in the future.

This disgraceful and abusive editorial, with other rebel influences, had the desired effect. The rebel authorities overruled, or rather overrode, this decision of the court, the tax was collected from all, and applied to the relief of rebel families alone. Through the influence, therefore, of this hollow-headed and corrupt-hearted editor and traitor, and the influence of other rebels, worse, perhaps, than himself, the destitute and suffering Union women and Union children of Bradley, were compelled to raise money and pay it to their rebel neigboring women who had encouraged their own husbands and sons to murder and drive out of the country the husbands, sons and brothers of these Union women and children. This was the rebellion in Bradley county. This was the doctrine of the editor of the *Banner*. Very probably this editor received his share of these perquisites. Very probably his share of these funds, raised by these destitute Union women and children, liberally paid him for this shameful editorial, and the part he otherwise acted in driving their husbands and sons out of the country. The tax thus extorted from the families of Doctors Brown and Hunt, in the absence of these men, and which, perhaps, fell into the hand of this editor, was doubtless a very liberal reward for the sufferings he had occasioned these families, and for the manner in which he vilified these Union men because they had to flee fromrebel oppression.

THE HANGING OF MR. E. G. GRUBB.

Mr Grubb, with his family, settled in the third district, perhaps in 1854. By trade Mr. Grubb was a blacksmith and was a good and useful citizen. No complaint was made against Mr. Grubb by any of his neighbors before the war, and the only fault that was found against him after the commencement of the rebellion was, that he was a Union man, and had a Union family. Three rebel citizens, all neighbors to Mr. Grubb, took particular pains to sound him upon his politics, and to watch his movement. Being unable to shake his loyalty to his country, and particularly being enraged at his boldness, and the freedom with which he expressed his Union sentiments, these and other rebels in the neighborhood commenced on him a course of persecution. Some time, perhaps in 1862, these rebels reported Mr. Grubb to Wheeler's cavalry as a dangerous Union man. The soldiers of Wheeler's cavalry had frequently called at Mr. Grubb's house, and had been entertained by him and his family at their table. About three o'clock one morning, eight or ten rebel soldiers, belonging to this cavalry came to the house of Mr. Grubb, compelled him to get up, arresting him in the presence of his family. Mr. Grubb was a man who did not succumb to the rebels, and from whom no recantation of principles could be extorted, not even to save his life. His wife, however, as well as other members of his family, entreated the rebels for his sake, endeavoring to make them tell what he had done, for which he was arrested, and what they proposed to do with him. Giving his wife no satisfaction, only, perhaps, that she would never see her husband again. They placed him upon one of their horses, and conveyed him away as a prisoner. After traveling some half a mile or a mile, they halted and commenced to examine Mr. Grubb for money, at the same time cursing and abusing him as a Lincolnite, and endeavoring to extort from him information in regard to Union property and other Union citizens. Anticipating the robbing, his money had been placed beyond their reach, and as to giving them information about his Union neighbor Mr. Grubb was ready to die sooner than be guilty of a thing of the kind. Failing either to get money or to compel him to make the desired revelations, they commenced preparations to hang him from the limb of a tree. They hung him by the neck the first time until he was nearly senseless, then asked him if he would give them the desired information. Being answered in the negative, they hung him the second time, and, perhaps, the third time, but with no better success, as to the desired information, and finally left him upon the ground, scarcely able to speak, and for some time unable to rise. Toward morning, Mr. Grubb so revived that he was enabled to drag himself back to his home, but will, perhaps, never entirely recover from the injuries he received.

14

MR. JOSEPH LUSK.

Mr. Lusk lived in the fourth district. He had been a resident of Bradley upwards of thirty years, and had three sons in the Federal army. Samuel and Lavender were both members of the 1st Tenn. battery. Joseph was Lieut. in Col. James P. Brownlow's 1st Tenn. cavalry.

In October, 1861, the notable Capt. Brown sent one of his rebel soldiers with instructions to demand of Mr. Lusk his private arms. The soldier had no sooner made known his business than Mr. Lusk sprang to one of his guns and leveled it at the rebel, ordering him instantly to leave his house, or he was a dead man. The rebel wheeled, and begging of Mr. Lusk not to shoot, escaped from the premises as hastily as possible. Owing to the ill success of this messenger, and knowing the determined character of Mr. Lusk, Brown thought it not best, perhaps, to make further attempts to rob the old gentleman of his guns; consequently, he was one of the few in Bradley whom the rebels did not plunder of this kind of property. On three other occasions Mr. Lusk drove rebels from his premises in a similar manner.

At one time, a rebel soldier or rebel citizen rode up to his dwelling, and was about to dismount. Mr. Lusk informed him that no rebel was allowed to dismount from his beast on his premises. The old gentleman having the weapons in his hands to enforce obedience, and his manner being imperative, the rebel, instead of dismounting, turned and disappeared in such haste that his animal sent the dust in clouds curling in the air behind him. On another occasion, three rebels were carrying off and burning the rails on one part of Mr. Lusk's plantation. The old gentleman attacked them single-handed and soon succeeded in driving them from his plantation.

The last visit, however, which the rebels paid Mr. Lusk was the most sorry visit for them. Mr. Lusk had been reported to the rebel soldiers as the owner of two or three valuable mules. Mules were very serviceable animals in the army, and three mounted rebels one morning made an attempt to rob Mr. Lusk of these animals. By some means Mr. Lusk suspected a visit of the kind and was prepared. Armed with his revolver and squirrel rifle, he met the rebels as they approached his house; and without any introductory ceremonies fired upon them, emptying one saddle, after which he rushed upon the remaining two with his revolver. This attack was so sudden and unexpected, and was prosecuted with such a courageous vengeance, that the two rebels left their dying companion, and fled as though a battery of grape and canister had been opened upon them. The wounded rebel died in a short time, and was buried, we believe, by Mr. Lusk's family. This transaction occurred not long before the Federals took possession of the country; and this was the last time any direct attempts were made by the rebels to disturb Mr. Lusk. The fate of the rebel soldier shot by him, caused his Union neighbors to fear that the rebels would attempt revenge on them, and probably some few left the neighborhood in consequence. Mr. Lusk, however, we believe, never permanently left his premises; and as the rebellion was then on the wane in Bradley, the rebels concluded to leave him undisturbed conqueror of the field.

DEATH OF AMOS MANES.

In many respects the death of Mr. Manes was one of the most heart-rending tragedies that occurred in Bradley during the war. His mother was a Union widow woman living in the fifth district. Young Manes and his brother William were soldiers in the Federal army. In their absence, their mother, like all other Union women in East Tennessee left alone in the midst of the rebellion, had to struggle with many difficulties. Two or three little boys, herself and a daughter, comprised her family in the absence of her sons. Thus situated, she not only found it a struggle to provide for herself and family, but being a strong Union woman, she had to suffer persecution from the rebels. James M. Henry, a neighbor, a man of very doubtful character, was her inveterate tormentor.

The little boys of widow Manes borrowed a harness of Henry's mother-in-law, and were trying to plow their corn. Henry stripped the harness from their beast and carried it out of the field. This was done not because he needed the harness himself, nor because he had any liberty from his mother-in-law to take it from them.

A field contiguous to the corn-field of Mrs. Manes was owned by Henry. The fence between the two fields was imperfect, and the little boys of Mrs. Manes were unable to repair it. Refusing to repair the fence himself, Henry, apparently with malicious intent to destroy the widow's corn, continued, unnecessarily, to turn animals into his field.

The husband of Mrs. Manes was a blacksmith, and followed the business till his death. In addition to the abuses just named and others that might be named, early in 1862, perhaps, Henry went to Mrs. Manes and informed her that Capt. Wm. Brown had requested him to bring her blacksmith tools to Cleveland. The tools being refused him, he told Mrs. Manes that Brown would have them if he had to come and get them himself. She replied that if Capt. Brown came into her house she would meet him with hot water, a shovel of fire coals, or anything else she could lay her hands on. Henry left without the tools. The blacksmith shop of Mrs. Manes stood on the main road, some forty rods in front of her dwelling. In a few days after Henry's application for the tools they were missing. Henry was suspected, and Mrs. Manes soon ascertained that some of the tools, at least, were in his possession. She sent her little boys requesting him to bring home her property. He gave the boys a part of the tools he had taken, sending word to their mother that those were all he had. This was not satisfactory. About the time the rebels were driven from Bradley, Wm. Manes came home on a furlough, when he, with others, called to see Henry about his mother's missing tools. All, or nearly all of them, were found secreted in Henry's cellar and taken home.

The foregoing events transpired before our army took possession of Bradley. In the spring of 1864, our forces were encamped at Blue Springs, a half or three-quarters of a mile from the plantation of Mrs. Manes. Henry, notwithstanding his previous willingness to assist Capt. Brown to steal the property of Mrs. Manes, and notwithstanding he had otherwise aided Brown in his iniquity, by taking to his own house and secreting goods belonging to Brown and his family—goods many of which no doubt had been stolen from Union people—now pretended to our authorities that he was, and always had been, one of the most reliable Union men in the fifth district. He and his family swarmed around Gen. Grose at his headquarters, feasted him with their good things till Henry had fully established himself in the General's confidence as a good Union man. This, however, was not the worst of Henry's conduct with Gen. Grose. It was now a good time for him to renew his persecutions upon Mrs. Manes. He reported her to the General, stating that she had secreted, and perhaps was then secreting, rebels in her house, and on every opportunity was giving information to rebel scouts. Also he managed to make the impression on the General's mind that Mrs. Manes had a son in the rebel army. The General was so deceived on this point by Henry, that, at one time when Wm. Manes was at home, he was about to arrest him as a rebel and put him to labor on the breastworks at Blue Springs.

Mrs. Manes was as good a Union woman as ever fought the rebellion in Bradley county. She protected and fed to the extent of her ability, for months, Union conscripts hiding in the woods near her house, and in every other way in her power aided the cause from the commencement to the end of the war. She gave two of her sons to the Federal army, and no slander on earth could have been more foul or more cruel than Henry's insufferable lies about her to Gen. Grose. All the grounds in the world that Henry had on which to base these charges, were that Mrs. Manes had a son-in-law, who at the commencement of the rebellion was a rebel, and who enlisted as a rebel soldier, or at least for some time was connected with the rebel army. He, however, saw his error, deserted and came home to his wife, then living with her mother, after which he had to secrete himself from the rebels. He was never harbored by Mrs. Manes while he was a rebel. She, her daughter also—the man's wife—as good a Union woman as her mother, were as much grieved that he had anything to do with the rebels as any others in a similar case possibly could have been. Convinced that he was thoroughly cured of his love for the rebels, Mrs. Manes nor her daughter did wrong in receiving him and endeavoring to keep him out of the hands of the rebels.

Gen. Grose, however, was so completely victimized by Henry's power to deceive, that he would not allow Mrs. Manes or any of her family to come within the Federal lines. In addition to this, he not only threatened to arrest her son, as already mentioned, but concocted and inflicted upon her a strategy of deception, by which he thought, perhaps, to entrap her and cause her to betray herself as guilty of that which Henry had charged upon her. He and his orderly, and perhaps a portion of his staff, rode in the night to the house of Mrs. Manes, waked the family, reporting themselves as rebel scouts. Thus deceived, or in other words, supposing that they *were* rebels, and fearing that their object there was to capture this son-in-law, then with them in the house, to give them no occasion to enter the daughter stepped to the door to answer their questions, while Mrs. Manes was concealing the son-in-law—the daughter's husband—behind one of the beds. The General's orderly inquired for the locality of the Federal pickets. The young lady replied, "they are down in the road," she, possibly, pointing in its direction. He next inquired the distance to the camp of the Federals. She again replied, "you can see their fires." This was the sum of what passed between the parties. Supposing her visitors to be rebels, and consequently trembling for the life of her husband, the daughter, of course, felt anxious to get rid of them, but gave them no information that would not have been given them by any other Union person similarly circumstanced. Gen. Grose,

however, supposing that he had been talking with the
mother, and already prejudiced against the family, rode
away, interpreting this interview as evidence of the truth
of Henry's statements in the premises. Henry being in
the secret of this strategy, and perhaps having had something to do with its origin, was promptly at the General's
headquarters the next morning. He inquired what dis-
coveries the General made the night before. The General
replied that he discovered about what he expected to discover, namely, that his representations of the Unionism
of Mrs. Manes were correct. Henry responded, "yes, and
it will be well to watch in that direction hereafter." Esq.
Bean, whose residence was near the General's headquarters, was present listening to this conversation. His curiosity being excited to know whom the suspicious persons
were that the General and Henry had been endeavoring
thus to entrap, he was told that they were Mrs. Manes
and her daughter. This, to him, was a strange state of
things. Consequently, he, Mr. Hiram Smith and Major
McCulley, and perhaps other Union men, consulted together, and ascertaining the extent to which these abuses
had been carried, went to the General and gave him a
detailed account of the facts in the case, disabusing his
mind in regard to the whole matter. Thus enlightened,
the General assumed a different bearing towards this family, rescinded his order which prohibited its members
from entering his lines, sending Mrs. Manes word to this
effect. Mrs. Manes, however, was a woman of spirit, and
felt that she had been too deeply injured to accept this as
a complete burying of the hatchet, and never, while the
General was at Blue Springs, could she be persuaded to
visit his camp.

The command to which Amos Manes belonged was,
during the foregoing occurrences, stationed at Nashville.
Shortly after these occurrences, we believe, one of the
orderlies of Gen. Grose — the same, perhaps, that was
mouth-piece for him at the house of Mrs. Manes — was at
Nashville, and there informed young Manes of the manner
in which Henry had reported his mother and sister. Be-

sides, his sister had informed him of the whole transaction by letter. It was reported that, upon receiving this information, young Manes threatened to revenge on Henry, stating, in effect, that when he should visit his home he would put him where he would report his mother no more. The probability is that he did make threats, and perhaps threats of this kind. It is to be remembered, however, that if he made threats at all, he made them under the influence of feelings that would very naturally arise in the breast of any person on the receipt of such news as that just referred to.

Young Manes and his brother William came home on furloughs, the last of June, 1864. Mrs. Manes advised her boys to have nothing to do with Henry, to let him alone entirely, and to avoid his presence. Being influenced perhaps by this advice, and their feelings on the subject having apparently subsided, neither of them, while at home, made any threats against Henry, or manifested any disposition to injure him for his previous abuse of their mother.

On the fourth of August, after being at home about five weeks, and having soon to return to his command, Amos remarked that before he left he would see Henry, and endeavor to collect an amount that Henry was owing him. His mother stated that if he had any unsettled business with Henry, to let it remain unsettled for the present, and attempted to dissuade him from calling on Henry; he replied that no danger existed, there would be no trouble. He and his brother William went to Henry's house, distant a mile, perhaps, from their own. It was very warm weather, the doors of Henry's house were open, and chairs were setting in the shade of the trees in front of one of the doors. After the usual salutations, the two with Henry being seated upon these chairs, Henry remarked that he supposed they " came to create a fuss." Amos replied that they did not come for that purpose, but to have a settlement with him of the business that was between him and himself. Henry then referred to the reports of his abuse of Mrs. Manes, stating that those reports were lies. This brought on words between himself and Amos, William remaining silent to the end. In the brief conversation that ensued, Henry, in an impudent and insulting manner frequently used the term "lie," applying it to those who had accused him of persecuting Mrs. Manes, including both Mrs. Manes and her daughter and, perhaps, giving the lie to Amos himself, until Amos raised his arm threatening to strike him. At this point Henry hurried into his house evidently to get his gun, the door remaining open behind him. The Manes boys then drew their weapons, Amos cocked his revolver, calling out to Henry not to bring his gun "out there." By this time Henry had reached his gun, and standing, perhaps, in the middle of the room he was in, firing through the door space, shot Amos through the heart, causing immediate death. William caught his brother as he fell, saying to Henry that he had killed his brother, but if he would put up his gun he would put up his revolver,

Henry was arrested and tried by our military authorities at Cleveland. He and his friends attempted to show that he shot Manes in defence of his own life. On trial, confident that he would be cleared on this ground, Henry manifested no remorse for his crime, but was self-justifying, bold and defiant throughout. He was sentenced to seven years imprisonment in the penitentiary at Nashville. Afterwards, very unjustly, no doubt, his sentence was commuted to three years.

No blot or stain was upon the character of the Manes family. All its members were respectable citizens, good and acceptable neighbors, and were true to their country. The same can be recorded of Mr. Henry's family, excepting Mr. Henry himself. Two of his sons were soldiers in the Federal army, and served with honor to their country and with credit to themselves.

Henry, at one time, had to defend himself in a law case. A relative was a witness against him, it was stated privately by this witness, that if on oath he should be compelled to state all that he knew against Henry, the people would hang the defendant. Henry possessed great tact and power to deceive. His fair and plausible exterior was sure to make a favorable impression at first, and continue to mislead those whose acquaintance with him was superficial. Some of his nearest neighbors, among the most reliable and respectable in the community, those who knew, and had dealings with him for many years, finally declined all commerce with him whatsoever, saying that it was impossible to give him any liberties, and prevent him from taking that which did not belong to him.

IMPRISONMENT OF MR. DANIEL MCDOWELL.

At the commencement of the rebellion Mr. McDowell lived in the ninth district. He was arrested on his way home from church, July 17th, 1863, by the notorious Capt. Snow of Hamilton county, Snow having with him at the time two other notorious rebel outlaws, Jack Roberts and David L. Walker. McDowell was taken to Cleveland and locked up in the county jail. After remaining there seven weeks, he and three other Union men then in the same jail, Austin Shiflit, Owen Solomon, and J. L. Kirby, made their escape and struck for the woods. Thomas Low was then jailer of the county, but had no control over these four political prisoners, they being watched while in jail by a rebel military guard. Low, however, with his blood hounds, and one of the guards, gave chase after the fugitives. Running them about four miles, Mr. McDowell having been sick, and being feeble was overtaken by the dogs, and to avoid being torn by them, took refuge in a tree. The dogs watched and guarded their prey perched above them in the tree, until Low and the guard arrived. Low ordered McDowell out of the tree, and told him that he must return to prison. McDowell argued that Low had no control over him as he was under the rebel guards; and after some dispute on the subject, McDowell offered Low fifty dollars if he would release him. Law objected to this, saying that that would deprive him of the opportunity to report to the public that he, McDowell, was caught by his dogs, or in other words, would deprive him of the opportunity of publicly establishing the character of his dogs, as being expert in catching Union conscripts. Mr. McDowell was compelled to return to jail. The other three escaped. Suffering in a miserable jail for some time longer, giving Low, perhaps, sufficient time to announce the success and skill of his dogs in catching Union conscripts, thereby inviting for them future employment in the same business. McDowell succeeded in bribing Low with one hundred dollars, also bribing the guard, he was secretly released. In the following winter, when the Federals took the country, Mr. McDowell complained of Low to our authorities. Low was tried and sent North for his treason, but Mr. McDowell's hundred dollars was never returned to him.

SIX SOLDIERS.

Isaac Richmond, William E. Fisher, Wilson Norton, Jacob Humbert, Wm. L. Hicks and Nicholas N. Keith, were among the first, and possibly, were the very first Union men who fled from Bradley, and joined the Federal army.

Richmond discharged his duty faithfully to the satisfaction of his officers, the honor of his country, and with credit to himself during the war. He and Fisher, it will be remembered, were those who captured their two neighboring rebels in the third district.

Fisher was at one time attacked by sixteen rebels. He fought them until he emptied three revolvers, killing one and wounding others, after which he was taken prisoner, throwing his revolvers down a precipice to keep them from falling into the hands of his captors. He was afterwards exchanged and served until the end of the war.

Norton, in a skirmish in Kentucky, killed two rebels at one shot and thereby saved the life of his Captain.

Humbert, at one time, with others, was charging upon the rebels in the village of Lancaster, Kentucky. A negro came running to him, pointing in a certain direction, and crying out "Yonder go de rebs, massa!" Humbert wheeled his horse, and charging in the direction the negro pointed, soon came upon six or seven rebels, making prisoners of the entire company. Charles Tibbs, son of Congressman Tibbs, was one of the number, recognizing Humbert. Tibbs was the first that approached him, with the left hand raised in token of surrender.

Nicholas Keith, was among the troops who captured Gen. John Morgan, in Ohio, July, 1863—was the soldier, or one of the soldiers, at least, to whom Morgan surrendered. Keith got Morgan's negro and nine hundred dollars in Confederate money.

Hicks having been home on a furlough, was returning from Cleveland to his command, through Bradley county, September 11th, 1863, the day Col. Bird's men were driven out of Cleveland by the rebels. Hicks fell in with Bird's men, and particularly distinguished himself in that conflict. Throughout the war Hicks never failed to be at his post, and never flinched from a hand-to-hand encounter with the rebels.

HOME GUARDS.

The "Home Guards" in Maury Co., Georgia, at their drill, June 1st, 1864, adopted the following resolutions:

"1st. *Resolved*, That we invite all ministers of the Gospel who preach among us, to give a lecture on the war, at their earliest convenience, or give their hearers unmistakable evidence that they support the Southern Confederacy.

2d. *Resolved* That no more negro preaching be allowed until the war is over. Negroes can hear white men preach if they wish to.

3d. *Resolved*, That these resolutions be presented to our preachers at their first meeting.

E. B. May. *Chairman*.

F. Summerour,	William Hosler,
W. T. Trimmier,	Jesse Thompson,
R. A. McDonald,	T. R. Bates,
John K. McDonald,	Samuel Stoveall,
Madison Bates,	James Vann,

Vigilance Committee."

CHAPTER XX.

THE RED FOX.

THOMAS SPURGEN was born in Green county, East Tennessee, and is perhaps a little over thirty years of age. On the 14th of November, 1856, he was married to Miss Nancy Jenkins, of Cock county, of the same State.

Mr. Spurgen is of medium stature, squarely built and well proportioned ; with a frame and natural physique indicating more power of endurance than nimbleness or elasticity of muscle. He has light, sandy hair, light, florid complexion, blue eyes, with firm, compact features ; is naturally cool, inhering the power of self-possession equal to any emergency. If he were going to shoot you he would get ready and do so, perhaps without a word, and with as little ado as he would hand you a cup of water or give you a chew of tobacco. His temperament is the nervous bilious predominating, with enough of the lymphatic to head off an effervescence of feeling under all circumstances, and at all times to prevent a flustering concern about future consequences, but not enough to impair the judgment or prevent a vigorous play of his well developed perceptives. Hence Mr. Spurgen is no coward nor anybody's fool. His organs of locality and memory are large ; this, with his perceptions and the endowment of purpose, make him a good woodsman and sure campaigner. Here lay the principal secret of his success as a pilot. A moderate ambition always kept him within himself. He never attempted too much, and always accomplished what he undertook.

This is a brief, but perhaps a truthful analysis of the subject of the portrait at the head of this chapter. Mr. Spurgen was facetiously and very appropriately styled the "*Red Fox of East Tennessee.*" Though a young man, he has now answered to the call of his country the second time. He served in the Mexican war sixteen months—was at the battles of Cerro Gordo, Chepultepec, and at the taking of Vera Cruz.

At the commencement of the rebellion he was living in the eighth district, Bradley county, and in a community almost exclusively of rebels. From the fall of 1861 till July, 1862, he operated in the north of the county, piloting Union men across the Tennessee, at the same time deceiving the rebels of his neighborhood both as to his refugee operations and his political sentiments.

In May, 1862, Spurgen determined to join the Northern army. At this time the Tennessee was lined with rebel pickets. Another Union man, Wm. Marr, wished to accompany him, and to lessen the dangers of escape, Spurgen resorted to strategy. The rebel commissaries at Charleston were greatly in want of beeves. This at once furnished him with a clue to the kind of strategy that would serve his purpose. Acquainted with cattle growers in the Sequatchie Valley—a valley on the refugee route to Kentucky—he forged a note purporting to have been given to him by one of these stock raisers, to be paid in cattle, and as maturing about that time. He also forged a letter purporting to have been just written by the giver of the note, informing him that his cattle were ready according to agreement, and that the writer wished Spurgen to come immediately and get them. Spurgen showed these papers to two of his rebel neighbors, Lorenzo Alexander and Ezekiel Spriggs, enquiring if they would assist him to get passes on them for him and his friend to go to Sequatchie for his cattle. These rebels replied that if he would sell them to the rebel commissaries when he should get them over, they would vouch for him; and as these commissaries were much in want of cattle, in view of such an agreement on his part they presumed he could get the passes he desired. To this Spurgen consented, and had no difficulty in getting his passes. Spurgen and Marr could now go to Kentucky and be protected by the rebels as far as the Sequatchie, instead of being exposed to be shot down by them as fleeing Union refugees. Reaching the Tennessee Spurgen produced his passes, explaining to the pickets the nature of his business, when they willingly allowed him and his friend to pass over. On leaving these pickets Spurgen told them that he would be back with his cattle in a day or two, and if they should be removed before that time he wished them to notify those who should succeed them of his coming, that they might have no fears to pass him back, for the commissaries at Charleston were anxious to get his cattle as soon as possible. It is needless to add that these river pickets never had the privilege of passing Spurgen and his cattle back into Bradley. The two rebel neighbors, Alexander and Spriggs, as well as the accommodating rebel authorities at Charleston, found themselves badly gored by Spurgen's horned cattle, notwithstanding these cattle kept themselves some fifty miles away.

Spurgen and Marr reached Huntsville, Scott county, East Tennessee, July 6th, 1862. Spurgen, and, we believe, Marr also, enlisted in the 7th Tennessee Infantry, then at that place, a regiment an account of which has been given in the history of the second Clift war. On the 9th of July, Spurgen was detailed to return to Bradley and recruit for Clift's regiment. He returned in safety, recruited a company of fifty or sixty men, piloted them to Huntsville, performing the trip in twenty-nine days.

The day after he arrived at Huntsville—the 9th of August—Col. Clift, as already related, was attacked and driven from his post. Spurgen participated in the fight, and distinguished himself as a successful sharp-shooter. He remained with his regiment and was with it in its peregrinations among the Cumberland Mountains, when it was endeavoring to join the Northern army.

About the twenty-fifth of August, Spurgen returned to Bradley for recruits the second time. He was again successful, piloting his company across the two States, Tennessee and Kentucky, delivering it at Cincinnati, Ohio. From Cincinnati he went to Louisville, Ky., where he was appointed by Gen. James Spears, a regular recruiting officer for the Army of the Ohio. He selected Bradley county as the field of his operations, and in a few days once more reached his home in safety. For nearly one year from his appointment Spurgen toiled unceasingly as a recruiting officer. At the expiration of this period, including the two trips already mentioned, he had completed thirteen tours from Bradley to the Northern army, piloting through the forests of Tennessee and Kentucky thirteen companies to our lines. The aggregate number of men in these companies was a little more than eleven hundred and fifty, about a thousand of whom enlisted in the Federal army. The remainder were persons, many of whom were unqualified to enter the service, who passed through with Spurgen simply as refugees. The average distance traveled each tour was about 275 miles.

At one time, returning to Bradley, Spurgen was captured, as he supposed, by Champ Ferguson's cavalry. A companion named McUen was captured with him. Spurgen, always equal to any emergency, soon managed a way of escape. The two were ordered to take the road in advance of their captors, Spurgen, observing that the rebels were deeply absorbed in conversation, apparently considering some important enterprise, and it occurred to him that this might afford them some advantage. Getting a short distance in advance of their enemies, at the right time, Spurgen and his friend darted into the bushes, and dropped themselves down a precipice, where it was impossible for cavalry to follow. Getting to a place of safety, they concealed themselves among the rocks and thickets the rest of the day and during that night.

Before dawn the next morning, Spurgen cautiously went back to the point where he was captured, to get a bundle of letters which he was taking through for Tennessee boys, to their friends in Bradley, and which he dropped under a bush, unseen by the rebels, a few moments before he was taken. Had Spurgen been taken with these letters, doubtless that would have been the end of his useful career as recruiting officer, and pilot. This was the only time that he was worsted by the rebels. No refugee or recruit was lost who committed himself to Spurgen's guidance, nor did any letter or other valuable fail of its destination that was entrusted to his care. His success could not have been the result of accident, but must have been the fruits of foresight, judgment, unwearied caution and industry. He scarcely ever conducted his companies successively through upon the same route. Many in Bradley, who received letters from their friends in the Northern army, through Spurgen's hands, were ignorant of the means by which they were conveyed. His rule was, that no letter or package given to him for conveyance should contain his name, or any allusion to him whatever, or any allusion to the fact, that Union companies were being piloted from Tennessee to the Northern army, by any persons whomsoever.

A soldier or refugee named Francisco, in the Northern army, desired Spurgen to bring a letter to his wife in Bradley. Spurgen knew that Francisco had a brother in Bradley who was a bitter rebel, and he hesitated. Francisco promised that his letter should contain only his own name and that of his wife, and should contain nothing by which she or any other person could obtain a clue to the means by which it reached Bradley. In direct violation of this promise, maliciously, or through sheer idiocy, Francisco stated in the letter that Spurgen was the bearer of it. He also instructed his wife in the letter to show it to his rebel brother. She received the letter, showed it to this rebel brother, who immediately rode to Cleveland and reported to the rebel authorities, that Spurgen was in the country as a spy. The rebel troops then at Cleveland being Mississippians, and not informed of the state of

15

things in Tennessee, did not fully credit the tale, or at least were dilatory in regard to the matter, and Spurgen in the meantime started with his company to Kentucky and was soon beyond their reach.

In the summer of 1863, when our armies neared the Tennessee River on their way to Knoxville and the field of Chickamauga, the necessity for piloting recruits from Tennessee to these armies, no longer existed; and Spurgen on the 20th of August, joined Col. Bird's command, then having reached the west side of the Tennessee, opposite the mouth of the Hiwassee. A body of rebels was at the time on the opposite side of the river, east of the Hiwassee. The 4th Ohio and 15th Indiana batteries were part of Bird's command. These batteries opened fire across the river upon the rebels quickly shelling them out of their camps. Spurgen and four others, Baker Armstrong, who was subsequently murdered by Gatewood, the noted guerrilla, being one of the four, were sent across the river in a skiff to reconnoiter for the ousted enemy. The rebels had not only vacated their camps, but fled, taking the main road leading west to Kincannon's Ferry on the Hiwassee, but having halted on the flats, east of the river, to gather corn, stationing their pickets a short distance east of them in the road. Our boys, following hurriedly, came suddenly upon these pickets, and boldly firing into them they fled, throwing their main body also into a panic, when the whole were driven pell mell across the ferry, in all the haste and confusion imaginable, although they outnumbered their pursuers perhaps ten or fifteen to one. The rebels continued their flight through Bradley, apparently with a view to join their main army at Chickamauga, followed by the five Federals to the heart of that county. Spurgen being now near his home, visited his family. In the meantime Bird ascended the Tennessee, crossed at Kingston, returning on the east side to the Hiwassee. From this point he sent a company of about sixty men to Cleveland. These were the first Federals that entered Cleveland, arriving on the 11th of September, 1863. They remained in Cleveland one night only, returning to their command by way of the ninth district. As they passed through, the Union people of this district entertained them with a sumptuous dinner at a place called Beeche's Springs. Spurgen joined them at this point, and with them returned to his post in the ranks. He remained with Col. Bird, then under the command of Burnside, until the spring of 1864, spending the most of the winter at Lick Creek, about forty miles from Knoxville. In May 1864 he was attached to Scofield's corps, and continued with it to the end of the war. He performed his full share of the services and toils of the Atlanta campaign, being in the battles of Buzzard's Gap, Resaca, Dallas, Pine Mountain, Kennesaw, and was at the taking of Atlanta. On this campaign he was twice slightly wounded, once in the face, again in the ankle. His services on this campaign obtained for him the complete confidence of his officers, and on the return of our army north after Hood, through this confidence he was entrusted with the most important duties of a soldier. He distinguished himself at the battle of Nashville, and particularly distinguished himself in the pursuit of Hood's scattered army, to the Tennessee river. He was at Clifton on the Tennessee when the 23d corps started on its transfer to the eastern army, and was one of the many who assisted to perform that wonderful movement.

Vigorous as ever, Spurgen filled his place in the ranks throughout the eastern strides and swift circumvolutions of this corps, in the glorious work of decapitating the last living head of the rebellion. He was at Fort Fisher a few days after this stronghold of treason fell into the hands of the Government; and after the surrender of Johnston, was mustered out of the service in Alamance county, North Carolina, being sent to Nashville, Tennessee, where he was paid off and discharged, July 25th, 1865. During his entire services, Spurgen never lost an hour from sickness or even from his wounds, he was always ready for duty, and always accomplished what he undertook.

At the close of Spurgen's career as pilot, Andrew Johnson and others, sensible that his services merited that honor and favor, strongly urged him to accept a commission. Not ambitious of distinction, and having too much sense to accept a post, which in his judgment he was in some respects unqualified to fill, he declined the honor.

Spurgen's worst enemies in Bradley lived in the seventh and eighth districts. Wm. Parks, Lorenzo Alexander, Ezekiel Spriggs and their families, were the bitterest of rebels, and especially after he failed to fulfill his contract in regard to the Sequatchee cattle, the two latter families sought every opportunity to report him to the rebel authorities. At one time, Mrs. Alexander called at Mr. Spurgen's house, and discovered that he was at home. When Mrs. Alexander left, Mrs. Spurgen informed her husband that he would be reported within fifteen minutes after Mrs. Alexander should reach her home. Mrs. Spurgen's perceptives, always awake when rebels were near, and perfectly able to look through their every external guise, were not mistaken on this occasion. In less than two hours after Mrs. Alexander left the house, a squad of rebel cavalry dashed up and enquired for Mr. Spurgen. His wife informed them that he was not at home. They, however, dismounted and thoroughly searched the house, as well as the entire premises, but the foxy piloteer, profiting by the good judgment of his wife, had vanished out of their reach; and his enemies once more failed to stretch the neck of the ubiquitous and thousand-eyed Union skipper of the mountains.

Spurgen had another inveterate enemy in the seventh district, in the person of the notorious Capt. W. McClellan. McClellan incessantly watched for an opportunity to capture Spurgen, but like all the rest of Spurgen's enemies, failed to bag his prey.

This infamous McClellan and his men, arrested two of the Hooper boys, Spurgen's neighbors, and started them for Charleston. The father knowing the desperate character of McClellan, followed the party with a view to intercede for his sons before the rebel authorities at Charleston. McClellan's men saw him pursuing, when a number of them met the old gentleman, tied a rope around his neck, telling him that he could now follow his Lincolnite sons to the gallows, with a rope around his own neck to his satisfaction. They dragged the old man forward, drawing and pulling him about by the neck in the presence of his sons, as though he was some obstinate brute that they were taking to the slaughter. On the same trip these rebels arrested another man named Wm. Bracket. Reaching Charleston the rebels hung these three men by the neck for the second and third time, each time until they were entirely senseless and nearly dead. One object was to extort information in regard to other Union men in their neighborhoods. Mr. Bracket in particular had been reported to them as aiding and secreting Union refugees, especially one whom they were very anxious to capture. Mr. Bracket had that morning given this refugee his breakfast, and although they hung him apparently within a breath of his life, more severely, perhaps, than they did the others, yet he nor the Hooper boys betrayed their friends.

What were the subsequent sufferings of these Union men at the hands of the rebels, or when or how they escaped is unknown to us. We know, however, that Mr. Hooper, his three sons, and Mr. Bracket all lived to see the rebellion crushed, and a part, at least, of their rebel enemies brought to justice.

Mr. Spurgen also, and his family, after suffering and toiling to destroy the hydra-headed monster, are now living in Bradley in the enjoyment of the fruits of the great victory, and with their feet upon the necks of their former enemies and persecutors.

This sketch of the military career of Mr. Spurgen should not be concluded without a few remarks on the part borne in that career by his wife. Certain it is, that this career would have been greatly impaired by any other than such a wife as he possessed. In 1862 Mrs. Spurgen moved from the eighth district into the ninth, locating in the midst of a Union neighborhood. Previous to this change particularly, her privations and sufferings, as a Union woman, can never be fully known by any person living but herself.

In March, 1863, the writer visited Mrs. Spurgen at her house in the ninth district. He had conversed with her but a short time before he was taught a lesson of suffering patriotism that he will not soon forget. She and her infant children had been afflicted with chills and fever for months, which together with her lone condition, with no home of her own, her destitution caused by the great scarcity of provisions in the country at that time, particularly the scarcity of medicines and other comforts that one in her state so much needed, with everything else that was against her, apparently would have crushed any spirit but her own. Reduced to a shadow, with features as pale as those of a corpse, and unable to speak without trembling from head to foot, she said that she and her children had suffered terribly during the winter, were still suffering, and she expected that they would continue to suffer during the war; that she greatly needed the presence of her husband; yet she desired him to remain in the army and do his part till the wicked rebellion was conquered.

Could those Northern mothers—mothers whom the country had blessed with everything the heart could wish, but who were muffling their sons in furs and packing them in warm overcoats, for secret transportation to the Canadas, the pineries, and the distant territories, to keep them out of the army while their country was struggling for existence—have witnessed the courageous and patriotic heroism of that frail and suffering creature, as exhibited during that conversation, the spectacle would have made these Northern mothers blush for their own disgraceful want of this great virtue.

The patriotism of Mrs. Spurgen, however, was by no means a solitary example of this virtue among the Union women hidden away among the hills of Bradley and other portions of East Tennessee. The fireside of many an humble Union cabin in this county, and thousands of them throughout East Tennessee, cabins lining the interminable valleys, spotting the vales, and standing out against the sky like specks, upon the mountain ranges, can furnish histories of female patriotism, heroic sufferings and sacrifices, unconquerable loyalty to the stars and stripes, equally praiseworthy with those virtues as exhibited by Mrs. Spurgen.

DEATH OF MICHAEL BAUGH.

Mr. Baugh lived, we believe, in the eleventh district, Bradley county, and was a staunch and bitter rebel. He was a man of some talent, and was somewhat active as a politician. His talent for abusing and insulting Union people was not excelled, perhaps, by that of Capt. Brown himself. Universally, when traveling past the dwellings of his Union neighbors, he would insult and abuse any who might be in sight or within reach of his voice. He would frequently tie his pocket handkerchief to the end of his cane, insultingly displaying it in the presence of Union people, in token of his love for the southern Confederacy, and as indicating the bloody triumphs the rebel flag had obtained in the field.

A Union family named Miller, lived in the twelfth district, in which there were three or four sons, who were active Union men. They were pretty rough characters, but were strong Union men. Baugh had frequently reported these Miller boys to the rebels, and had made strong efforts to have them arrested and punished. He had, perhaps, otherwise misused and injured them.

On the 20th of April, 1863, Baugh was found dead in the road about seven miles north or north-west of Cleveland, having been shot by some unknown person. The general impression was, among Union as well as rebel citizens, that the deed was performed by some one of the Miller boys.

Mr. Thomas Low, the jailer, who with his dogs hunted and captured Mr. McDowell, as already related, and two or three other rebels, with these same dogs, spent a number of days hunting the Miller boys among the White Oak Mountains, with a view to capture them and bring them to trial for murdering Baugh. Mr. A. K. Potts was chartered to guide this company of men and dogs in the search, but its efforts were fruitless.

Upon the supposition that the Miller boys were the murderers of Mr. Baugh, this was the only case in Bradley county that came to our knowledge in which any rebel citizen was murdered by Union men. Other rebels in Bradley were wounded by Union men, but in no other instance, as we could ascertain, was murder charged to Union people of the county, even by the rebels themselves.

CHAPTER XXI.

WILLIAM LOW.

At the opening of the rebellion Mr. Low had lived in Bradley fifteen years; and at the time was acting as constable in the sixth district. Being a civil officer, his politics immediately became the subject of severe criticism, which soon ended in his expulsion from office as one of the obstinate and fool-hardy favorers of the Lincoln Dynasty.

In October, 1861, Mr. Low was suspected of bridge burning; and on this suspicion was arrested by Mr. C. L. Hardwick, a pompous rebel merchant of Cleveland,—a man who in the heat of his rebel zeal spent a portion of his nights locked up in his store, smelting lead and manufacturing rebel bullets with which to kill Union men and Yankees; and to use as ready arguments to bring such men as Mr. Low to a sense of duty. After being dragged about town and through the rebel military camps by Capt. Brown and this rebel Hardwick for some days, Mr. Low was sent a prisoner to Knoxville. On his way he was kept under a strong guard of soldiers, who allowed him to be insulted and abused as a "d——d Lincolnite, tory, traitor, bridge burner," etc.

Also, as was their custom to treat all Union prisoners who became the victims of their pleasure, Mr. Low, at the different stations on the road, came in for his share of the complimentary greetings of the secesh ladies. These sensitive creatures, sneering with disgust, and pointing the finger of scorn, were horrified at the sight of a "Yankee bridge-burner"—"sneaking traitor"—"mean Lincolnite," and showered upon Mr. Low their rebel execrations and personal insults, as though he was some stark specimen of existence, whose very presence was contamination.

After confining him two weeks in the Knoxville jail, unable to prove him guilty of bridge burning, he was allowed to return to his home.

The time of Mr. Low's arrest by this Cleveland merchant—this bullet making and bullet-headed traitor—was the period of the greatest excitement in the country in regard to the burning of the bridges on the East Tennessee & Georgia R. R.; and when great numbers were being arrested, and many being hung on suspicion of complicity in that affair.

During this period even two Union men dare not be seen conversing together on the streets of Cleveland. Mr. McDowell, of the tenth district, about this time was arrested by Congressman Tibbs, for stopping a moment as he passed the court house window to speak to Mr. Joseph Hicks, the county recorder. At the time of Mr. Low's arrest the Union men were afraid to stir from their houses. Mrs. Low's own brother, whose door was but a short distance from her own, dare not offer her the least sympathy, not even to visit her to speak a word of comfort, or to assist her in the concerns of her numerous family.

The jail in which Mr. Low was confined was overflowing with Union prisoners. Many had to be guarded at railroad depots, hotels, &c. Mr. Low remarked upon his own confinement that, feeling himself innocent of the crime of bridge burning, and guilty of nothing but loyalty to his country, he found it rather humiliating to have the keys of the Knoxville jail turned upon him as though he was a thief or a murderer; yet, the disgrace was not without its counteracting benefit. Being closely locked up in the Knoxville jail, he spent the two weeks without any injury to his purse, living entirely at the expense of the Confederacy. Other Union prisoners in Knoxville at this time, less disgraced than himself in the circumstances of their confinement, on being released were confronted by their landlords with very considerable bills of entertainment, which they were compelled to pay before they were allowed to leave the place.

Having reached his home, Mr. Low was again applying

himself to support his family, but the end of his troubles was not yet. In November, 1861, his son, Powell H. Low, sixteen years of age, was arrested and pressed into the rebel ranks. In July following he deserted, and through many privations and narrow escapes found his way back to his home. His old enemies, however, were soon upon him the second time, when he fled to the woods and mountains, in which, and in different Union houses, he secreted himself a number of months.

In the spring of 1862, young Low joined one of the refugee companies, reached the Federal lines, and at Nashville enlisted in the 4th Tennessee Cavalry, in which he faithfully fought the rebellion till it was crushed, and is now at home enjoying the fruits of his victories.

In 1861, before young Low was pressed into the rebel army, he was requested by a rebel ruffian to drink with him to the health of Jeff. Davis. Young Low refused, intimating his preference for Abraham Lincoln. With an oath the rebel instantly struck at Low's breast with a knife, inflicting a dangerous wound in the arm, from which the blood flowed freely, requiring the utmost skill of Low's physician to arrest it. The wound was dangerous, and disabled him for five or six weeks.

In the fall of 1865, after the political tables in East Tennessee were turned, Low and his old antagonist met in the streets of Cleveland. The Jeff. Davis toaster was called to an account by Low, and informed that his unprovoked attempt four years previous to take his life must now be atoned for. Like all other cowards when they have not the advantage, this infamous brute stood speechless and idiotic before his accuser, too mean and low to make a manly confession, and too big a coward to utter a word in self defence. Unable, by abusing him with his tongue, to insult him or provoke him to move or speak, and disliking to shoot him down while thus crouching like an insensible stock before him, Low fell upon him with his loaded cane, and whelting him over the head as he would a sullen and incorrigible spaniel, soon cudgeled him out of the streets of Cleveland. His flight, after he was beyond the reach of the shillalah, was accelerated by a shower of rocks, in the midst of which his receding skeleton made a similar show to that of old Jeff. Davis himself, hobbling away from the Yankees in a flurry of petticoats.

The name of this rebel offender unfortunately has been mislaid, otherwise we should be happy to give him as well as others, that historical christening that would leave his name as well as his conduct on record, for the benefit of himself and friends and their posterity.

Leaving young Low to enjoy the savor of his good name among his Union friends, and to profit by the advantages his patriotism and virtues have given him over his rebel enemies, we will return to the other members of the family.

From Mr. Low's acquittal at Knoxville, until the spring of 1863, with prudent management, he was permitted to remain at home. Being under forty-five, he now became subject to the rebel conscript law, having to make the best of the difficulty. He fled to Nashville, where he remained a few months, but finally stole his way back, once more reaching his home attempting to remain and provide for his family. His old enemies, however, were as merciless as ever. He, Mr. John O'Neil, Mrs. Low's brother, and a Mr. Batt, all citizens of Cleveland, fled to the tenth district. They concealed themselves in artificial refugee caves, near the residence of Mr. Elisha Wise, a Union man, arrangements being made, among others, with the family of Mr. Wise for their supplies. Miss Rebecca Wise participated very cordially and very laboriously in the humane work of fulfilling these stipulations.

The ground home of these refugees, was nearly west of Mr. Wise's house, which stood on the south side of an east and west road, and about twenty feet from it. Four or five feet to the rear or west of the main building, stood a small out-house, frequently used as a cook room. Having stolen from their caverns, these refugees, about eight o'clock one evening, with the family of Mr. Wise, were supping in this cook room, with Susa, a little negro girl on the road fence as a picket. Suddenly twenty or twenty-five rebel cavalry came dashing down the road from the west. The little girl gave the alarm, but through mistake made the impression that the rebels were coming from the east. The refugees bounded from the cook-room, Mr. Low in advance, and attempted to strike for their caves in the woods. These caves being west from the house as just explained, the same direction from which the rebels were coming, Mr. Low, before he saw them, the night being rather dark, ran almost into the midst of his enemies, and while but a few steps from them was halted and fired upon at the same instant. The shot, however, was harmless, with the exception of scratching his boot and knocking the earth and gravel against his shins. Thus headed off, the refugees wheeled, Mr. Low darting into the main building, and taking shelter in a refugee hiding place, prepared by Mr. Wise against such emergencies, the others, sinking back into and screening themselves as best they could in the cook-room. The rebels were instantly in possession of the premises, and soon succeeded in dragging Mr. O'Neil and Mr. Batt from their imperfect concealment, very much to their mortification and chagrin. In finding Mr. Low, however, they were less successful. Although he was on the lower floor of the house, which was only about twenty feet square, divided into only two rooms, with an angular stair-way in the end and corner of one of the rooms, while the rebels were all around him, and frequently not more than six inches from him; yet it was impossible for them to find him. After fifteen or twenty of them had scoured the building from top to bottom, for half an hour, leaving as they supposed, not an inch of it uninspected, and after peering up the chimney also, they gave up the search, concluding that Mr. Low had given them the slip to the bushes before they got the building completely surrounded.

Thus vanquished in regard to their third man, they took their two prisoners and departed, leaving Mr. Low standing there nearly in the middle of the floor, no doubt greatly to his satisfaction, as well as a good deal to his surprise.

To understand the ingenious device by which Mr. Low was concealed, the reader has only to imagine the lower part of Wise's house made into two rooms, and a stairway at the end of one of the rooms, having a double partition between it and the room from which it was taken, or in other words; a stairway with one partition fastened to the end of the stairs, and another perhaps sixteen inches from this, further in the room, forming a space between the two sufficient to enclose the body of a person. When on the stairs one would see the partition fastened to the end of the stairs. When in the room he would see the one sixteen inches from the stairs, or sixteen inches from the one fastened to them.

The rebels took their two prisoners to Cleveland, from which place they were sent to Knoxville. Fortunately both proved themselves clear of the conscription, Mr. Batt from being a tanner, then manufacturing leather in Cleveland, Mr. O'Neil, from previously being connected with business belonging to the county.

After the departure of the rebels, Mr. Low emerged from his confinement, and receiving the congratulations of the family on his narrow escape from death, repaired alone to his haunts in the mountains. He remained in these retreats until our lines encircled Bradley, when he was once more privileged to sit upon his own threshhold, with the great viper, together with all the little vipers, lifeless at his feet—his family all saved, and with him joyfully gazing at the stars and stripes waving above his dwelling in the town of Cleveland, while his lock-jawed rebel neighbors, marched quickstep to the tune of Yankee Doodle, on their way to swear themselves back into the fold of the old Government.

This sketch would be incomplete without reference to the part borne by Mrs. Low and other members of the family in contending with Mr. Low against the rebellion.

The history of the rebellion in East Tennessee will never be effectually written, the secret of her miraculous resistance and long endurance will be an unexplained mystery, until the noble examples of patriotism, the invincible and suffering constancy throughout the struggle of her phalanx of Union women and children, are by the hand of some studious and lively chronicler, given to the world.

The better half of man is his wife, the next better portion are his children, and with all these unflinchingly to stand by him in a good work, the Devil might as well hang up his fiddle, for we know of no just cause on this earth, that an army of households thus marshaled, could not carry.

The patriotic conduct of Mrs. Low and other members of her family, is recorded as honorable and praiseworthy, not only to themselves, but as being a *fac-simile* of the noble conduct of hundreds of other Union women and their children in Bradley county, conduct equally meritorious, and which would be equally interesting and instructive to narrate.

Mrs. Low was a Union woman from principles of right as well as from motives of policy. Right and wrong with her, were naturally the pivotal points of action, and blessed with a high sense of honor and feelings of strong self-respect, she was never long in deciding that rights were to be defended and wrongs resented, irrespective of consequences. Naturally possessing these qualities in a high degree, Mrs. Low was not easily deceived in the moral quality of human enterprises and human institutions, nor was it her doctrine in order to prevent the breaking of a few limbs weakly, to temporize or vascilate, after opinions in regard to enterprises had been permanently fixed. The rebellion was thus by her instinctively seen to be the embodiment of crime, when she as quickly decided that its votaries, notwithstanding their numbers ought to be treated as criminals, a course of reasoning which at once decided her position, a position which she immediately took, and that without any trembling hesitation in regard to consequences. Mrs. Low felt her way to be right, and a way that was right although it might be studded with thorns, she felt, was not very likely, time and eternity both considered, to lead to a disastrous termination.

Without any very elaborate philosophizing upon the subject, but rather from an intuitive sense of right and natural love of justice, the foregoing were the only wheels of logic Mrs. Low had to turn, to place her in the position thus described, in regard to the rebellion, a position which she found equal to all emergencies, and which carried her safely through all the troubles of the war.

In this position, Mrs. Low had nothing to fear but the possible extent or fatality of calamities to herself and family, fatalities common to the bloody struggle, and from which Providence alone could exempt her. Her husband might be hunted down and murdered by guerillas, or hung or imprisoned for his loyalty; her son might be slain by bushwhackers, or shot down in the ranks fighting for his country, but all these were calamities for which her position provided, and which she at the beginning balanced against the crime, and probable safety of taking sides with the rebellion. Bad as her fate was, or worse as it sometimes promised to be, Mrs. Low at no time had any apology to make for the stand which she or her family had taken, and when the bolts came thick and fast—her husband threatened to be hung at Knoxville, her son dragged from home, pressed into the rebel ranks and made to assume the attitude of a traitor to his country, her premises plundered, her property appropriated and destroyed by the rebel cavalry, her children tremblingly gathering about her, and looking to her for protection and support, with fear on every hand, no one daring to advise her, nor pretending to know what an hour might bring forth, there were no signs of recantation, none of that hypocritical dissembling, or appearing to side with the rebels; but she openly declared her sentiments and announced her position as a Union woman, defying the malignant ingenuity of her enemies, and unflinchingly accepting the storm smiting and wrathful as it was.

If intense personal suffering could have justified prevarication or dissembling, Mrs. Low could have been among the first to claim such an advantage. The repeated injuries inflicted upon herself and family by the rebels, with her clear and sensitive view of the possible consequences, were a two edged sword, night and day lacerating her very vitals—an inward anguish that none could have felt more keenly than herself; and that for weeks and months with none but her children about her, sent her to a tearful and sleepless couch, yet, with a high minded sense that she was suffering for the right, disguising her sorrow she moved among her persecutors with an air of defiance and self-respect, and with looks of withering scorn that not only evinced her self-control, but gave those enemies to understand that she comprehended the insignificance of their moral worth, and the meanness of the treatment she was receiving at their hands.

Mr. Low concealing himself in the tenth district, in the spring of 1863, moved his family into that section. Early in the following fall the rebels stationed a regiment on Condy's Creek, not far from Mrs. Low's dwelling. The men of this regiment collected from the surrounding farmers about three hundred swine. When the battle of Missionary Ridge opened the country to our armies the flight of these rebels was so percipitate that Mrs. Low found herself suddenly in possession of nearly all the swine in the north of Bradley county. Our forces soon took possession of Cleveland, and Mrs. Low dispatched her son, Lafayette, twelve years of age, by night, to inform the Yankees of the valuable prize the rebels had left on Condy's Creek. A secesh family named Carr, discovered the boy traveling towards Cleveland, and mistrusting his business reported him to a rebel, or rather bushwhacker, at that moment present, who threatened and attempted to shoot him down in the road. He, however, escaped, reached Cleveland, and the Federals immediately took possession of the acceptable booty. Shortly after a rebel bushwhacker named Grigsby, meeting Lafayette accused him of reporting the swine, and of being sent by his mother to do so. The boy stoutly denied the charge telling Grigsby that he had been misinformed upon the subject. Grigsby replied that he believed he was lying, and if he knew positively that he was the guilty party, he would shoot him down in his tracks. After being denounced by Grigsby as the son of a d———d Lincolnite traitor, and as belonging to the vile race of Tennessee rebels, the boy was allowed to pass on.

In the summer of 1863, as well as previously, an abundance of letters, photographs, and other valuables sent by Tennessee soldiers in the Northern army to their friends in Bradley, were deposited by *Red Fox*, and other refugee pilots in the north part of the county. While on Condy's Creek, Mrs. Low and her family performed their share of distributing these valuables to their owners. Immediately after the arrival of one of these invisible messengers from the north, Union men women and children would be seen hunting stray cattle, going to mill, or hurrying to find the doctor, or in search of seed grain, or would be on some other errand of pressing necessity. Miss Mattie Low, Miss Rebecca Wise, Misses Jane and Nancy McPherson, with many others that might be named, participated in this work of patriotic affection. The Misses McPhersons had three brothers in the Northern army, one of whom lost his life at Knoxville. Miss Low and Miss Wise, each had one brother in the Federal ranks representing their interests in the Federal cause. Personal experience therefore, in the importance of their mission, prompted these ladies, notwithstanding the country was full of rebel citizens and rebel soldiers, to distribute these letters to their owners, and many a heart was made glad while many were made sorrowful by the intelligence received at their hands.

Notwithstanding Mr. Low and his family suffered incredibly as well as sustained heavy losses of property by the rebellion, yet the great calamity so much feared was providentially escaped. The end of the rebellion was reached and the lives of all were spared, a blessing in view of which all their temporal losses, and sufferings were

16

not to be considered.   Having thus survived the storm, Mr. and Mrs. Low and their family are now living in Cleveland, in the enjoyment of all, if not of an increase of their former happiness.

The most appropriate sequel, perhaps, to the present chapter, is a paragraph having some reference to one of the principal actors in persecuting Mr. Low and his family.

C. L. Hardwick, the specimen of humanity who has been already introduced as the rebel that arrested Mr. Low, has escaped the law, but with some relief to the many he injured, has not altogether escaped the merciless goadings of the historical quill.   The writer had the privilege of a squint at this diamond-eyed Union persecutor, as he among other rebels was crawling about the streets of Cleveland in September, 1865.   His activity in laying up other rebel crimes, besides that against Mr. Low's family, for himself to answer to in a future day, so emptied his purse in the summer of 1865, before Mr. Low could get a dash at his old arrester, that any redress by law for Mr. Low is, perhaps, impossible.   Reduced to bankruptcy by his rebel crimes, Mr. Low can afford to let him pass, so far as his money is concerned, as that, could he fleece him of it by the hundred thousand, would not compensate for the deadly stab he inflicted upon himself and family.   Let him and his money perish with each other, but let him not perish or escape until the anathemas of the Union families, whom he afflicted, compel him either to make a public confession of his faults, or until these anathemas drive him from civilized society.   Though destitute of the means to pay in the unsatisfactory thing of money, he has not, nor has been destitute of the opportunity to make amends by an humble and manly acknowledgement of his errors, in a public manner before the people.   Now that the war is over, and its surprising results are before us, no rebel, unless he is yet wilfully hardened can fail to see in these results, the sin of his past career and its injustice to those who suffered by it.   One such act of genuine repentance on the part of Mr. Hardwick, would do him greater honor, and would do more to restore him to the confidence of considerate men, than all the money he could count in a life time. Until this is done, let Mr. Hardwick not complain about the libels of history, or talk about the exaggerated rhetoric of those whose duty it is to trace out and set before the public and the world, the conduct of individual rebels. Until he has done this, let his shame become so public that it will meet him at every corner, and face him in every rail car in which he rides, and on every highway that he may travel the rest of his life. Language can hardly do this man injustice until he has made these amends not only to Mrs. Low, but to others who suffered at his hands. While the rebellion was rampant, giving him the liberty to slay as he pleased; and Mrs. Low and her children with other Union families, then not a stone's throw from his presence, were writhing in tortrue and trembling with fear for the results to them of his tyranny, in full view of the sufferers, he could composedly sit and stroke his aristocratic whiskers in the fashionable rebel doors of Cleveland. Go vile insect! Go thou unseemly creature, branded with the mark of the Southern beast, and followed by the scathing tale of your infamous career, until an humble confession on your knees, as far as it can, shall make restitution at least to one whose nature could suffer so deeply from your villainy, as to give you hope that it might now be moved by your repentance, and whose forgiveness would allow the world once more to call you a human being.

CHAPTER XXII.

MURDER OF FANTROY A. CARTER.

FANTROY A. CARTER was born in Danville, Pittsylvania county, Virginia, December 15th, 1819, and came to Bradley county, Tennessee, in 1842. August 29th, 1844, he was married to Miss Ellen W. P. Soul, neice of Bishop Soul, so long and favorably known as one of the Bishops of the Methodist Church.

At the breaking out of the rebellion Mr. Carter was found an uncompromising Union man. When the railroad bridges were burned on the 8th of October, 1861, in East Tennessee, by the Federals, Mr. Carter was very unjustly accused of complicity in that matter; and upon this accusation was arrested by Capt. Brown, and forced into the rebel army. He was put into the 36th East Tennessee Rebel Infantry, and into the company of Wm. A. Camp. This company was composed almost entirely of Union men, pressed like himself into the ranks. Through the influence of these Union members, Mr. Carter was made Lieutenant of the company.

As mentioned in another place, this regiment was ordered to the field near Knoxville. In justice to Mr. Carter, and a- an illustration of his case, and that of thousands of others in East Tennessee, we give a short extract from a letter written by him to his wife at Cleveland, while his regiment was at Cumberland Gap. The letter bears date March 12th, 1862:

"Yesterday there was an alarm—the report came that the Yankees were closing in upon us. We could see them distinctly; they looked like there were two or three thousand. The stars and stripes could be plainly seen—they looked very natural to one who has always been taught to love and reverence them, next almost to the Supreme Being. When I saw them floating in the breeze, feelings ran through my mind which will be forgotten only when this body of mine is laid beneath the clods of the valley. I could have stood there and gazed at them till the next day, without eating or sleeping.

"The time I have yet to serve the Confederacy as a volunteer is nine months from this good day; then I will again be a free man, and once more be permitted to speak the sentiments of a freeman, without the fear of any. Then, probably, I can the better appreciate what freedom is.

"I have understood that there is a great deal of excitement in and around Cleveland. If such is the case I wish you to remain at home; do not become alarmed, you have done nothing for which you need to run; therefore I charge you particularly to stand your ground; no difference who runs or who does not. If I am in the Southern army it will not hurt you; there are plenty of witnesses in Cleveland who are friends of ours, who know my condition, and know what placed me in my present situation."

It is melancholy to reflect that Mr. Carter in this extract expresses not only his own feelings, but the feelings of thousands of other Tennessee boys who were then in a similar condition with himself. It is still more melancholy that so great a multitude of these boys, like Mr. Carter, and young Stonecypher who died at Knoxville, were not permitted to live to enjoy their own and their country's freedom.

As mentioned in another place, the 36th Tenn. was ordered to Georgia — returned to Cleveland and disbanded. Mr. Carter accompanied his regiment on this tour, but resigned when it was disbanded, being in the rebel service only about seven months.

From his resignation, June, 1862, till September, 1863, Mr. Carter was at home. Though a Union man, and freely expressing himself as such in company with confidential Union neighbors, yet, having served in the rebel army, he had to conduct himself with reserve in the presence of rebels, as the result of which discretion, he was permitted during this interval to live with his family comparatively free from molestation.

When our army reached the Tennessee River on its way to Chickamauga, Union men in Bradley enjoyed the privilege of enlisting to fight the rebellion without having to flee to Kentucky to find a Federal command. In view of this, Lieut. O. G. Frazier commenced at Cleveland to recruit a company of horsemen. Mr. Carter united with Lieut. Frazier to raise this company, with the mutual understanding that Frazier should be Captain and Carter 1st Lieutenant of the company.

From the time Bird's men came into Cleveland—September 11th, 1863—till after the battle of Missionary Ridge, Cleveland was taken and retaken, and thus alternately occupied several times by rebels and Federals.

Enlisting as a Federal soldier, and engaging in recruiting this Union company, exposed Mr. Carter to the malice of Cleveland rebels. They called him the traitor, tory, Lincolnite, &c.; and reported him to the rebel soldiery when in their turn they occupied Cleveland. Mr. Carter was living at the time about three miles from town, in rather a thickly wooded country; and knowing the rebel hatred against him, kept himself secreted in the thickets whenever he thought danger was near.

Venturing one day from his hiding place to go to Cleveland, he was met by Dr. Thomas Brown, a bitter old rebel citizen, who, the moment he saw Mr. Carter, wheeled and rode back towards Cleveland. Having been acquainted with Brown, and knowing his character, this sudden movement excited Mr. Carter's fears that rebel soldiers were in town, and that Brown had gone to report him. He returned to his home as soon as possible, related the circumstance to his wife, when she advised him to flee to the woods. He however delayed a little, and shortly a troop of rebel cavalry was seen approaching from the direction of Cleveland, and this same old Brown on the same horse, one of the company. Mr. Carter started for the woods, but was discovered, and surrounded by the rebels just as he struck the edge of the timber, when one of them leveled his carbine and shot him through the heart. Closing around him, two of the rebels dismounted and robbed him of his money, his watch, tore his gold studs from his bosom, and endeavored to wrench his gold ring from his finger. The ring was not easily removed, and in this they failed.

Mr. Carter was murdered perhaps a hundred yards from his own dwelling. Mrs. Carter, her children, and her two sisters, were present, saw the rebels spur their animals and converge upon her husband as he entered the wood, and nothing but the undergrowth of bushes skirting the

MURDER OF FANTROY CARTER.

timber shut off the foul deed from the gaze of the entire family. Mrs. Carter and her family, bewildered and filled with terror, looked on from her door; and in a moment the fatal report of the rebel gun, followed by the lull in the general clamor of their commingling shouts and yells, and savage blasphemies, urging each other on to take the life of that innocent man, told that her husband was murdered. Mrs. Carter and her two sisters ventured across the narrow field and met the fiends emerging from the timber. They told Mrs. Carter that they had "killed a d——d Lincolnite over the fence there," and she could go and attend to him. She asked one of them to assist her to bring the body out of the bushes, but this was refused.

In savage glee the murderers left the premises and returned to Cleveland. The party consisted of about twenty-five or thirty armed men. None but the following were, perhaps, personally unacquainted with Mr. Carter: Wash. Brooks, Cam. Brooks—cousins—Capt. Peters, and the bloodthirsty Doctor who guided the others to the retreat of his victim.

As the gang, on their return, entered Cleveland, Capt. Peters, though his thirst for blood had been satiated, at least for the time, was, nevertheless, through the exertion this had cost him, thirsting physically, and called at the house of Dr. Jordan for a drink of water. The doctor and his two daughters came out and were supplying his wants, when he began to boast of what he had done. He said he had "just killed a d——d Lincolnite down in the woods by the name of Fant. Carter." The doctor replied that if it was Fantroy Carter, he had "killed a mighty fine man." "Well, *he* was the man, a d——d traitor, that had turned Lincolnite, and such men ought to die;" and exhibiting his carbine, added, "there is the gun that did the deed." It is a pity that the doctor and his daughters did not administer to the wretch a dose that would have put an end to his thirst for Union blood as well as for the common beverage of life.

By some of their own company it was subsequently

disclosed that when the two men robbed Mr. Carter after they had shot him down, one of them opened his bosom, looked at the wound, saw the blood flowing, and remarked that "it was a d——d good shot!"

These men it appears belonged to Capt. Everett's company of Hoge's regiment, then a portion of Wheeler's Cavalry.

In connection with this affair, or about the time it happened, this same gang of murderers boasted that, in one of their trips through Kentucky and Tennessee, the sabres of their company alone drank the blood of sixty Union men.

After three days Mrs. Carter succeeded in getting the remains of her husband buried in the cemetery at Cleveland. Fear seized the entire Union population of Cleveland and its vicinity, and scarcely any one dared to assist her. Mr. Carter's own brother, who was then either a rebel soldier or a rebel employee, was not allowed to leave his post to assist in the burying. Another brother, when news of the murder reached him, remarked that "Fantroy was his brother, but any man who would turn traitor to his country ought to suffer."

How little did this Mr. Carter reflect, when he made this remark, that it was a sentence of condemnation against himself, rather than against his murdered brother. His murdered brother, when alive, possessed the identical virtue, which he in his remark was contending for, consequently he died an innocent man, while he himself was the traitor that deserved to suffer.

Mr. Carter was killed on the 23d of September, 1863. The deed was known in a few hours after it was committed, to the entire community, rebels and Union people; yet not the least rebuke was administered to the perpetrators by their superiors, but the villains were allowed to boast of it as publicly and as much as they pleased. Nor was any expression heard from any of the leading rebel citizens that the deed was by them either, disapproved. The murder was no more disapproved by rebel citizens of Bradley than it was by the rebel soldiery. Mr. Carter was universally known as one of the best of men, and this, perhaps, was spoken of and admitted by rebels in Bradley, at his death: yet, that there was any injustice in his death, was not, as a general thing, admitted by the rebel citizens of the country.

Mr. Carter left a wife and five children dependant, principally, if not entirely upon their own exertions for support. The following are the names of the latter: Maria V., Anna L., Frank W., Florence E., and Charles Fantroy. In addition to these, two maiden sisters of Mrs. Carter—Misses Maria and Jane Soul—were also members of the family, and equally with the others suffered under the blow, and were left to bear this distressing bereavement.

Old doctor Brown who acted the bloodhound in this fearful tragedy, subsequently left for Dixie. If justice has not yet demanded his life, and he should ever again display himself in Cleveland, it is hoped that he will be summarily called to an account, and the gallows allowed to settle its claims with this rebel monster.

Frank, the son, who was perhaps twelve years of age at his father's death, was at the time captured by his father's murderers. The rebels ordered him to follow them, and he struck in behind them, but soon, when unobserved, darted to one side and fled through a cornfield, making his escape. While in their possession he heard the report of the gun but a short distance from him, which killed his father.

Mrs. Carter and her two sisters, from the fact that the Union people of Cleveland dare not befriend them, and because the rebels would not, struggled three days almost entirely alone with the remains of Mr. Carter, to get them buried. They had scarcely left the grave, however, when they were summoned before the rebel Provost Marshal, and requested to take the oath of allegiance to the Confederate government. Not manifesting a disposition to comply, they were told that they would not be allowed to leave Cleveland until they did so. Mrs. Carter, as we have seen, lived three miles from Cleveland, having temporarily only left her house for the interment of her husband. Detention, therefore, would occasion her the loss perhaps of all she left at home, besides the mortification and suffering of being held in durance by the murderers of her husband. Mrs. Carter and her two sisters were, therefore, compelled to submit, and reluctantly subscribe to the hated rebel oath.

This was the kind of sympathy extended by the rebel authorities of Cleveland to Mrs. Carter and her two sisters, in their sorrowful and heart rending bereavement. These rebels had murdered the husband and brother of these defenseless and harmless women, had given them three days in which to bury his remains, then with their feet yet stained with the clay that covered his coffin, bewildered and nearly senseless from what they had passed through, these stricken creatures were made to stand before their persecutors and swear allegiance to the very power that had so heartlessly bereaved and crushed them.

MRS. CARTER AND HER TWO SISTERS TAKING THE REBEL OATH.

With a knowledge of this fact before us, it will be difficult for any argument to counteract the truth of the statement, that the murder of Mr. Carter was, as a general thing, justified by the rebel element of the country.

In our judgment it is not too severe to designate the leading rebels of Bradley, such as the Tibbses, Donahoos, Sugarts, Tuckers, Browns, McNellys, Hoyls, Hardwicks, Grants, Johnsons and others, as in a measure responsible for this murder, and as those who with the immediate perpetrators, will have to give an account to God for the slaughtering of that innocent man.

The death of Mr. Carter stands among the most lamentable and unprovoked murders committed by the rebels in East Tennessee; and will go far in the judgment of history to deepen the general blackness of the rebellion in Bradley county.

W. M. WILLHOIT.

Mr. Willhoit was principal of Flint Spring Academy in the fourth district, Bradley county. In November, 1861, while his school was in session, the Academy building was surrounded by a squad of rebels led by Stephen Gregory, and himself and a number of his pupils captured. They were taken to Red Clay St., put into a guard-house and kept until next morning. While in this guard house, Mr. James Huff, in order to insult Mr. Willhoit and his students, came in among them with his overgrown dog, and made the dog go through with a performance which he called cursing Abraham Lincoln.

The next morning the prisoners were offered their choice of three things: to go into the rebel army, be sent to southern prisons, or buy their liberty with money. Mr. Willhoit accepted the latter. He was afterwards appointed rebel enrolling officer in the fourth district. Not wishing to act in that capacity he and forty others fled North. Guiding the company across the Tennessee, and to the crest of Waldron's Ridge, Mr. Willhoit arranged for the others to proceed, but returned himself to Bradley for another company. He raised the second company and conducted it also safely across the Tennessee, when he returned to Bradley as before for the third company.

Reaching the Tennessee with his third charge, he found that John Morgan had just heavily picketed the river, and that it was impossible for him to cross. He secreted his men in the White Oak Mountains and waited for an opportunity to get over. While here, two men pretending to be rebel deserters were sent to him by Union friends. After being with him one day, one of these men slipped away, reported him to the rebels, in consequence of which he and his men were all captured. They were taken into Georgia and delivered to John L. Hopkins, general conscripting officer of that State. For the consideration of seventy dollars Hopkins agreed to give them a trial, but afterwards forfeited his word and sent them all prisoners to Macon.

After being in the Macon prison a few months, through the influence of friends at home, we believe, Mr. Willhoit and his entire company were released and reached home in safety.

CHAPTER XXIII.

MURDER OF THE TWO CARTERS.

THE subjects of this chapter were not related to Mr. F. A. Carter, whose history has just been given. These were Levi and Robert Carter, father and son, having lived in the north part of the county for many years.

Mr. Levi Carter, the father, was a blacksmith, was between fifty and sixty years of age—an exhorter, or local preacher in the Methodist Church, and had always borne a good moral and Christian character. Robert, the son, was a young man, having a wife and two children, and was a quiet and respectable citizen. Both were strong Union men, but not of that extravagant zeal nor abusive deportment justly to render them offensive to the rebels; nor had they ever been guerrillas or bushwhackers, as accused by the rebels. Possibly and even probably, they had acted as pilots to Union refugees escaping from the county. Even in this, however, they had never been extensively engaged.

These statements reveal the full extent to which these men had offended against the Confederacy, and the only real causes of complaint which their immediate rebel neighbors could raise against them.

On the 27th of September, 1863, Mr. Carter and his son were met in the road in the ninth district by five mounted rebel bushwhackers. Four of these bushwhackers were well known to the Carters, having been raised, perhaps, in the county. Their names were James and George Roberts, brothers, Felix Purviance, and Polk Runnions. The other—the fifth—was supposed by many to be a man by the name of Tenor. He called himself the "Texan Ranger." James Roberts, the leader of the company, was known to be one of the most lawless and bloodthirsty men in the country.

When the two parties met, the Carters, recognizing the Roberts boys, and perhaps the others, and knowing that they would at least be arrested, attempted to flee. James Roberts drew his revolver and fired, wounding old Mr. Carter severely in the arm, bringing him down, or at least checking his speed so that he was soon taken. Young Roberts was also soon taken, when both were conducted to the house of Esq. Stanfield near by.

Old Mr. Carter was severely wounded, and having bled considerable was becoming faint, and requested to lie down. This was refused, he and his son being told that they had to go before Gen. Wheeler at Georgetown.

After James Roberts had finished reloading his revolver, the five rebels mounting their animals, the prisoners were ordered to take the road before them, and headed in the direction of Georgetown, they were driven away. All passed the house of the next neighbor, but a short distance from Esq. Stanfield's, in the same order, traveling in the direction of Georgetown, old Mr. Carter bleeding, apparently faint, and getting forward with considerable difficulty. This was the last time that all the parties were seen together by Union persons. A half-mile, perhaps, beyond where they were last seen by this Union family, the road on which they were traveling struck into the main Georgetown road, where the five bushwhackers found that Gen. Wheeler had left Georgetown, and was then with his troops passing along this main road in the direction of Knoxville. They also ascertained that Gen. Wheeler was at that moment stopping for dinner at the house of a Union widow lady by the name of Grissom, upon this main road about a quarter of a mile to their right. Receiving this information the rebels wheeled their prisoners to the right, conducted them within about two hundred yards of Mrs. Grissom's house, where they halted them, dispatching one of their own number to Mrs. Grissom's to report to Gen. Wheeler, and receive instructions in regard to the disposition of the prisoners. This messenger found Gen. Wheeler surrounded by his staff, sitting upon the porch of Mrs. Grissom's house.

When the Carters were captured they were carrying on their arms a quantity of Osnaburg grain sacks, which they picked up in some vacated **Federal** camps near the Hiwassee River. It was **noticed**, when the company left Esq. Stanfield's, that the rebels **kept possession of** these Federal sacks, taking sacks **as well as prisoners** along with them from Stanfield's.

The following affidavits of Mrs. Grissom and her two married daughters, will be a sufficient history of the terrible fate that immediately resulted to the two Carters:

"STATE OF TENNESSEE.)
BRADLEY COUNTY.   )

"On this, the 15th day of April, 1864, personally appeared before me, John Stanfield, an acting Justice of the Peace of said county, Emily Grissom, Matilda McUen, and Mary McUen, and made oath in due form of law to the following facts:

"Mrs. Emily Grissom.—I had been personally acquainted with Levi Carter and his son Robert for several years before they were murdered.

"On the 27th day of September, 1863, two or three hundred rebel soldiers came to my house from towards Georgetown. They arrived about 12½ o'clock P. M., and remained about one hour. There was an officer in command whom his men called Gen. Wheeler. They were cavalrymen. About fifteen of these soldiers stepped up to my table and eat their dinners. Gen. Wheeler did not eat.

"Between a quarter and a half hour after they arrived, a cavalryman came dashing up from towards Georgetown, and enquired for Gen. Wheeler. The man whom they called Gen. Wheeler was then sitting on the porch of the house; being pointed out to the cavalryman, he said to Gen. Wheeler, 'We've captured two bushwhackers, and have them just above here in the road.' Gen. Wheeler asked the man where they caught them. He replied, 'Just above here, on another road.' 'Well,' said Gen. Wheeler, 'we generally hang bushwhackers.' Gen. Wheeler then looked around and up to some trees near the door, and said, 'I do not see any convenient limb here to hang them on; I think we better shoot them. Yes, I reckon we better shoot them, that is the way to do with bushwhackers.' General Wheeler then inquired if the prisoners had any arms? The cavalryman replied, 'No, only a pocket knife,' at the same time raising his hands and showing the knife to be about the length of his forefinger and hand to the thumb. Gen. Wheeler replied that, 'It does not look like they were bushwhackers if they had no arms.' The cavalryman then held up an Osnaburg grain sack to Gen. Wheeler's view, saying, 'Yes, they are bushwhackers, for they had with them over a hundred of these Yankee sacks.' This was the substance of the conversation, and the man wheeled and dashed back the way he came. Gen. Wheeler and his men then made sport of the cavalryman, laughing at his foolishness in calling these men bushwhackers when they had nothing but a jack knife, and because they had grain sacks, saying that he ought to be made Colonel for catching such bushwhackers, &c.

"In a few minutes after the man left, we heard the report of a gun in the direction he went; and apparently in the same place a loud, shrill scream, as though the person who uttered it was in great distress. We heard no more cries of distress; but immediately the firing commenced again and continued till four or five shots had been fired. There was then a cessation in the firing of about twenty minutes, after which it commenced the third time, apparently further in the woods away from the road, and lasted till four or five shots more had been fired. About a quarter of an hour after this last firing, the same cavalryman came back and told—two others coming with him—that they had killed the two bushwhackers. Wheeler and his men were talking and laughing, and did not seem to care for what they had done. They also seemed to enjoy the firing which we heard, or at least were not at all disturbed by it. Gen. Wheeler and his men left soon after this cavalryman returned.

"About an hour after the man reported that they had killed the bushwhackers, as soon as we dare, all three of us went up the road nearly two hundred yards, and by following the tracks made by the horses of the rebels, found the dead body of old Mr. Carter about thirty yards from the main road. The body was very bloody, it having been shot through about five times. One bullet went through his suspender on the left breast.

"We found his son, Robert, perhaps two hundred yards from the body of his father, further in the woods. Before Robert was found, his own wife came, and was the first to discover his body. It was some time after his wife came before the body of Robert was found. His wife would call him in a peculiar manner, saying 'if he is not dead but hiding away, he will hear and will answer me. He has had to lay in the woods all summer, and if I call him as I have done before when hunting him, in a low tone, he will know my voice and will not be afraid to answer me.' In calling him in this manner, she at one time imagined that she heard him answer, and going in the direction she imagined his answer to be, she saw him lying upon his face, ran to him, turned him over, but found him dead. The body was pierced with five or six bullets, mostly in the region of the heart. There were no gunshot wounds in the head, but both eyes were cut out, eyelids and all, apparently with a sharp knife. The eyelids, flesh and all, to the bone, were cut away, leaving the sockets very large places or large hollows, presenting a very ghastly appearance. I, and one daughter—the other being gone for water—with the help of Robert's wife, carried his body and laid it by the body of his father, where we watched them till dark.

"When we saw that the eyes of Robert had been dug out, we looked all around upon the ground, thinking that the murderers had thrown them down near the body, but they could not be found. The hands of old Mr. Carter were tied behind him with the strands of a hempen rope.

"Sworn to and subscribed before me, this 15th day of April, 1864.

JOHN STANFIELD,

"Justice of the Peace for Bradley County, Tennessee, by Emily Grissom, Matilda McUen and Mary McUen, of Bradley County."

The murder of these innocent men, under the license and in the presence of a rebel General, by their own neighbors,—those who knew them to be guilty of nothing but loyalty to the old Government,—caused a thrill of horror throughout the country; and the Union people began to feel that none of them, however prudent or sagacious, had a lease of their lives for a single hour! Many who had hoped to weather the storm, and live at or near their homes till deliverance should come, now fled from the county or buried themselves in dens or artificial caves in the mountains.

Not only that night but the next morning, a diligent search was made for the eyes of young Carter, the entire ground of the bloody scene being thoroughly canvassed by Robert's own wife and others, yet they could not be found. It was currently reported and universally believed among Union people in the county, that James Roberts, the leader in this terrible work, took the eyes home in his pocket and showed them to his mother! As he entered his home, he informed his mother that he and others had killed the two Carters. She expressed her fears that they had not entirely finished them! He swore that these "Lincolnites" were both dead; and to convince her that the work was complete, at least in regard to Robert, he pulled the eyes out of his pocket, threw them into her lap, exclaiming, "Well, by G—d! there are Robert's eyes, any how!" So far from being shocked at the sight, she replied that she hoped he would bring to her the eyes of more of the "Lincolnites!"

The writer spent considerable time to reach the origin of this report. The Union parties supposed to have a knowledge of the facts were absent, and their testimony could not be gotten. Facts were elicited, however, abundantly sufficient to justify the statement that, in substance, the report was correct. There can be no question but that James Roberts took the eyes of Robert Carter home and showed them to his mother; when she approved of the whole proceedings, and encouraged him not to slack his hand in the same kind of work for the future.

Wicked men, and especially wicked cowards, love to boast of their wicked and cowardly exploits. The statements in regard to this murder, by no means all originated with Union people, nor alone in the neighborhood where it was committed. In less than three days after the deed was done, it was, by means of Wheeler's men

17

and the five bushwhackers themselves, with all its attendant circumstances, known throughout the adjoining counties.

In regard to the final disposition of these eyes, it was reported that they were preserved in spirits, and kept by the rebels as a memorial of their valor and their victory.

We find an allusion to this barbarism, by Mr. G. W. Hickey, Union candidate for office in Cherokee county, North Carolina, in an address which he delivered to Union people of that county.

We extract from his address as follows:

"In East Tennessee. near Georgetown, a band of these men ran upon an old man and his son. by the name of Carter—the old man was a preacher of the Gospel—the young man had a wife and children. They shot the old man. killing him. then threw down the young man and cut out his eyes with knives. put them into their pockets. and afterwards into a bottle of brandy to preserve them. They then let him up and told him that he might go if he could make his escape. They still pursued him and overtook him. about two hundred yards from the former place and shot him down dead."

It was with the utmost difficulty that the bodies of these murdered men could be buried. Not a Union male person dare come nigh the spot, nor have anything to do with committing the remains to the earth. With the assistance of a negro who was prevailed on to come with his cart, the two Mrs. Carters, aided by Mrs. Grissom and her daughters, and perhaps by one or two other Union women, were compelled to bury their own husbands.

From developments made by the perpetrators themselves, it was ascertained that the eyes of young Carter were cut out of his head while he was yet alive, and before he had, to any extent, been otherwise injured. He was thrown upon the ground, held down by a posse of these demons, while another of their number dug out his eyes, perhaps with his own knife, taken from him when he was captured. After this he was allowed to rise, and told to make his escape if he could. Then with a hellish fiendishness that language cannot describe, these incarnate devils mounted their animals, and at the word given by Jim Roberts and others, they would simultaneously, as a game of diabolical sport, charge upon him with their

horses, driving him against the trees, or causing him to
stumble over the logs, or trampling him under their horses'
feet! This was enacted time after time! The ground

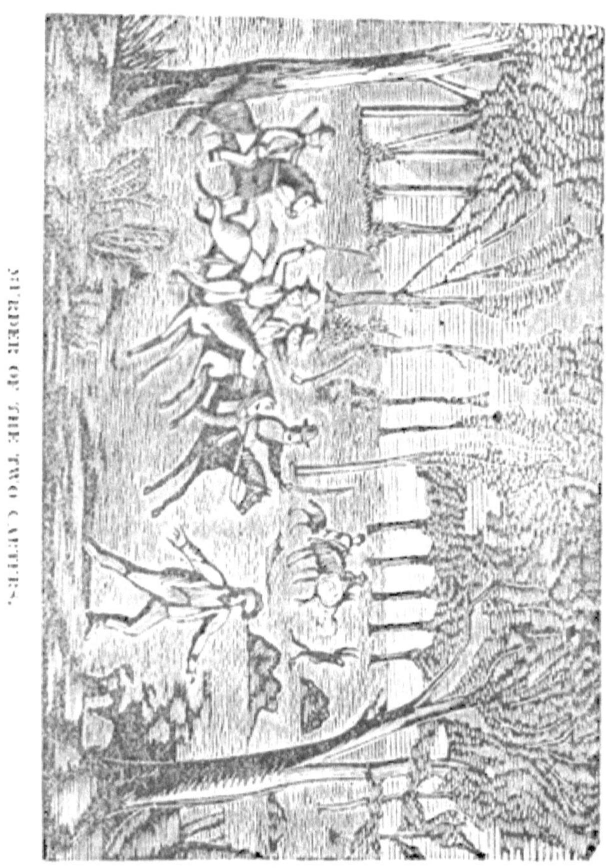

between where the bodies lay, in some places was
tramped and torn, and the bushes twisted and broken
from the heavy and compact dashing of their animals.

After driving him in this manner, a hundred and fifty
yards or more, his eyeless and ghastly face covered with
blood, and his lips pleading for mercy, and when he could
rise no more, they extinguished what life remained by
piercing his heart with bullets from their carbines and
revolvers.

Mrs. Grissom stated that it it was evident that some of Wheeler's men joined these five bushwhackers in murdering the Carters. Gen. Wheeler was then making his way up the Tennessee to a point convenient for crossing, preparatory to his big raid down the Sequatchee valley, and through Tennessee in the rear of Gen. Rosecrans' army at Chattanooga.

In the dusk of the evening of the day, and near where the Carters were killed, a stranger, a rebel cavalryman, accosted two young ladies, and enquired if they knew Robert Carter. Being told that they did, he next enquired if they had heard from him that afternoon. They replied that they had not. "Well," said he "I suppose that I have seen Robert Carter since you have; I helped to kill him this afternoon, and there," holding up his navy. "is the revolver that performed the deed!"

James Roberts, the leading criminal in this horrid transaction, was a young man, perhaps between twenty and twenty-three. Previous to this, his career as a rebel, guerrilla, bushwhacker, murderer, thief, robber, and actor in all other kinds of villainy, had carried him well nigh through the entire catalogue of human crime.

Previous to the death of the Carters, a Union soldier named Duncan, fell into the hands of Roberts. Duncan seeing himself overpowered, in an honorable manner, threw up his left hand in token of surrender, which was no sooner seen by Roberts than he took deliberate aim at Duncan and fired! Duncan fell, the bullet striking him near the eye, but instead of penetrating the skull passed between it and the scalp, round to the back part of the head! The blood flowed freely, and to all appearance, when Roberts came to him, he was in the agonies of death. Supposing that the ball passed into his brain, and that further injury was unnecessary in order to his death, Roberts robbed him of his watch, his money, and all other valuables that he could easily find upon him, then, as a last trophy, pulled off his boots and left him.

Some hours after, it occurred to Roberts that a more thorough examination of Duncan's body might put him in possession of more money.   He went to the spot where he fell, but to his surprise and mortification his victim was not there.

Duncan, shortly after Roberts left, came to his senses, and was not long in so far recovering, that he dragged himself away, and got out of danger. In a few days he reached the Federal lines, and finally recovered. As soon as he was fit for duty he took his place again in the ranks in defence of his country ; but the poor fellow, in about a year after he was shot by Roberts—was killed in Kentucky, loosing his life by the same class of abominable outlaws to which Roberts belonged, the guerrillas and bushwhackers. He was a brave Tennesseean, and now sleeps among the honored dead of that State, who poured out their blood in contending against the most damnable set of tyrants that God ever suffered to oppress mankind.

After the murder of the Carters, this Roberts continued his life of crime, scouring Bradley and Hamilton counties, until within a short time of the battle of Missionary Ridge, when his fortunes changed, and his career of blood was brought to an end.

He and another rebel guerrilla named, we believe, Green, were traveling together, either in Bradley or Hamilton, when they saw a man cross the road before them and enter the house of a Union man named McNeil. Roberts knew that a son of this family was in the Federal army. Supposing the person that crossed the road to be this son, home on a visit. Roberts at once determined to kill him. The two entered McNeils house and demanded of the old gentleman his " Lincolnite " son. McNeil replied that his son was not at home. Roberts told him that he was a liar, for he had just seen him enter his house ; and as he finished this remark, drew a chair to knock Mr. McNeil down.   The old gentleman sprang for the door, and opened it just in time for the door to receive the blow instead of himself.   Both followed, chasing Mr. McNeil around the house, Roberts calling out to his companion, d—n him, kill him!" At this moment the man whom they saw enter the house, sprang

with a gun from a place of concealment, took the opposite way round the house, met the parties and shot
Roberts to the ground. Roberts' companion fled and
escaped. The contents of the gun entered the breast of
Roberts, and it was thought that he must immediately
die. The man, however, commenced to reload his gun with
a view then and there to complete his destruction. When
the loading of the gun was completed, Roberts was still
alive, and the man was preparing to send his spirit into
eternity. Mrs. McNeil, not wishing to see him murdered
lying helpless at her door, interfered in his behalf, argu-
ing that as his wound was mortal, and he already beyond
doing them or any one else more harm, as bad a man as he
was, it was not magnanimous nor Christian to deny the
poor wretch the few remaining moments that were left
him. Through these entreaties the man was prevailed on
not to shoot him the second time.

The mother of Roberts was sent for, who came and conveyed him to her own home. When his mother saw him
apparently dying, she turned to the family in an angry
and upbraiding manner, and enquired why they did not
leave their house and flee when her son entered, why they
remained to contend with and murder her boy?

Soon after the battle of Missionary Ridge, the country
from Chattanooga to Knoxville fell into our hands, and
Roberts was found by the Federal soldiers, some of them
Tennesseeans who were acquainted with his history, at
home in the condition just described. The Tennessee soldiers visited Roberts daily, determined, if they saw the
least prospect of his recovery, to take his life.

His mother, his sister, and his physician, doctor Atchley, told these soldiers that Roberts was sinking and
could not possibly live but a short time. Roberts himself when these soldiers were present, would feign great
exhaustion to help on the deception. Instead of sinking,
however, Roberts was actually recovering, and as soon as
his physician considered his strength sufficient, he was in
the night, pitched into a wagon, and by his sister and
this doctor, with a negro to drive the ox team, stealthily

conveyed through our lines to Dalton, a distance of some twenty or twenty-five miles. Dalton being yet in the hands of the rebels, Roberts considered himself now safe from the vengeance of those whose friends he had murdered.

At Dalton, Roberts was cared for by his sister at the house of a rebel named Thomas Renfrow. After being here some time, Renfrow and his father fell into a quarrel in the room where Roberts lay; and struggling together over a loaded gun, to see which should have it, the gun accidently discharged, and in such a position that the contents lodged in the bosom of Roberts, entering not more than two inches from his former wound, and causing instant death.

This account of Roberts' fate at Dalton, was given to the writer by Mr. John Gilbert, who lived in the spring of 1864, at Blue Springs, Bradley county. Mr. Gilbert was living at or near Dalton at the time this accident to Roberts was said to occur, and related the circumstance as a fact. Mr. Gilbert is a Baptist minister, and on this subject could have had no possible object in stating an untruth. Many Union people of Bradley regarded the report as a fabrication coming from Roberts' friends, and circulated in order to put an end to further efforts on the part of Union men and Federal soldiers to take Roberts' life. It is barely possible that Mr. Gilbert and others were deceived by Renfrow, and that Roberts is still alive. Roberts was taken to Dalton, perhaps, in December, 1863, and had not been heard from since by the Union people of Bradley, late in the fall of 1865, and the strong probability is, that this youthful scourge of his fellow beings, was at Georgia, removed from among men.

George Roberts, younger than James, who, as stated, was also concerned in killing the Carters, was no mean accomplice with his older brother in crime. He fled to Dixie before our army in the winter of 1863–4, and is, i justice has not overtaken him, probably, somewhere in Georgia.

The father of these boys died about five years before

the war, and was said to be as fine a man as lived in the country. Sometime in the winter of 1864–5, Mrs. Roberts followed her husband and her deceased rebel boy to the other world.

Purvines and Runnions, two of the other accomplices in this crime, were citizens of Bradley. Purvines, in the fall of 1865, was yet at large. Runnions was arrested and incarcerated in Bradley county jail for his participation in this murder, but subsequently broke jail, and is now, so far as is known, also at large.

Mrs. Carter, made a widow and bereft of her son by this talismanic butchery, died about a year after, measurably from the grief and mental bewilderment of being the victim of such a tragedy.

Young Mrs. Carter, Roberts wife, when she discovered her husband, and turned him over, seeing that he was not only dead, but struck with the ghastliness of his mangled and bloody face, pitched over him, falling upon her own face on the ground, and wild and beside herself in a paroxism of grief, clawed with her hands around his body, smiting her head and face against the earth, besmearing and covering herself in his blood, until restrained, and measurably brought to her senses by the efforts of Mrs. Grissom and her two daughters.

CHAPTER XXIV.

ARTIFICIAL CAVES.

ONE of the most sublime moral spectacles elicited by this gigantic rebellion, was that intuitive and inextinguishable faith given to the Union people of East Tennessee, amounting, almost, to a positive foreknowledge that deliverance ultimately would come to them and their country.

Through the perfidy of Gov. Harris and other Tennesseeans in power, the State was submerged in the dark waters of the rebellion, carrying down with it and strangling fifty thousand Union men in East Tennessee alone—Union men encouraged by as many Union women, both determined to trust in God and wait through suffering for His providential deliverance. Notwithstanding the formidable power with which the people of East Tennessee were overrun from the south, with the barrier of Kentucky's *neutral rebellion* on the north, they nevertheless stood firm, and willingly accepted the storm. The scourge and the prison were sure for the time, but faith and hope were amply strong to anticipate the future victory.

From the commencement of the rebellion in 1861, till the winter of 1863–4, East Tennessee struggled, fought, looked and waited for relief. Relief neared and retired, neared and retired again; and it was not till the battles of Lookout Mountain and Missionary Ridge—fought respectively on the 24th and 25th of Novembea, 1863—that the clench of the beast was loosened from the throats of the loyal people of that part of the State.

Our victories at Forts Henry and Donelson—the former on the 6th, and the latter on the 14th, 15th and 16th of February, 1862—opened the Confederacy, and our armies swept through Nashville and south to the Tennessee, taking possession of Dixie from Corinth to the gates of Chattanooga.

The reverberation of General Negley's cannon, the deadly missiles of which on the 7th of June, 1862, were driven through the streets and buildings of Chattanooga, swelled and re-echoed over fifteen Union counties, thrilling with delight the hearts of their loyal inhabitants, and awakened in them a hope that the period of their captivity had expired.

On the 10th of June, 1862, Gen. Buell moved from Corinth, sweeping in a circuitous southern route to Athens, Tenn., where he unjustifiably delayed to reorganize, and enforce or restore discipline among his troops, by which error he lost Chattanooga, Gen. Bragg in the meantime occupying that town from Tupello, Miss.; after which Buell quietly settled down upon Battle Creek, his men whiling away their leisure hours exchanging newspaper congratulations with the rebels on the south side of the Tennessee River.

On the 2d of August following, Gen. O. M. Mitchell, at his own request, in consequence of the strong rebel sympathizing influence against him for his effective course, was relieved of his command of the Third Division of Buell's army; and thus ingloriously terminated his brilliant campaign in Tennessee.

On the 22d of the same month, the rebel Gen. E. Kirby Smith, with his corps, left the vicinity of Knoxville, passing through Big Creek Gap, to invade Kentucky. On the 20th, two days earlier, Gen. Bragg started with his army from Chattanooga, passing over Waldron's Ridge, a spur of the Cumberlands, also to invade Kentucky, with particular designs on Louisville. Gen. Buell was now compelled to abandon Tennessee, and follow Bragg in a parallel line with him, having fears that his real designs were to strike Nashville. As Buell's army disappeared to the north, leaving the people of East Tennessee once more entirely at the mercy of the rebellion, hope died within them, to be revived only by events beyond their ability to foresee.

The disappearing of Buell's army from Battle Creek and along the Tennessee, in August, 1862, sent a gloom over the land like the pall of death itself; yet the faith of these people did not waver. They believed that these armies would return, and that light would again dawn upon their country.

Esq. McPherson, of Bradley, thus describes his feelings on receiving the news of this retreat of Buell's army to the north: This to him, he stated, was the darkest hour of the war, in regard to East Tennessee. In the spring of 1861, he estimated that in one year the country would be redeemed. At the time of Buell's retreat it had been scourged a year and a half already, apparently ruined; and yet the Northern army was now compelled to fly to Nashville and Kentucky, allowing the rebellion again to swallow up the whole people like a flood! This was a state of things for which none of his former calculations had made any provision; and although his faith yet remained, he very forcibly felt himself now reduced to faith alone. He still felt that Tennessee would be saved; but the time when or the manner how, were matters that no longer entered into any part of his hopeful theory.

It was after the retreat of Buell to Kentucky to circumvent Bragg, that the Union people of East Tennessee went into the hottest of the furnace; and the manner in which they endured the flame can be accounted for upon no other principle than that patriotism is one of the strongest passions of the heart; and that the faith and hope of Esq. McPherson were an illustration of the faith and hope of the whole eighty or hundred thousand Union sufferers in East Tennessee.

The Union people of East Tennessee were under the yoke from the spring of 1861 till the winter of 1863-4. As this yoke from time to time was tightened upon their necks, in that proportion were their efforts increased and their expedients multiplied to baffle the tyrants and live through the ordeal till deliverance should reach them.

In the summer of 1862, the first rebel conscript law was passed, and East Tennessee very suddenly felt the pressure of this Confederate war mandate. Under its vigorous enforcement, fight for the rebellion, or evade the conscripting officer, were the alternatives before all Union men between the ages of eighteen and thirty-six. Perhaps not one in a hundred of these Union men—and there were many thousands of them in East Tennessee, northern Georgia and northern North Carolina—tamely submitted to the former alternative; but immediately from this entire region, thousands of them were seen floating like autumn leaves in the direction of Nashville and Kentucky. Rebel conscripting officers went into a vigilance committee of the whole. Powder and lead, horseflesh and bloodhounds, manipulated and driven on by demons incarnate, with citizen spies and reporters as a general picket guard, were brought into requisition, and many an unfortunate refugee, far from home, with his face towards his country's flag, was brought down by the fatal bullet, or sunk under the weight of the deadly bludgeon.

While in this extended field of strife it was universally the helpless refugee who bled, yet the general victory remained with him. Hate and hell nerved the arm of his thundering pursuer, but God helped the cause of the pursued. The loyal element of the country was not idle nor taken by surprise. A network of Union relays and reliefs, of underground railroads and invisible camps of instruction and rendezvous, with secret places of refugee entertainment, lofts of silence, under-floor cells, natural caverns and dark places along the creeks and ravines, artificial caves in the woods, with every other conceivable place of personal abstraction, at once sprang into active being, and were systematically used from one end of the country to the other. While rebel hate did its worst, this system, being effectually carried on by an army of skillful citizen managers, and home guards secretly connected with two-hundred-mile pilots, disguising their regular trips to Kentucky,—the internal machinery being strung together by fraternal gripes, patriotic pass-words, Union signs and signals, and Lincolnite symbols, known and committed to heart from parent to the youngest child of every family, black as well as white,—under the blessing of Heaven gave the general victory to the Union people, and sent the strength and flower of the land to the aid of the Government by helping to swell the ranks of the Union army.

During these three years East Tennessee was nominally in the hands of the rebels, but virtually it was controlled by the Union people. They were not the outward authority, yet they were the secret and governing power that held and moved the State. By the treachery of Harris and a leprous Legislature, East Tennessee was cut loose from the government dock; but thanks to her Union men, women and children, by these means they sprang to the rescue and virtually kept her moored within the harbor.

The most memorable of all the strategies resorted to by the Union people of East Tennessee to evade the rebel conscription, were the subterranean houses or artificial caves. One of these places is illustrated on page 263, a refugee inmate being represented as receiving food from the hand of a Union woman.

The localities of these places were the most unfrequented forests, and usually upon hill-sides, where cavalry would not attempt to travel. They were perpendicular excavations in the earth, square or oblong, to a convenient depth for a human residence, and of a size to suit the number proposing to occupy. The excavating completed, strong poles were lain across, the ends being let down a foot or more below the surface. These were then covered with strong planks, rails or stout poles, forming a roof, when the depression above was filled, beaten down, turfed over and covered with leaves, and made to correspond with the surrounding surface. Sometimes, to make the deception entirely complete, shrubs of pine and other wood were planted on the roofs after they were finished. A trap-door was attached to one corner of the roof, the outside of which was usually first covered with pitch, then rock moss and leaves imbedded in the pitch, to give the door the appearance of the rest of the surface. These roofs were finished with such permanence, that a cavalier might ride over one of them and not suspect the cavity beneath him.

The writer visited and entered two of these subterranean refugee homes in the twelfth district—one near the residence of Mr. Amos Potts, the other near that of Mr. Israel Boon. In the tenth district also he examined three of these places, near the farm of Mr. Elisha Wise.

Bradley contained at least from fifty to seventy-five of these Union dungeons. They were the most numerous in the north part of the county, ranging from five to seventeen miles south of the Tennessee River. Notwithstanding their number, and the extent to which they were occupied, these places were constructed and inhabited with such secresy, that no instance of Union men being captured either in building or occupying them, came to our knowledge.

Tailoring, shoemaking, basket making, coopering, and all sorts of carving in wood, were improvised in these houses, especially by such as were heads of families—those who, notwithstanding their own sufferings and the pressure of the times, felt the claims of providing for their wives and children. Numerous samples of boots, shoes, wooden buckets, wooden dishes, baskets, and other manufactures, such as chairs, canes, ax handles, &c., &c., were shown to the writer, all of which were the products of these strange exilements, the producers being nerved by a sense of duty, and by affection for those from whom they were exiled by rebellion and treason. The writer is in possession of a small oaken market basket, produced in one of these factories, which he proposes to keep while he lives, as a memorial, so far as it goes, of the truth of these statements.

Union women and children secretly conveyed provisions, mostly in the night, to their husbands, sons, brothers and fathers, immured in these dungeons.

ARTIFICIAL REFUGE CAVE.

CHAPTER XXV.

MR. AMOS POTTS.

MR. POTTS was among the earliest settlers of Bradley, being at the commencement of the rebellion upwards of sixty-five years of age. His home was in the twelfth district. Mr. and Mrs. Potts were people whose industry, frugality, and unscrupulous honesty, had procured for them through life a competency of this world's blessings; while their exemplary moral and Christian character, and their natural inoffensiveness as members of society, secured for them not only the respect and confidence, but the love and esteem of all who knew them. They were the very opposite of those whom considerate judges of human nature would suspect of intentional wrong, or whom any one could think deserving of punishment for political opinions.

Mr. Potts served in the War of 1812, under Gen. Jackson, and like all others in advanced age, who serve their country in early life, at the opening of the rebellion, felt a proportionately stronger attachment than he otherwise would have felt for the government he once defended, and, upon the same principle, also felt an unusual veneration for the flag under which he fought and risked his life fifty years before. Accordingly when the rebellion showed its bloody hand, Mr. Potts and his whole family were not long in declaring themselves loyal to their country.

Mr. Potts, with his children and grand-children around him, formed a nucleus of twelve or fifteen persons, in the twelfth district, who did their share during the war of throwing obstructions in the way of the rebellion.

Albert Potts, an unmarried son, living with his father, in the fall of 1861, was arrested at the instance of Capt.

Brown, and given his choice to enlist in the rebel army or be sent a prisoner to Tuscaloosa during the war. One or the other of these propositions must be immediately complied with. Albert reflected upon the consequences to himself of going to Tuscaloosa, and balanced these against the chances of desertion in the other case, and finally, with a mental reservation which he thought justifiable under the circumstances, told Capt. Brown that he would enlist. Shortly after his enlistment his regiment was sent to Knoxville, where young Potts took the benefit of the first opportunity, and left Capt. Brown to manage both his Tuscaloosa prison and rebel army to suit himself. He returned to his home but soon fled to Kentucky, and after an absence of over two years, stole his way back, reaching home in June, 1863, and by concealing himself in the woods and caves eluded his enemies until our army took the country. Mr. Langston, a son-in-law of the old gentleman, was driven into the woods, but at length fled to Nashville, where, in the employ of the government, he sickened and died. Mr. A. K. Potts and his son William, resorted to the same strategy of living in the woods, and fleeing North to escape from the rebels.

Notwithstanding the eagerness with which these men were pursued by traitors, all but Mr. Langston escaped and lived to see the rebellion conquered.

Four or five times in two years these families were plundered of everything on their premises the rebels could find that struck their fancy.

On the 25th of December, 1863, a company of convalescent Federal soldiers passing from Chattanooga to Knoxville, camped for the night a short distance from Mr. Potts' dwelling. A squad of rebel cavalry led by a fellow named Tyner, was on the same day making a plundering cavalry dash from Dalton into Bradley, and ascertaining from rebel citizens that these Federals were passing through the country, Tyner headed his column in the direction of their trail, which he struck about four miles south of Mr. Potts' plantation, and followed it until he reached Mr. Potts' house. Feeling themselves not strong enough, perhaps, to justify an attack of the Federals, the rebels wreaked their vengeance, what little time they dare remain, upon old Mr. Potts, accusing him of feeding the Yankees, abusing him and his family and robbing the house and premises.

Three Union boys named Winkler, brothers, were at the house of Mr. Potts when the rebels dashed up. Two made their escape, the other being lame was captured but a few rods from the house. A leader among them named McDaniels, immediately commenced to abuse Winkler, cursing him and drew his revolver to shoot him. Winkler being lame and unarmed was unable to make any defense. The old gentleman, the old lady, and their daughter, Mrs. Langston, begged McDaniels not to take his life. This appeared the more to enrage McDaniels, who with his revolver cocked, was endeavoring to aim it at Winkler's face. Mrs. Langston and the old lady threw themselves before Winkler, pleading with McDaniels not to shoot, both being able so vigorously to resist his attempts, that after struggling with him three or four minutes he desisted.

Failing to kill Winkler, McDaniels drew his revolver on old Mr. Potts, threatening to shoot him if he did not immediately deliver up his best saddle, an article, he said, which he greatly needed. The old gentleman refused, when McDaniels thrust his revolver against him, pushed him across the room and through the door into the yard, cursing him continually, and ordering him to deliver the saddle without delay. Though about seventy years of age, and exceedingly frail, instead of being frightened, when fairly out of doors, the old gentleman commenced to halloo for the Federals at the top of his voice. This seemed to operate favorably upon his cowardly assailant, who, on looking toward the Federal camp, was diverted from stealing Union saddles to making preparations for retreat.

Another circumstance besides the hallooing of the old gentleman, tended to hasten the retreat of the rebels. Miss Rebecca Potts, the daughter of A. K. Potts, confronted McDaniels when assaulting her grand-father, and told him that she would go herself and report him to the Federals. One of the rebels informed her that if she left the house she would find herself overtaken with a bullet. Unintimidated, she started in full view of the whole party, ran to the Federal camp and reported the rebels. They left, however, before the Federals could attack them.

The lame Winkler boy being unable to travel, and the rebels having no horse for him to ride, he was left behind. Another boy, however, named Mitchell, whom they there captured, was taken to Dalton, but he subsequently escaped.

Before reaching the house of Mr. Potts, while on the trail of the convalescents, the rebels captured thirteen of their number, those who had fallen behind their companions, and were resting in the houses by the way. These with young Mitchell were hurried off to Dalton that night, some of whom no doubt suffered and possibly lost their lives in the horrible pens at Andersonville or other rebel prisons in the South.

Although the rebels were at Mr. Potts' but a few minutes, yet they stripped the house and premises of what they could find that suited them. As to McDaniels, besides his abuse of Mr. Potts, and robbing Albert of his money and other valuables notwithstanding the extent of his cowardly threatening, the haste of his departure was such that Mr. Potts is still in the possession of his saddle.

One of the most remarkable visits, however, that Mr. Potts received from his rebel friends during the rebellion, was that of a rebel, who at the time said his name was Husten; but whose right name probably was Hunley, a rebel colonel. He, with two others, on the 25th of September, 1864, came to Mr. Potts' house enquiring for horses. Mr. Potts owned a fine young horse, a large clay colored animal, already evidently reported to Hunley by rebels in the vicinity, as appeared from his conversation. He found where the horse was kept, and demanded of Mr. Potts the keys to the stable. Mr. Potts began to expostulate with him upon the injustice of taking his property in the way he proposed, when Hunley instantly went into a rage, clutched the old gentleman by the throat and choked him to the ground. The old lady being present when the conversation about the keys commenced, and seeing that the rebel was becoming angry, thought it best to give up the keys, and hurrying into the house to get them, she was returning with them through the door as the old gentleman went down under Hunley's grasp. She quickly handed him the keys. He took them without saying a word, and deliberately went to the barn and took

COL. HUNLEY CHOKING OLD MR. POTTS.

the horse. With the attention of the old lady, Mr. Potts soon began to recover, and as Hunley was leading the animal past the door, was able to tell the thief what he thought would become of such men as himself, and saying that it was his prayer, that God for the future would deliver him and his family from the hands of all bloodthirsty men of his class. To this address Hunley returned no reply, but got himself through the gate as hastily as possible and left with his booty without so much as a look of thanks toward its owner.

This was the last that Mr. Potts saw of this rebel colonel, but this is not the sequel of the transaction. The next day, ten or twelve miles from Mr. Potts' plantation, Col. Hunley turned the horse loose, or rather left him with Mr. Abram Slover, desiring Mr. Slover to send him back to Mr. Potts, or send Mr. Potts word where he could find him, Hunley representing to Mr. Slover that he simply borrowed the animal to use for a short time in driving out a lot of stock that he had purchased in Bradley. Mr. Slover immediately delivered his trust to its proper owner, when both Mr. and Mrs. Potts were as greatly surprised and rejoiced at the appearance, in this way, of their favorite animal, as they were the day before afflicted to loose him.

The only solution that could be reached in reference to this sudden change in Col. Hunley, was that a guilty conscience commenced a controversy with him on the subject of his treatment of Mr. Potts.

The most ripened villain could hardly avoid an hour of returning consciousness after thus abusing such a man as Mr. Potts, a man nearly seventy years of age, and one whose very countenance and tone of voice indicated him to be among the most innocent and harmless men in the world—one that never wilfully injured a hair on the head of a human being. That Col. Hunley was pursued by the ghost of his outrage upon such a victim is not remarkable; and the fact that he yielded and restored the property, is evidence that, though the outward hardening had fearfully progressed and was fast turning his nature into a stone, an impressible point remained in the centre which the petrifaction had not fully mastered.

After this by various strategies Mr. Potts kept this valuable animal out of the hands of the rebels until the next July, a period of about ten months, when he was again taken in a similar manner. Martin McGriff, Bud Beagles, and Reuben Boyd were the individuals who committed the robbery the second time. McGriff was raised in Bradley and was then living in Cleveland.

The three came to the house of Mr. Potts together,

McGriff acting as the leader. Mr. Potts was not at home, and McGriff enquired of the old lady where her husband kept his clay-bank horse, adding th t her sons were tl e Federal army fighting against the Confederacy, and he should take the horse if he could find him. They soon found the animal and took him away.

McGriff was mistaken in supposing that the old lady's sons were at that time in the Northern army. Albert, with three of the Winkler boys were then concealed in the barn, and saw him bridle the horse, and could have shot him while in the act, and would have done so had they known that only two other rebels were present, and had it not been for the revenge which they knew would be visited upon the family in consequence, the whole country then being at the mercy of the rebellion. Mc-Griff was a notorious rebel, though in justice to the family it ought to be stated, that he had brothers who were good Union men, and who lectured him at the time on his villainy in thus robbing one of the most worthy and inoffensive citizens of the county. These Union brothers tried to prevail on Martin to return the horse but without avail. He was seen riding him about the country, and once or twice rode him past Mr. Potts' house. In order to screen himself from the odium of being called a thief, McGriff reported that he purchased the animal of Mr. Potts, and paid for him $600.

The old gentleman never obtained his horse, and never fully ascertained what disposition was made of him. Mc-Griff, doubtless disposed of him to great advantage, as he was universally conceded to be one of the finest animals in the country.

In relating this affair in the winter of 1864, the old lady remarked that she felt the loss at the hands of McGriff much more than at the hands of Col. Hunley. When the horse was taken by Hunley the case was fruitful of other troubles, so much greater and so much more calculated to excite her fears, that the idea of property was forgotten, and she was even glad to see the animal go if that would save their lives and rid their premises of such a monster as Hunley. But when she saw him taken by one of their own neighbors whom they had never injured, but had always been ready to befriend, it was an injury and a loss that stung her to the heart. She also remarked, that when McGriff led the animal by the door, he showed himself so high and lofty, was so full of life and looked so grand, that it brought to her mind how long and hard she and her whole family had struggled, and in how many ways they had tried to secrete and save him, and remembering in connection, at that moment all their other troubles of the rebellion, she went into the house and wept over the loss, feeling almost as though one of the family had been taken away.

After the war Mr. Potts prosecuted McGriff for damages and mulcted him in the insignificant sum of three hundred dollars; when every principle of justice dictated that it should at least have been one thousand.

This, as one instance, will illustrate the justice that is likely to be awarded in cases where the mildness, amenities and advantages of civil law, and the customs of trial by civil law, can be resorted to by criminals whose offences were committed, not in defiance of *existing* civil law, but only after they, as a body of traitors in insurrection and rebellion against their government, have annihilated all civil law in the premises. What is government but law? What are national and municipal governments but systems of civil law, to which all concerned are alike subject? The man, therefore, or the body of men, who destroys the government destroys the civil law in the most effectual manner possible. He uproots the very source and support of the civil law.

The difference between the private offender in time of peace, and organized and active traitors is, that the first simply offends *against existing* law. He does not attack the law itself, but commits his crime *against* it, leaving the law standing and in force to arrest and punish him if he cannot keep out of its way. The traitor, however, in the very first instance of his career, lays violent hands upon the law itself. He attacks and demolishes its very citadel.

He does not deign to keep himself out of the way of the law, but he puts the law out of his own way, by putting it out of existence. The government and its time-honored system of laws growing out of it, he sweeps aside as chaff, after which he roams his country an unrestrained freebooter, with no civil power in existence to impede his course.

This was exactly the condition of things, not only in Bradley, but in the whole of East Tennessee, for three years. McGriff's offence, therefore, against Mr. Potts, was not committed against civil law, for no civil law existed in fact or held jurisdiction, or even claimed to hold jurisdiction, in the country at the time.

The principle is, that organized rebellion in a State—rebellion rising to such a magnitude as to compel the State to grant her rebel subjects belligerent rights—annihilates civil law, and consequently the jurisdiction of civil law within the territory under military occupation, till a resort to arms settles the dispute.

Government, or civil jurisdiction in the rebel States, was the very thing in dispute while our great contest was going on, and the concession of belligerent rights to the rebels was a mutual agreement between the parties to decide that question by the sword. Government, or civil jurisdiction of the disputed territory, by this mutual agreement, was placed in the condition of a stake, a thing pending between the parties, to be won or lost by either party, as the case might be; and while so placed was in fact the property of neither, but as much, by the agreement, the property of one as the other. It finally fell to us, but it might have fallen to the rebels; and while by mutual agreement it was thus exposed or subject to the chances of their success, as well as to the chances of ours, it was not ours any more than theirs, so far as the agreement was concerned. Indeed, while thus pendent, it was ours no more than theirs in any sense: for in this agreement we yielded up our right to it on all other grounds, and hoped for it and expected it only on the abstract conditions of the agreement, namely: that we won it by the sword.

In regard to each party, therefore, ownership, government, or civil jurisdiction of the disputed territory, under this agreement, was a mere contingency of the future, and while thus a future contingency in regard to both, was practically as well as theoretically out of existence. The civil power on our part was withdrawn, and Government represented itself there by a more potent element— the military. In other words, its jurisdiction in that territory passed from its civil to its military branch. The military is a branch of all civil governments, and when from insurrection or rebellion, a State cannot be represented in any of its territory by its civil power, and this consequently is withdrawn, it represents itself there as fast as it can by its military branch; and in the very nature of such changes—in the very nature of such military occupation—the jurisdiction of this branch is complete and unlimited in the premises, as well as final in its action, extending to the conduct of every individual within the rebellious territory as fast as occupation takes place. In the very nature of the case this must be so, or the organization is a myth, and its objects can never be accomplished. Rebel territory, as fast as we could possess it, and the people within it, became subject to military authority, as they were before to that which this had superseded. McGriff's crime against Mr. Potts, therefore, was not an offense against the civil law, but against the military law then in force in Tennessee, in place of the civil law, claiming and exercising jurisdiction over him and his conduct, as well as over all others in those parts of the State that had been redeemed.

Offenses against law or government, are civil or military according to the power against which they are committed—the power exercising jurisdiction in the premises at the time. The military was the only authority then in Tennessee representing the Government, consequently it received and took cognizance of McGriff's offense in that branch. But this is not all. This offense was not only against and in defiance of the military as the *only* authority then having jurisdiction in Bradley, but it was the act of a military foe against the strength of these authorities —opposing and obstructing their operations. It was committed against Mr. Potts because he was loyal to the Government—a Union man and an enemy to the rebellion; because he was considered as aiding and abetting these authorities in putting the rebellion down. In fact, because he was considered part and parcel of the power then endeavoring to crush the rebellion. The Union people of Tennessee *were* a part of the power working to accomplish this object. Our military authorities looked to and depended on them for aid in various ways. They depended on the Union people for information, for supplies, and to act as their guides through the country, and to co-operate with them in every way they could, which they did. When these Union people were damaged, injured and weakened, these authorities and their operations suffered by it. Crimes, therefore, like that of McGriff's against Mr. Potts, were offenses against the Union people as a part of the military itself,—offenses, therefore, bearing against these authorities themselves, and against their operations, consequently over which they had unlimited and final jurisdiction.

As a matter of war policy, with a view to defend themselves, to husband and increase their strength and forward their operations, McGriff's case was theirs to dispose of.

These remarks have not been made as indicating, nor are they an attempt to prove, that reorganized civil courts, after the war, can have no jurisdiction over cases of this kind neglected, or that could not be reached by the military.

For instance, the citizen murderers hung in Murfreesboro by Gen. Thomas, in the spring of 1862, had they escaped the military then having jurisdiction over their crimes, would have fallen subject to the authorities succeeding the military; and, had they ever become known, justly could have been punished by the civil law. Jurisdiction of crime in that county changed after the war; but the guilt of these criminals, had they not been de tected them, would have lasted through all such changes. Their crime was committed against *natural rights*—a right which no changes among men can destroy; consequently their guilt could not be annulled by mere changes in the jurisdiction of justice.

Military law should have been applied to all offenses in Tennessee similar to that which we are considering, as soon as possible after our military authorities occupied the country.

The object of these remarks is not merely to establish the fact of military jurisdiction where civil law is withdrawn—a thing generally conceded—but to make it plain that it was the imperious duty of our military authorities, immediately on taking possession of Tennessee, to redress the wrongs inflicted on Union people by their rebel neighbors. This was what the Union people of Tennessee had a right to expect, and this in fact is what they did expect. Had a military court of perfectly suitable men been appointed in Chattanooga as soon as our forces took the place, within a month after the battle of Missionary Ridge, every Union family in Hamilton, injured by rebels owning real estate or personal property within our lines, might have been redressed, or placed in security of redress, very many of whom will now never get justice till they get it at the Judgment Seat above.

A military commission of five honest, industrious and positive men appointed in Cleveland, to hold their sessions ten hours each day for two months immediately following our entrance into the county, would have repaired more losses, redressed more wrongs, punished more offenders, and administered more justice very important to be administered, than will now be effected there while the rebellion can be remembered.

Who can assign any good reason why all, or all that could have been reached, of the cases in East Tennessee, similar to that of McGriff's offense against Mr. Potts, should not have been called up and disposed of at once by military courts? Who can assign any good reason why all such cases, or the most of them, should be dis-

layed two years, till civil courts could be organized in which to adjudicate them? No matter whether the persons of the offenders could have been immediately reached or not, full restitution at least should have been made by our authorities to all Union parties injured by rebels, where property could be found to confiscate.

SHOOTING OF MR. WM. THOMAS.

Mr. Thomas lived in the eleventh district, Bradley county. He was a poor man, yet not wanting in the poor man's blessing, being surrounded, we believe, with nine children. He resided upon the famous White Oak Ridge, of Union refugee fame, the boundary line between Bradley and Hamilton. He operated upon this ridge as a pilot, aiding Union refugees to cross the Tennessee.

In October, 1863, on his way home from Cleveland, Mr. Thomas, after traveling about three miles, passed Larkin Taylor, Jacob Edwards, rebel guerrillas, and Mr. Andrew Carson, a citizen, conversing together by the road. Mr. Thomas saw the three that day, and was seen by them in Cleveland. They were conversing near Mr. Carson's home. Carson was a strong rebel, and had made efforts before that time to have Mr. Thomas arrested. Mr. Thomas knew that Taylor and Edwards pretended to belong to Capt. Snow's gang of cut-throats in Hamilton; and feared from what he saw in Cleveland, and from seeing the three conversing by the road, that they were meditating evil upon himself, and suspected a visit from Taylor and Edwards that night, as he presumed that they were then on their way to Hamilton, which would lead them near his house.

Mr. Thomas reached his home, retiring that night with his family as usual, but making preparations for emergencies. He was well acquainted with Taylor and Edwards. Two or three hours, perhaps, after he and his family retired, he heard a suppressed call at his gate, which was near the door. He made no reply, waiting for the call to be repeated, the second and perhaps the third time: hoping if it was from Taylor and Edwards, to recognize them by the voice. Being foiled in this—they perhaps assuming a fictitious voice—and thinking that it might be Union refugees sent to him for aid, he opened his door, and was in the act of stepping down upon the ground, which brought him into a position to see the visitors sitting upon their horses, whom he instantly recognized to be Taylor and Edwards. Feeling satisfied that they designed to kill him, he attempted to draw himself back into his house, when one and perhaps both of them fired, and he fell upon his own threshhold. One shot took effect and completely severed his thigh bone. The murderers fled, and the next day were tracked into Hamilton, and near to Peter Munger's dwelling, a Union man, whose carding mill and cotton gin—after appropriating to themselves all the woolen rolls they could find in the factory—they set on fire. The fire was discovered in time to save the buildings, but much of the property inside of them was destroyed.

Edwards, we believe, left Bradley, and is, doubtless, still at large. Taylor was arrested for this crime after the war, and imprisoned in Cleveland. In 1865 he was discharged for want of evidence.

That Taylor and Edwards were the persons who attempted to murder Mr. Thomas is beyond peradventure. No honest men, acquainted with the circumstances of the case, can arrive at any other conclusion. Great efforts were made by Taylor's friends and his lawyer, Mr. M. Edwards, to impeach the statements of Mr. Thomas in regard to his attempted murder. The positions taken by Taylor's friends and his lawyer in regard to these statements, were slanders as foul and unjust as their authors were dishonest and unprincipled.

Taylor, Edwards and Carson, notwithstanding this and all the other crimes they committed during the rebellion, go unwhipped of justice, while Mr. Thomas, through their thirst for Union blood, will spend the rest of his days a ruined and helpless man. His family also, unless Government shall afford him relief, socially and pecuniarily, will feel the blow, perhaps through life.

UNION METHODIST MINISTERS IN BRADLEY.

Traveling—Wm. C. Daily, J. L. Mann.

Local—Anderson Trim, John Brower, Elijah Still, A. F. Shannon, W. D. Smith, Asa Stamper, Isham Julian, W. W. Hames, P. H. Reed, Peter Swafford, Wm. B. Ballenger, G. Blackman.

All the foregoing ministers suffered their full share of persecution from the rebels. Mr. Daily and Mr. Mann, however, being traveling ministers, were pursued with a proportionately greater virulence than the others; both being called to an account for their disloyalty to the Confederacy by the Holston Conference, Mr. Daily at its annual session at Athens, Tennessee, 1862, and Mr. Mann at its annual session at Wytheville, 1863. Mr. Mann was expelled from the Conference. He fled north and was appointed chaplain of the 9th Tennessee cavalry in which he served sixteen months. Mr. Daily and Mr. Mann are now successfully serving under the auspices of the M. E. Church, in their former field of ministerial labor—Bradley and its adjoining counties.

The following named ministers were also dealt with for their loyalty to the old Government, by the Conference at Athens.

W. H. Rogers, W. H. Duggan, Jesse A. Hyden, Patrick H. Reed, John Spears, James Cumming, Thomas N. Russel, and Thomas P. Rutherford. Bishop John Early presided at both these Conferences.

REBEL METHODIST MINISTERS IN BRADLEY.

Traveling—A. G. Worley, Presiding Elder. J. W. Belt, G. McDaniel, T. K. Glenn, and H. B. Swisher.

Local—A. L. Brooks.

CUMBERLAND PRESBYTERIAN UNION MINISTERS IN BRADLEY.

Hiram Douglas, Jacob Lawson, Robert Carden, Washington Smith, Richard Parks.

MURDER OF MR. EARBY COOPER.

Mr. Cooper was murdered on the 15th of December, 1864. About an hour after he and his family retired for the night, five or six men called at his door, assuming to be Federal soldiers, and were admitted into his house. They pretended to be in search of rebels, and told Mr. Cooper that they mistrusted him as secreting rebel soldiers on his premises. He replied that no rebel soldiers had ever been harbored about his house. Pretending to doubt his statement, they requested the privilege to search for themselves. After searching within, all but one, taking the light, went out doors, ostensibly to search the premises without. Mr. Cooper, his wife and two or three children, and a brother, Dempsey Cooper, who was stopping with him him for the night, and the one rebel, remained in the house in the dark, with the exception of a faint light that glimmered from the embers on the hearth. By this time Mr. Cooper was convinced of the real character of his visitors, and managed—though the one rebel was present—to express his fears to his brother Dempsey, and both prepared for the worst.

In a few moments the rebels without returned to the door, one with the candle in his hand. The door was opened by Mr. Erby Cooper, when they, standing upon the step, inquired if he was Eraby Cooper. Either delaying to answer, or answering evasively, the whole company commenced to fire upon him, he standing his ground and returning the fire with his revolver.

After firing six or eight shots the rebels yielded the ground and fled. Mr. Cooper pursued them over the yard fence a few steps from his door, where he fell, from which place he was taken up dead a short time afterwards, having been pierced by five or six bullets. A trail of blood was found the next morning along the path taken by the rebels in their flight, but to what extent they were injured by Mr. Cooper, was never, we believe, fully ascertained by his friends.

The moment the struggle commenced at the door

between Mr. Eraby Cooper and the four or five rebels, the rebel inside, and Mr. Dempsey Cooper, closed in a hand-to-hand fight with their revolvers, near the bed where Mrs. Eraby Cooper and her children were lying. Mr. Cooper's revolver proving to be out of order, and not discharging regularly, he dropped it, clenched a chair, and felled the rebel to the floor. As the blow was given, however, he received a shot that made it impossible for him to follow up his advantage. The rebel soon recovered, and the door being by this time clear, sprang to his feet and fled. Though severely wounded, Mr. Cooper finally recovered. Whom these rebels were, was, we believe, never ascertained. They were unknown to the Mr. Coopers, and as it appears that they did not know which was Mr. Eraby Cooper, the Coopers must have been unknown to them. It was doubtless a similar case to that of the murder of Mr. Richmond, the perpetrators being evidently hired and sent to perform the foul deed, by malicious rebel citizens who thirsted for Mr. Cooper's blood on account of his activity as a Union man.

Mrs. Cooper and her children narrowly escaped with their lives. Rebel bullets from the door, some of which possibly passed through the body of her husband, struck near the bed where she and her children were lying. As the contest between Mr. Eraby Cooper and the rebels at the door, and that between Mr. Dempsey Cooper, and the single rebel within, commenced and was raging at the same moment, one can easily imagine the frightfulness and horror of the scene through which the family of Mr. Cooper, that night, was compelled to pass. The case also may illustrate the fearful extent to which the Union people of East Tennessee were made to suffer by the rebellion.

APPENDIX.

It is true that our great American rebellion was unlike anything else of the kind in history; and that the Government as well as our commanders in the field had to proceed in regard to it, almost entirely without precedent to guide them. The policy of the Government, and of the different department commanders also, had to be improvised as the way opened before them, and particularly was this the case in regard to the border states, where rebels and loyalists were so intermingled; where the tares and the wheat so persistently spring up together, that it was difficult to remove the tares without destroying the wheat likewise. Making, however, all due allowance for the unprecedented difficulties of the case, it is questionable whether **our** military authorities in the border states, particularly those in Tennessee, **and more** particularly still in East Tennessee, acted with that discretion which might **have** been expected—justly and wisely discriminating between rebels **and** loyalists, and **upon this** basis dispensing awards punitive and **compensative, which the nature of the case not** only justified, but the good of the cause positively **demanded.**

It is doubtful whether any department commander operating in the West, with the exception of Gen. Fremont, and any division commander with the exception of Gen. O. M. Mitchell, and possibly a few others, developed and pursued that line of policy, very perceptibly the most advisable at the time.

Nashville was surrendered to Gen. Buell by R. B. Cheatham, its mayor, Feb. 25, 1862. The following is Gen. Buell's proclamation to the people of Nashville and Davidson county on that occasion.

HEADQUARTERS DEPARTMENT OF THE OHIO,
NASHVILLE, TENN., February 26th, 1862.

The General Commanding congratulates his troops **that it has** been their privilege to restore the national banner to the Capital of Tennessee. He believes that **thousands of** hearts in every part of the State will swell with joy to see that **honored flag** reinstated in a position from which it was removed in the excitement and folly of an evil hour; that the voice of her own people will soon proclaim **its welcome, and** that their manhood and patriotism will protect and perpetuate it.

The General does **not** deem it necessary, though the occasion is a fit one, to remind **his troops** of the rule of conduct they have hitherto observed and are still to pursue. We are in arms not for the purpose of invading the rights of our fellow-countrymen anywhere, but to maintain the integrity of the Union, and protect the Constitution under which its people have been prosperous and happy. We cannot therefore look with indifference on any conduct which is designed to give aid and comfort to those who are endeavoring to defeat these objects; but the action to be taken in such cases rests with certain authorized persons, and is not to be assumed by individual officers or soldiers. Peaceable citizens are not to be molested in their person or property. Any wrongs to either are to be promptly corrected and the offenders brought to punishment. To this end all persons are desired to make complaint to the immediate commander of officers or soldiers so offending, and if justice be not done promptly, then to the next commander, and **so on** until the wrong is redressed. If the necessities of the public service should require the use of private property for public purposes, fair compensation is to be allowed. No such appropriation of private property is to be made except by the authority of the highest commander present, and any other officer or soldier who shall presume to exercise such privilege shall be brought to trial. Soldiers **are** forbidden to enter the residence or grounds of citizens on any plea without authority.

No arrests **are** to be made without the authority of the Commanding General, except in cases of actual offence against the authority of the Government; and in all such cases the fact and circumstances will immediately be reported in writing to Headquarters through the intermediate commanders.

The General reminds his officers that the most frequent depredations are those which are committed by worthless characters who straggle from the ranks on the plea of being unable to march; and where the inability really exists, it will be found in most instances that the soldier has overloaded himself with useless and

19

unauthorized **articles.** **The orders already published on this subject** must be enforced.

The condition and **behavior of** a corps are sure indications of the efficiency and **fitness of** its officers. If any regiment shall be found to disregard that propriety **of conduct** which belongs to soldiers as well as citizens, they must not expect to occupy **the** posts of honor, but may rest assured that they will be placed in positions where they cannot bring shame on their comrades and the cause they are **engaged in.** The Government **supplies** with liberality all the wants of the soldier. The occasional deprivations and hardships incident **to** rapid marches must be **borne with** patience and fortitude. Any officer who **neglects** **to** provide properly for his **troops, or** separates himself from them to seek **his own** comfort, will be held **to a rigid** accountability.

By command of GENERAL BUEL.

           JAMES B. FRY, A. A. G., Chief of Staff.

Official : J. M. WRIGHT, A. A. G.

This proclamation is **dignified and commanding, and, in some** respects, even **able.** In fact it is too **able, respecting matters on a scale altogether** too general, **overlooking the peculiar and most vital points of the case.** It argues in the writer a **great, an overgrown, but dead heavy talent, and a** moral **nature** that never particularly concerns itself with the individual **actualities** of human life. What it combines and enforces is eminently proper in all armies and on all occasions, but the most important combinations and enforcements **in** the premises are not made at all. **The position of Gen. Buell and** his army at the time Nashville **was surrendered into** his hands was the **most** peculiar, remarkable, and vitally important, **of the position of any General** recorded in history. Gen. Buell, however, **utterly failed to apprehend this** great fact, and, accordingly, the great *fault* **of this proclamation is** *want of discrimination.* It is a document, consequently, **fraught with very glaring** and destructive omissions. As a moral production, or **production responsible to moral** right, its fault is looseness of moral principle. It **betrays either moral ignorance and** obtuseness of moral perceptions, or the **absence of a consciencious** regard for known truth—the absence of a consciencious **regard for the known rights of** all and justice to all. It was dictated either by **a misapprehension or disregard of, or** rather indifference to, the *spirit* of the **rebellion,** particularly as it existed in Nashville. This proclamation disappointed **and discouraged, if it did** not positively mortify the Union people of Nashville and **the surrounding country,** while it encouraged and strengthened the hands of rebel **citizens.** It assured the rebels that their position as such, and what they had done **as such in persecuting, robbing, murdering** and driving the **Union people out of** the country, were **not to be looked upon as crimes nor as meriting any punishment, or as subjecting them to any inconvenience** by proscription, or **restriction** of **their liberties or of their business.** It makes not the least distinction **in** any **respect between guilty rebels and** virtuous Union people. It takes **no** notice of **the important fact of the existence** in Nashville at that time of two opposite **parties, the sole issue between them** being the Rebellion—one rebel the other loyal, **one friends the other enemies to the Government.** No notice whatever **is** taken of the Union **people; the fact of their** existence **appears** to have been purposely **passed over through fear of giving offense to the rebels.** Policy, as well as duty, **demanded that the integrity with which these Union people** had stood by the **Government should be proclaimed in this order and put in the** strongest possible **contrast with the treasonable and criminal conduct of the rebels.** A special recognition **in this order of the Union people of Nashville and** Davidson County, as a **body, and as having distinguished themselves as the friends** of the Government, **briefly eliminating the actual moral virtue of their** position, and the services they **had rendered the country, would have been a mark** of distinguishing favor justly **due, and which these Union people had a right to expect.** This not only would **have gratified the Union people, but they would have felt it** a full recompense for **what they had suffered if not for what they had** lost, thereby being encouraged **in their loyalty for the future, while this, alone,** would have reflected a cutting **rebuke to the rebels, causing them to smart under** the contrast thus **drawn** between **their treason and the loyalty of their Union** neighbors. Gen. Buell, however, was too **great a man; his military conceptions** were altogether too **vast,** if not too **vague, to allow him to descend to these** insignificant particulars, **particulars** that would have **touched the hearts of** the people, and that **would have** evinced that his policy **was to be shaped and moulded** from the bottom **upwards,** making its foundation **the actual substratum** of the materials **among which he** had to work.

Gen. Buel, in this **order, could use** the **most** opprobious terms **in** expatiating in advance upon the **possible** delinquencies of his private soldiers; but it contains not a word of **reprimand or** even advice **to** rebel citizens all around him in regard to their infinitely greater crimes already committed, a subject so eminently befitting it, crimes which had compelled these soldiers to leave their homes and expose themselves to fatigue, starvation and death, to rescue the country from that destruction which from these crimes it was in the most iminent danger. He could forbid the private soldier to enter the grounds of rebel citizens without authority, which was all proper enough in itself, and could read him **a** lecture of fortitude and patience in bearing up under the hardships and privations of the war, though he might be reduced to *hard tack* alone, indicating by a cold abrasion of language, that the abundance of rebel wealth in the country was not to be irregularly appropriated to relieve his wants in any case, however unusual or trying.

The error of Gen. Buell as a christian commander, was that he connived at crime as a means of destroying the spirit of it, instead of punishing it promptly and firmly, yet mildly, as a conscientious and humane officer, feeling the responsibility of having in charge the interests of the country, and the welfare of the people with whom he was dealing and those under his command.

Fort Donelson surrendered on Sunday morning the 16th of February 1862. **On** the following Sunday morning, the 23d, about 9 o'clock, just one week, almost to an hour, from the surrender of Donelson, the Federal troops arrived in Edgefield opposite Nashville. The news of this great rebel defeat reached Nashville the same morning the fort surrendered, in consequence of which a panic seized the rebel inhabitants of that city unequaled by any thing of the kind before known in the history of the country. Nashville rebels were smitten dumb with fear, and stood appalled at their condition. They felt themselves guilty, and very naturally expected to be punished for their crimes, when our army should arrive. Especially did they look for retribution to be visited upon them for the outrageous manner in which they had persecuted, tortured, and despoiled their Union neighbors. They expected that the Union people would enter complaints against them to the Federals, and that they would at once have to pay bitterly for these outrages. Under the influence of these forebodings, all the rebels that possibly could, immediately on receipt of the news from Donelson, fled from the city 'n all the haste and confusion imaginable, taking refuge in Dixie. Those who could not fly but were compelled to remain and meet the consequences, were completely humbled in view of the ordeal that was approaching them. They were perfectly conquered, whipped and subdued. The spirit of rebellion was completely frightened out of them. During the interval between the victory at Donelson and the arrival of our troops at Nashville, their haughty and insolent bearing towards their Union neighbors entirely forsook them. They became perfectly respectful, and approachable, almost universally manifesting penitence for their abusive treatment of the Union people with a disposition to be forgiven and to have old friendships restored. This was the wholesome effect upon Nashville rebels, and this was the submissive spirit which they manifested while they were in prospect of the daily arrival of Federal troops into whose hands they expected to fall, and by whom they expected to be dealt with according to their sins. No sooner, however, did this Federal army arrive, and, was this order of Buell's published, his policy instantaneously becoming known throughout the country, causing the rebels unbounded relief and joy, giving them to see that they had suffered all their fears for **nothing**, that they were in no danger of being punished either for their rebellion or their injustice to the Union people, and that the complaints of those Union people **were** given the cold shoulder and treated with contempt, their authors in some cases even rebuked by Federal officers, and consequently, that they could do the same things again with impunity, than this door of renewed friendship with Union people was backed out of by the rebels *instanter;* and the evil demon of rebellion again took possession of them, and they went to plotting treason, the overthrow of our armies and the destruction of the country with ten fold more wickedness and bitterness than before. They also assumed towards the Union people their former insolent bearing, the same haughty air and hateful look, made the same venomous flings, coupled with the same bitter spirit of persecution that characterized their course before Nashville was taken. These, though briefly stated, are historical facts, facts that can be attested to-day by hundreds of Union witnesses in Nashville.

Now, had Buell possessed the penetration to fathom the depths of this malignancy, instead of administering the opiate of a milk and water proclamation to eradicate it, his policy, without being vindictive, would have been based upon the principle that the treason of these rebels was a crime. His action towards them would have corresponded to their own convictions of their guilt, when the prospect of falling into our hands and of being subject to the prosecutions of the Union people, whom they had injured, had brought them to their senses. A marked distinction should have been made between rebels and Union people, and adopted as the rule in point of liberties, privileges and advantages, till circumstances warranted a generalization in these respects. Forty-eight hours after Buell's arrival in Nashville would have been sufficient to furnish him with a perfect list of the names of all the friends and enemies of the Government in Davidson county. Six or eight such men as Lawyer East, John Trimble, Esq., Post Master Lindsey, Mr. Hickey, H. C. Thompson and John L. Stewart, of Nashville, and Mr. Joseph and George Weekly, of Edgefield, with two from each of the other districts, selected by these, the whole to act as a committee of information, in two days would have given an unexceptionable list, of the personal loyalty and treason of Nashville and the surrounding country. Two or three individuals only acting as vouchers for the people of the whole country, and that for months together, left room for great abuses. Twenty or twenty-five, all more or less acquainted with the people, deciding upon the political status of an individual, would have precluded the possibility of personal favoritism, and thus hundreds of worthy persons who were denied the passes, would have been granted them, and *vice versa*. All Union men in the country vouched for by such a committee, before our army had been in Nashville three days, might have been given standing and unlimited passes for the term of the war or at least during their loyalty, judged by the same committee, to go and come as they pleased, without further molestation from the authorities. Instead of this, however, the Union people, notwithstanding what they had already suffered from the rebellion, must be subject alike with the rebels, to the very great annoyance and damage of getting their passes renewed every few days, for three years. No possible harm could have resulted to the cause' from the unrestrained liberty of these Union people, any more than from the unrestrained liberty given to Federal soldiers themselves when sent out as spies.

Unlimited permits, also, for the transacting of business, should at the same time have been granted to all Union families and firms, subject of course, to the necessity and pressure of our military operations; while the rebels in their business should have been restricted, circumscribed and narrowed down to a point of absolute necessity. Such was something like the distinction that should have been made between rebels and Union people, and made at once after our authorities possessed the country, not only in Nashville, but in the whole of Tennessee, and particularly in East Tennessee, as well as particularly in Nashville.

Such a course, not only would have been just, but it would have resulted greatly to the benefit of our cause. It would have afforded the Union people opportunities to repair the damages which they had sustained by the rebellion, and would have encouraged them to be active in co-operating with our authorities, obtaining information, &c., information that would have essentially aided our authorities in making general progress against the rebellion.

On the other hand, restriction would have been no more than justice to the rebels for their rebellion, and as retaliatory punishment for the same treatment on their part towards the Union people, and especially in as much as it was absolutely necessary to restrict both them and their business in view of our own safety. Justice thus administered to the rebels in Nashville, not tyrannically, nor insultingly, nor in a vindictive spirit, but in a proper manner, mildly but with firmness, and administered at the right time, when they themselves felt that they deserved it, the rod would have done them good; and the spirit of rebellion would have been conquered and annihilated at that time in Davidson county, as it will now not cease to exist while the present generation continues.

These remarks illustrate the principle or policy that should have been pursued by our authorities in regard to rebels and Union people throughout the State of Tennessee, or in fact wherever the persecuting spirit of the rebellion had made Union people suffer.

The Union people of Tennessee, and particularly of East Tennessee lived and suffered for three years in hope, and that hope was the Northern army. The arrival of the Northern army was to them the prospective hour and culmination of their patriotic bliss and of their country's deliverance. This was an event for which they looked, longed, waited and prayed, with an intensity proportionate to their trials, and what they considered to be the importance of the expected triumph. Many Tennessee boys had fled to the Northern army, and were anxiously and faithfully helping to push our lines to include their own homes. It was a common remark among Union people in Tennessee, while they were suffering under rebel oppression that, "When our *friends* arrive," referring to the Northern soldiers, "the tables will be turned. We shall be recognized as friends to the government, our position and our sufferings both will be appreciated, and we shall not only be protected, but our rebel neighbors will be called to an account for the wrongs they have inflicted upon us." As fast as the Northern soldiers did arrive in Tennessee, Union hands and Union hearts were open to receive them, Union tables were spread to supply their wants, and everything in the possession of the Union people that could administer to their comfort was at their disposal. At the sight of the Northern army the Union people laughed and cried for joy.

Mr. John L. Stewart, one of the most enthusiastic Union men in Nashville, had been bitterly persecuted and tortured by the rebels. During the long week of suspense between the fall of Donelson and the arrival of the Federal army in that city, Mr. Stewart could scarcely eat or sleep for his anxiety to see the Federal soldiers take possession of Nashville. When, on the morning of the 25th of February, 1862, the fleet of government transports headed by a gun-boat, with all her guns frowning upon either side, was descried from the Capitol ascending the Cumberland and nearing the city, each transport with the Stars and Stripes visible at mast head, as they steamed up to the landing with banners flying, their decks burdened with dense regiments of blue coats and the shrill martial music waiting out the notes of Hail Columbia upon the morning air, Mr. Stewart was completely overwhelmed and carried away with the sight, the effect being more than he could bear. The national glory and Union triumph that was in the scene, bringing deliverance to himself and his friends, gave him a burst of joy that quite bereft him of his senses, sending him wild and insane with delight. To make use of Mr. Stewart's own language, for the whole day and even for a week he could compare himself to nothing but a shouting Methodist at a camp-meeting, so great and unbounded was his joy, from the effects of which he did not fully recover for a month.

The case of Mr. Stewart may illustrate upon general principles the spirit in which the Union people of Tennessee, Union women and children, particularly of East Tennessee, were prepared to hail and welcome the Federal army to their doors.

Now, **the facts** in the case **do n**ot warrant the statement that our armies, as they took possession of Tennessee, fully appreciated this feeling among the Union people. Reciprocated Federal friendship to this feeling fell considerably below the point of its actual existence on the part of the Union people, from the department commanders **down, from** the beginning to the end of the war. Had Gen. **Buell** given the **example at** Nashville, shaping his policy in that direction—**enjoined the practice of it upon his** officers, thus infusing the true spirit into his **army among officers and men, the** principle, doubtless, would have remained in **the army and more or less transfered** itself to successive commanders and successive armies. **As it was, a great** proportion of the good, or in other words **a great proportion of the disposition in** our army to defend and administer strict **justice to the Union people, and keep the** rebels in their proper places, was lost for **want of this active encouragement in the** department commanders, and for want **of that system which such authoritative** encouragement would have induced in **regard to the subject. Individuals, here** and there, saw the disgraceful evils and **abuses, and desired to correct them but could not,** only to the extent of their **individual authority.**

From this cold **indifference to loyalty and** loose manner of dealing with treason **in the beginn**ing, the **evil branched off and** showed itself in other forms equally **injurious** and mortifying **to the Union** people. Classing all together with little or **no** distinction, as equally **virtuous,** was an indirect invitation to our officers to **mingle** with all as equally **virtuous** and equally desirable company, and this ex**posed them** to the temptation of mingling most with those who made the greatest **efforts to** win their favor, **and** could hold **out** the most profuse and gratifying **inducements** to secure **it. The** rebels, **at the** approach of our armies, feared the **conseq**uences to themselves **and** their property, and having been corrupt enough to plu**nge** the country into trouble, they **could** now resort to treachery and meanness **to** get themselves out of difficulty. On the arrival of our armies, rebels were **the** first to obtrude themselves **upon** the notice of our officers and continued the most constant and **obsequious** in their attentions upon **them.** Rebels invited these officers **to their houses and to their** parties, introduced **them to** their wives and daughters, feasted them **at their tables,** heaped upon them their good things of which they generally **had plenty. By these and** other means they labored industriously **to ingratiate themselves into the favor of** these officers, and in many cases were too successful. **Having intrenched** themselves in the confidence of these officers, **or rather having bought their favorite sin,** these rebels were perfectly **at home** and perfectly **independent. They** could get passes and permits simply **by asking** for them, **when modest Union** men had to produce vouchers to obtain them. **They** could get **protection pap**ers for their property and Federal guards to stand at their doors, **when upright** Union men seldom requested either. Union **people were** infinitely **above the** hypocrisy and disgraceful truckling resorted to **by the rebels to** secure **the protection of our armies.** Union people had too **much self-respect to descend to such meanness** to court acquaintances or **curry favors, especially favors that were in** reality a matter of due; **and had they been disposed to enter this mire of com**petitorship, very frequently **would have labored at a great disadvantage. They had been pil**laged, robbed, **and had had their sub**stance laid waste perhaps by these very rebels, **till not enough remained, in many instances, for them**selves and families. The rebels **by their treason and friend**ship with the rebellion had escaped these misfortunes. The rebels possessed fine **houses, elegantly furnished rooms and sumptious boards which were weighty arguments in their favor, and against which the Union people,** in their **circum**stances, **felt little disposed to strive, especially considering the** moral character of the **contest.**

It was **patent throughout the country, and** during the first and second **years of** the war, **was the universal news**paper **topic** from Boston to Chicago, **as well as** the universal **theme of** army conversation that Tennessee was filled with suffering and outraged **Union** people. These Union people were not unadvised of this fact. They were perfectly aware that their situation was fully known to the Government **and** the army, and very naturally expected that Government kept an eye to their condition. They also supposed that one of the principal objects for which the army was sent into that country was their relief; and that on the arrival of our armies, their grievances would be redressed. They did not presume that it would be necessary, on the arrival of those armies, for them to board and swarm upon our officers at once, and load them not only with their complaints but their physical dainties, in order to be recognised and appreciated. The rebels, however, having the impudence to take this course, thus stealing the march not only upon the Union people, but even upon these officers themselves immediately secured their confidence, then engrossed their attention and procured their protection, while Union people disappointed and mortified, stood at a distance, and looked on with disgust.

Rebels were frequently known to boast that it was better to be a rebel, than a Union man. To be a rebel, they asserted, gave them indemnity from loss while the rebels held the country, and left them something with which to bribe yankee officers, and buy indemnification of the Federals on their arrival, and have an abundance for themselves besides; with the other advantages of escaping entirely the storms and persecutions universally endured by the Union people.

It is **not** intended by these remarks to convey the idea, that these abuses became absolutely the rule through out the State of Tennessee, during the war; but it is safe to assert that they were **so** frequent in **many** localities, owing to the looseness of the general policy in this respect, **and owing to** the number of Federal officers in the **army**, whose principles and **patriotism were as** loose as those of the rebels, that **these** abuses lost the character of **positive** exceptions to the rule, and more or less in every county in the State, mortified and disgusted the Union people.

While we appeal to the Union people of Tennessee for the truth of what we have said upon this subject, we nevertheless do not offer it as an adequate defence of their cause, either in regard to the diabolical cruelties of their immediate enemies, or the indifference of many, and the perfidy of some of their friends. The sufferings of the Union people of East Tennessee, and the horrors of Andersonville, Bell Island and Libby, are the two mountainous—distinguishing and diabolical wrongs of the rebellion, and are subjects that will not be exhausted by the historical themers of the coming century.

At the commencement of this article Gen. O. M. Mitchel was spoken of as a commander in Tennessee whose policy was an exception to the fault we have here complained of. No writer ought to touch this subject without leaving it distinctly recorded that Gen. Mitchel as clearly, if not more clearly than any other commander in Tennessee, saw this subject in its true light. Had his policy upon this subject, inaugurated during his brilliant campaign from Nashville through Tennessee to Alabama in the spring and summer of 1862, been adopted as the general rule, the evil we have here spoken of, to any appreciable extent, never would have existed. The eminent justice of that policy, however, created him enemies whose relentless opposition cost him his command of the Third Division of the Army of the Ohio, and in all probability was the initiatory step that cost him his valuable life. He saw at a glance the depths of the wickedness of the rebellion, from which stand point a policy in regard to it in Tennessee was dictated that emphatically announced him as the friend of the Union people of the State, and could not, in any proper sense of the term, announce him as an enemy to her rebels. Had he been permitted, as he earnestly requested of the Secretary of War in the fall of 1861 to march with his command from Louisville through Cumberland Gap to Knoxville, with a view to relieve East Tennessee, the result could scarcely have been other than a national blessing, as well as a merciful relief to the suffering Union people of that part of the State. After having been granted his request by the Secretary of War, Mr. Cameron, President Lincoln, influenced by the miserable jealousy and selfish complaints of other Generals in the Army of the Cumberland, was induced to countermand the order; and thus that important expedition was abandoned, and the valuable services of Gen. Mitchel as prospectively connected with it were lost, and East Tennessee for three years left to be consumed by the venom of the destroyer.

It may with propriety also be stated in this connection, that, had a similar proposition made by Gov. Brownlow a short time after this, been accepted by the government, and the number of men furnished him that he desired, East Tennessee doubtless would have been released early in 1862.

GATEWOOD RAID THROUGH POLK COUNTY.

John P. Gatewood, the noted guerrilla, murderer and bushwhacker of Northern Georgia and Tennessee, was born in Fentress county, East Tennessee; and at the commencement of the rebellion was, perhaps, twenty years of age, being the youngest but one of **six brothers.** The names of the other brothers were, Henry, Berry, Milton, William and Lytle. The father and sons were all rebels, and all but the youngest, Lytle, one way and another connected with the rebel army. Milton was drowned in the **Tennessee River** sometime during the war. Two others, perhaps Henry and Berry, were in Johnston's army when he surrendered to Sherman in Virginia. **Another, probably William,** was, during the last of the war, a guerrilla, and it was **understood operated as such** with his brother John in Tennessee and Georgia.

John P. Gatewood, if not **some of his** brothers, received his first schooling in rebel crimes under the tuition **of** Champ Furguson in Kentucky, being a member of his company perhaps one or two years. He appeared in Tennessee and Georgia in the **summer** of 1864, **being sent by the rebel** General **Wheeler** to recruit for the rebel service in the rear of Sherman's army during the Atlanta Campaign. He soon distinguished himself, and was not long in becoming generally known in that section as the leader of one of the most savage and bloodthirsty guerrilla gangs that was ever collected, or that ever operated in Tennessee or Georgia. He established his general headquarters, probably in Gordon county, Georgia, about fifty miles south of Chattanooga, and for a period of eight or nine months, until Johnston's surrender in Virginia on the 26th of April 1865, he infested upper Northern Georgia and South East Tennessee, robbing, plundering, and murdering the Union people till his name became the horror of every household in the land.

His distinguished raid into East Tennessee, which was made through Polk county, was perpetrated on the 28th of November, 1864. On the night of the 28th Gatewood, with his company, camped in Maury county, Georgia, a few miles south of the Georgia and Tennessee line. Early on the morning of the 29th, his column, in two or three divisions, struck Tennessee, the two right divisions entering Polk county, while the left division entered Bradley county, and passed through the third and thirteenth districts, boarding and pillaging the premises of Mr. Wm. Humbert, and robbing other Union families of those districts, converging in its route to a point of conjunction in Polk county with the other two divisions.

Gatewood himself headed what was supposed to be the center or main; and either before or shortly after all came together in Polk county, at the head of his column he rode up to the house of a Union man by the name of Horace Hill. Mr. Hill was sitting upon the fence in front of his door. Gatewood approached near to Mr. Hill as though he proposed to converse with him in a friendly manner, but suddenly drew his revolver, placed it close to his head and fired. The ball passed nearly in a straight line through the head from one ear to the other, causing instant death. Mr. Hill fell backward from the fence into his own yard, and expired in the presence of his own family. Michael Hill, a nephew of Mr. Horace Hill, was also on the premises at the time and was also attacked by the rebels. He, however, being armed, returned their fire defending himself as best he could, retreating at the same time. He kept the rebels at bay till he reached the Conasauga river, leaped in, swam across and escaped unhurt.

While Mr. Horace Hill was yet lying by the fence, either already dead or dying, the rebels invaded the premises, captured two colored boys, while a part of their number entered the house, pulled the fire from the hearth out upon the floor, apparently making an effort to set the house on fire. After committing three outrages, by which the rest of the family became nearly dead with fear, taking the colored boys as prisoners, the fiends left the premises, directing their course toward Benton, the county seat of Polk county. One of these colored boys subsequently escaped and returned. He reported that Gatewood was slightly wounded in the arm by Michael Hill. He stated that he saw Gatewood washing the blood from the wound in a stream, shortly after leaving the premises of Mr. Hill.

About four miles from where they murdered Mr. Hill, the rebels met four Union refugees from Cherokee county, Georgia. The parties were within sixty yards of each other before either saw the other. The refugees fled across a field to their left. One of them, Mr. Elihu Morse, unobserved, dropped behind a pile of rails and escaped. The other three were soon captured. In the meantime Gatewood and his Lieut., Jasper Graddy, had passed forward about a quarter of a mile to the residence of Mr. Pettit, and were talking with the family at the gate. The three refugees were brought within a few rods of where he was standing, and halted in the road. He watched them as they were brought up, and about a minute or two after they were halted, he suddenly wheeled, and drawing his revolver, rode upon the prisoners, and with an unerring aim, successively shot two of them through the head. His men also at the same time commenced firing upon the helpless victims, and instantly the three, in their gore, were struggling in the agonies of death in the road. As soon as the men fell, Gatewood waved his revolver over his head and cried, "Hurrah for the brave Tennesseans!"

The murderers robbed the persons of their victims of the money and other valuables which they could find upon them; stripped off their shoes and a portion of their other garments, and left them. Shortly, however, two of the rebels returned, kicked and turned the bodies over, examining them for money the second time. One of the rebels in the meantime remarked that he believed that they were not all dead, but were possuming, and that he thought it safer to shoot them till no possibility of their recovery remained. His companion replied that whether any of them were yet alive or not their wounds were mortal; that they were all shot through the head and must certainly die; and he proposed to let the unfortunates linger and suffer as long as possible. Before the point was decided two or three other rebels returned to the spot and joined in the conversation as to the necessity of shooting the bodies the second time. One of those who last arrived, notwithstanding the school of blood he was in, had not, it appears, lost all humanity. He stated that there had been too much shooting already for that morning, and he was opposed to any more savage mangling of the dead men before him. This advice prevailed, and the bodies were soon left without receiving further injury.

The names of the three victims were Chriswell Morse, brother to Elihu Morse, who escaped—and L. C. and J. W. Hapgood, brothers, all men of families—leaving wives and children in Cherokee county, Georgia. J. W. Hapgood was shot through the head, and probably died instantaneously. He left a wife and two children. L. C. Hapgood and Mr. Morse came to their senses before the straggling rebels returned to them, and though feigning death, as some of these rebels suspected, were able to hear the conversation in regard to shooting them the second time. Half-an-hour, perhaps, after the rebels left them, they ventured to rise, and dragged themselves away to places of safety. They were taken to Cleveland, received into our hospital at that place, and both finally recovered. Mr. Hapgood was struck on the left eyebrow, the bullet passing into and carrying away the eye, ranging downwards and through just above the roots of the tongue, and passing out below and a little behind the right ear. Mr. Morse was struck on the left cheek, the ball passing downwards through the neck, lodging in the left shoulder, where it still remains. Although they recovered, both are crippled and badly injured for life.

The writer saw Mr. L. C. Hapgood in the fall of 1865, in Bradley county, and received these statements from his own lips.

Shortly after this scene of butchery, about eight o'clock A. M., Gatewood's Lieutenant, Jasper Graddy, captured a Union man named Robt. F. McClary. Graddy and McClary were schoolmates when boys. Gatewood ordered McClary to dismount from his horse, a fine animal, and directed it to be given to one of his own men. McClary was then put upon a dull and very bad riding mule, placed in the rear of the column under strict guard, and made to keep up with the company. He was immediately robbed of his money—twenty dollars in greenbacks—by one of the number, whose name was Johnson, a Kentuckian. McClary appealed to Graddy, requesting him to compel Johnson to return his money. Graddy replied that Johnson was a very bad man, that he could do nothing with him, and that the theft could not be remedied.

The rebels were universally well mounted and well armed. Many of them wore, and almost all had with them, the blue Federal overcoat. They passed from one place of robbery and butchery to another generally on a gallop. Gatewood rode at the head of the column the entire day, and Graddy was most of the time at his side. At one time Gatewood ordered McClary to be brought to the head of the column, where he compelled him to ride between himself and Graddy for several miles. The object appeared to be to ascertain where the best horses and mules belonging to Union people could be found. Mr. McClary's answers were not altogether satisfactory, and cursing him as a d——d know-nothing, Gatewood ordered him to take his place again at the foot of the line.

The first halt of any note that was made by the raiders after McClary was captured, was at the Widow Armstrong's, a Union lady. A mile, perhaps, before they reached the house of this lady, they passed the house of a bitter rebel named Griffith. As McClary, being at the foot of the column, passed Griffith's, he noticed that Lieut. Graddy had halted, and was talking at the gate with two or three of the Griffith women. In a few moments, however, Graddy overtook them, and dashed by to reach his place at the head of the column. The information that Graddy received at Griffith's, encouraged the rebels to believe that their prey was sure; and as they came within sight of the widow's plantation, Gatewood ordered his men to charge. The order was passed along down the line in loud and vociferous repetitions by the men, when like so many infuriated demons, almost the entire column immediately swarmed upon the premises of Mrs. Armstrong, leaping their animals into the yard and surrounding the house with an eager fury and hellish hate, as though they proposed instantly to murder every thing upon the plantation. Baker Armstrong, a single man about thirty years of age, and son of the widow, and A. C. Parks, particularly, were the Union victims for whose blood Gatewood and his men were thirsting. Both of these Union men, with a Federal soldier named Raper, a member of the 5th Tennessee Cavalry, were at Mrs. Armstrong's house when the rebels dashed up. Mr. Armstrong fled across a field in the rear of his mother's dwelling, but was soon overtaken and surrounded. Seeing himself overpowered, he threw away his revolver, raised his left hand in token of surrender, and began to walk towards his enemies, when one of them dismounted and commenced firing on him. Thus attacked, he wheeled and made another effort to escape. Rebel bullets, however, soon brought him down. After receiving three or four shots, two in the back part of the head, and in the neck, he fell, pitching forward upon his face. By this time his mother was within a few feet of him, begging of the rebels to desist. The dismounted rebel, however, sprang before her, fastened his hand in the hair of the dying man, pulled him over, with his face upwards, and placing his revolver near his lips, in spite of his mother's efforts, emptied the contents of it into her son's mouth, mangling and blowing away his face in the most shocking manner conceivable. Without uttering a word the fiend then walked away, bearing, as Mrs. Armstrong and her daughter afterwards asserted, more emphatically the countenance of a demon incarnate, than any other human being on whose features they ever gazed.

Mr. Parks fled to the chamber, and by some members of the family was covered in a pile of cotton; and his life was saved. Raper was taken prisoner. All this occupied but a few moments; although the search for Parks was continued for sometime. Gatewood, finally abandoning the effort to find Parks, ordered his men into line, crying out that they must be on the move, for more work of the kind remained for them to perform. Raper was ordered to mount his horse, and take his place at the foot of the column in company with Mr. McClary. Proceeding perhaps a quarter of a mile, with his column on the move, Gatewood approached Raper, d——ing him furiously, enquiring why he ran when he and his men approached him. Vociferously adding, "I will put an end to you," and instantly blew out his brains with his navy revolver. The poor man fell from his horse with a heavy gulch to the ground. The blood gushed from his wound, streaming completely from one wagon track to the other across the road. He was but a few feet in advance of McClary when he fell. After performing this deed Gatewood approached McClary, cursed him, and told him if he did not promptly keep his place in line, and keep up with the column, he would serve him in the same manner. Then looking back to some of his men yet in the rear, he instructed them to shoot the d——d Lincolnite that lay in the road till they were certain he was dead; after which he dashed forward to his position at the head of the line. As Raper was considered already dead, he was shot no more, but was left in the middle of the road, while his horse was kept by the murderers.

Half an hour, perhaps, after the rebels had disappeared, a daughter of the Griffith family, one of the women who were seen by McClary talking with Grady, entered the dwelling of Mrs. Armstrong, and impudently, and in a spirit of exultant satisfaction, told Mrs. Armstrong that she was the person who informed the rebels that they would find her son and Mr. Parks at her house.

The name of the wretch who murdered Armstrong, by some, was supposed to be King. It was also supposed that his murderer was known to Armstrong, and was recognized by him at the time, and that the reason that he shot him in the mouth as related, was through fear that Armstrong might yet be able to speak, and would inform his mother whom his murderer was.

Between Mrs. Armstrong's and Benton, a distance of seven miles, Lieutenant Grady, as usual, was seen to stop at three or four rebel houses, as was understood, to obtain information of his Union victims, and of Union property which the rebels wished to capture. In this way he halted at a Mr. Sloan's, where he was seen talking, probably to Mrs. Sloan herself. Grady also stopped at the house of a rebel named Patterson, where it was thought that the person who came out and apparently gave him directions, was Mr. Patterson. He also halted at the dwelling of Mr. Wm. Higgins. Here he was seen conversing with both men and women belonging to the premises. All these were rebel families living, if we mistake not, between Mrs. Armstrong's and Benton.

Two miles from Mrs. Armstrong's the rebels invaded the premises of Mr. Parks, father, we believe, to A. C. Parks, who had escaped them at the house of Mr. Armstrong. Here they captured a Union man named Gurley. They inquired of McClary if their prisoner was A. C. Parks, whom they were in search of at the house of Mrs. Armstrong. Although they were answered in the negative, they immediately murdered their victim by shooting him through the body with a carbine or an Enfield rifle. McClary could not distinguish the individual who committed the deed, but from the report and from the movements of the murderers within his view, judged the weapon used to be a carbine or an Enfield rifle. Mr. Gurley was a man of a family, and, we believe, from the North, at least he was a stranger in the country. McClary passed the body of Mr. Gurley, also left in the road. The back part of his head was literally blown to pieces.

Reaching Benton, the rebels took possession of the town, refreshed themselves and their animals for a short time, robbing and plundering the Union citizens to their satisfaction. While here, one of their number—Columbus Moony—murdered Thomas Kincer, a Union man of the place. Mr. Kincer was at work in his shoe shop. As the rebels came upon him, he fled into a house nearby, and begged of the woman of the house, for God's sake to shut the door. His murderers, however, were close upon him, and found him in the act of disappearing under the house, having removed a loose plank in the floor for that purpose. Being a moment too late, with his head and shoulders yet exposed as the rebels burst in, he raised his left hand surrendering himself a prisoner and begging for his life. Moony, however, instantly shot him while in that helpless condition, the bullet passing through his left hand raised in token of surrender, and striking him in the throat ranged downwards towards his breast, and he died in less than five minutes, with his body partly concealed under the floor.

This was the sixth victim whose spirit that day had been hurried into eternity, by this moving swarm of blood-stained demons incarnate.

Samuel Brown, whose history has already been given, son of the notorious Capt. Brown, was one who pursued Mr. Kincer, and was standing by Moony's side, when Mr. Kincer was murdered. In the history of this Brown, it was stated that he murdered a Union man, whose name could not then be given. We have since discovered that the name of this victim was Smith Irwin, of Polk county.

On leaving Benton, Gatewood, directed his course back towards Georgia, taking the Ducktown Road. About eight miles from Benton, the rebels met a small company traveling with two or three teams. Alvin Jones, a lad perhaps fifteen, with a U. S. Plated belt buckled about his waist, was sitting upon one of the wagons. Discovering the Federal belt, Gatewood, approached Jones, cursing him for being a bushwhacker, at the same time discharging two revolver shots into his body. Gatewood then ordered him to get out of his wagon, which he did. He was then robbed of the rings from his fingers, and other valuables. By this time the boy began to faint from loss of blood, and was unable to stand. Gatewood, pointed to a stone but a few feet from Jones, and cursing him, told him to lay his head upon that rock and die. The boy obeyed, layed his head upon the rock as directed, and breathed out his life in the presence of his murderers.

The rebels then turned their attention to robbing the other members of the company, plundering their goods, &c. In one of the wagons they found a cask of whiskey. This immediately absorbed the attention of the whole crew. They threw the cask upon the ground, bursted one of its heads, and transferred its contents to their canteens by sinking them in the liquor, as it was in the cask. A portion of it was at once transferred to their stomachs, from which receptacle it soon made its way to the brain, a transfer that was visible from the increased spirit of fiendishness that entered into many of them before they left the ground.

Four miles from this point, the rebels suddenly came upon six Union men. A part, and perhaps all of the Union men were armed. They, however, fled up the bluff of the Ocoee river. The rebels exhibited themselves to their view with their blue overcoats, calling out for them to come down—that they were Yankees also, and wished to see them. One of their number ventured down to the rebels. They treated him with the whiskey they had just pillaged, appeared very friendly, showed him their Federal uniforms to convince him that they were Yankees. They then requested him to go back to his companions and tell them to have no fears, but to come down—that they were all friends, and that they wished to have a talk with them about the rebels in the country. Thus deceived, he went back to his companions, and unsuspectingly and very unfortunately, they all came down to the rebels. They were immediately taken prisoners, stripped of their arms, after which the rebels simultaneously commenced to shoot them down. Four of them, Samuel Lovel, Harvey Brewster, Thomas Bell and James Nelson, were killed dead upon the spot. Two, Peter Paris and Jasper Parton made their escape. Paris fled back up the mountain and although he received four wounds, escaped, and finally recovered. Parton started from the very midst of the rebels, made his way through them, leaped into the Ocoee river, swam to the other shore, and although he received five or six wounds subsequently recovered.

McClary stated that he never saw a lot of hunters or a pack of hounds wilder with excitement, and more furious after a buck, than these demons were in their efforts to head off and destroy Parton while he was escaping from them. They swarmed around and after him, some on their horses, and others on foot, firing upon him a perfect blaze continually. At one time their shots brought him down, and he rolled completely over, and apparently under their horses' feet, but rose again, and made his way through them.

Throwing the four dead bodies together in one pile near the road, the rebels passed on. One mile from this scene they murdered another union man, a refugee fleeing north, whom they also left dead by the side of the road. His name, perhaps, was Johnson.

McClary, through entreaties with Gradily, at the foot of the column, perhaps unknown to Gatewood at the time, was released, we believe, just before the rebels murdered Johnson. Seeing himself free once more from such hands, after such a day's ride, and such a day's scene, McClary must have felt himself a happy man.

Mr. Johnson was the twelfth victim at least, that had fallen lifeless that day up to that hour, at the hands of these men, besides those escaping wounded. At this point we find our notes confused, and in regard to Gatewood's further transactions of that day cannot speak with positiveness. Reports stated that sixteen or eighteen men in Tennessee and Georgia lost their lives as the result of that day's raiding by Gatewood. Evidently more mischief was committed by him that day after the death of Mr. Johnson, and possibly more lives were taken. He crossed the Ocoee, it appears, at Grier's Ferry, and ascending the river some distance, camped for the night upon its bank.

The next morning, as Gatewood passed into Georgia, the work of murder was resumed. Early in the morning, the rebels invaded the premises of a Union man named Gasaway. Mr. Gasaway fled and escaped. Gatewood himself attacked a young man whose name was Barnes. He chased Barnes into the woods, and overtaking him, commenced to fire upon him. Barnes caught hold of a sapling and begged for his life. Gatewood, however, continued to fire, aiming at his head. Holding on to the sapling Barnes managed to evade the shots. The fourth shot, however, struck him in the eye, carrying it away entirely—the bullet passing down and lodging at the roots of the jaw. Gatewood, supposing him mortally wounded, placed his foot upon his neck, pulled off his boots and left him. About two hours afterwards, he was found by his friends sitting up, though entirely senseless, wiping the blood from his face with his hand up into his hair. The print of the the heel of Gatewood's boot was found upon Barnes's neck. He subsequently recovered.

Gatewood and his company took their booty a short distance south into Georgia, where they sold their stolen horses and mules, about forty in number, to the

... among themselves. The purchasers were ... fifteen ...
... to go South, disposed of the property, return and ... bought ...
... the proceeds might be equally distributed among all the ...

... Gatewood's command on the day of the raid consisted ... about ...
... there were boys from ... From ... I ...
be obtained the names of a few, which, as it boots ... I will mention ...
his brothers, perhaps William; Jasper Gradly, the ... depot ...
Kentuckian who robbed McClary; Columbus Massey, the one w ...
Samuel Brown, son of Capt. Brown, of Bradley; Frank Green, of Bradley;
Stuart, from Kentucky; Marion Gillian, both Georgians, and Ja ...
believe, from the third district, Bradley county; ... Henderson, ...
son, Hawkins, Maston, A. Young, Freeman Gates ... whom ...
called Hall, from Kentucky; Bowman and Rucker.

Gatewood and his men, while the fruits of the Polk county raid were bei
posed of, quartered upon the plantation of a Union man named Smi ...
about sixty miles from Cleveland. Gatewood himself, during the ...
at the house of a rebel named Holland. The whole company, however, soon ...
for Walker county, Georgia.

In April, 1865, or shortly after the surrender of Johnston in ... ...
and most of his company, knowing that their conduct deserved death, and that
their lives would be unsafe in Georgia, or anywhere else in the ... ...
after the war, left for Texas, taking one of their number, a murderer, ...
Cherokee county jail, as they passed. They reached the Mississippi river in
safety. A report returned, however, that they were attacked by some federal
forces on the bank of the Mississippi, and that Gatewood was killed. This was
simply a report; and this scourge of the human race, may probably ... ...
gaged in his work of blood and crime, somewhere in the South.

Gatewood was married, shortly before he left Georgia, to a lady in Cherokee
county, whose name was Kane.

When Gatewood's men, were murdering Baker Armstrong on the Polk county
raid, two Union citizens were about starting from the Armstrong neighborhood
to go to Cleveland, Bradley county. Before they left, they heard of Mr ...
Armstrong's, and learned that it was the work of rebel raiders. They hurried
to Cleveland, and informed our military authorities, that the rebels were mak
ing a raid through Polk county. These informants must have reached Cleve ...
as early as 3 o'clock P. M., and probably before. The rebels could scarcely have
left Benton, when our military at Cleveland, were informed of the affair. Towards night, some hours after our commander at Cleveland received this ...
he started out an insignificant force of cavalry, which proceeded leisurely tow ...
Ducktown. The party affected nothing further than to strike the upward ...
of the raiders into Polk, and to ascertain some facts in regard to the raid. ...
our authorities at Cleveland possessed the least spark of the spirit that fired ...
bosom of General Marion and Ethen Allen, in the days of the Revolution. ...
wood and the most of his men would have paid the debt of their crimes u ...
gallows before daylight next morning. Gatewood's camp on the Ocoee, ...
of the raid, could not have been but about forty miles from Cleveland.

During the seven or nine months, that Gatewood was in the country, he perpe
trated other and similar raids into Tennessee. His name became emphatically
the terror of the land, especially in Georgia. That such a scourge of God and
man was permitted to remain in the country for this length of time, with his gen
eral headquarters not more than thirty or fifty miles from Chattanooga, while our
forces at that place and Cleveland, numbered during the whole period, from
three to five thousand men, was as great a disgrace to our arms, as the presence
of such an enemy was terrible and destructive to the country; and ... ...
commanders in those places at that time to be remembered by the Union people
of Northern Georgia and East Tennessee with feelings at least of great disrespect.

The parents of Gatewood, before the war, for many years perhaps, were members of the Methodist Church. This son, it appears, in some respects, was a precocious child as well as a precocious youth. When a lad, and going to mill on
horseback, with a view to frighten the neighboring women whose houses he
passed, he would suddenly drop helplessly from his animal's back, with his face
fall to the ground, feigning death from the stroke of some terrible disease. This
and similar traits when a boy, were the foreshadowing of the desperate character
of the man. He was the pupil in blood of Champ Ferguson; but if he is spared
and God sees fit to afflict our race by prolonging his days to the number that was
allotted Champ, other things being equal, he will infinitely outstrip his illustrious
prototype in a life of crime. Hundreds of Union victims, probably, fell by his
hand alone during his stay in Georgia. He reminds one of West's picture of
death with the lightning forks of destruction in the monster's fingers.

REBEL RAIDS FROM GEORGIA INTO BRADLEY COUNTY.

After Sherman started upon his Atlanta campaign, in the spring of 1864, with the exception of the principal towns and principal railroad stations, Bradley and its adjoining counties were left unprotected and exposed to rebel guerrillas and bushwhackers, who, in the rear of Sherman's army, collected into bands and immured themselves or established their headquarters in the fastnesses and mountains of northern Georgia and northern North Carolina. Depredations by this class of men commenced in the county as early as August, 1864, and were continued till the following April or May. During this interval Bradley was invaded, more or less extensively, not less, perhaps, than ten different times by rebel bands emerging from Georgia and the mountains of North Carolina—bands composed of the most lawless and wretched men in existence.

The raiders would strike the southern line of the county usually about sundown, and on a circuitous route penetrate during the night, sometimes even to the north part of the county, robbing and plundering Union families, shooting and murdering Union men; and sweeping the county of stock, would make their way back into Georgia generally about daylight the next morning.

In one of these raids the rebels attempted to murder a minister whose name was Hames. Supposing their shots to be fatal, they left him. He, however, subsequently recovered from his wounds. At another time the raiders murdered a Union man near Georgetown, whose name was Hunter. Mr. Hunter was murdered on the night of the 5th of February, 1865. His life was taken in cold blood, and for no cause, only, as was supposed that he was an unusually active Union man, and had previously, perhaps, reported as rebels some of the raiders to our authorities.

On the 1st of February, 1865, another Union citizen, named Alfred Johnson, fell in the south part of the county, by a band of these rebel murderers. Mr. Johnson was beaten to death with bludgeons, and left by the rebels, his head being broken literally to pieces. A small company from the 5th Tennessee Cavalry was sent from Cleveland to reconnoiter for the rebels, and perhaps to recover or bury Mr. Johnson's body. Being yet in the vicinity, the rebels attacked these cavalrymen, killing one of their number—Decatur Wier—and causing the others to fly. The remains of Mr. Johnson were finally buried by Union women. The following are the names of those who performed the humane work: Mrs. Coly, widow, Mrs. Arthur Oar, Mrs. Jno. Mitchel, Miss Mary Ann Mitchel, Miss Mary Willhoit, Miss Elizabeth Willhoit, Miss Margaret Huffine, Miss Myra Jones, Miss Queentine Jones, Mrs. John Bell.

One of the most remarkable of these raids was made, perhaps, in November. The raiders penetrated as far north as Georgetown, some six or eight miles north of Cleveland. It was during this raid that they murdered Mr. Hunter. Numbering about one hundred and seventy, they were enabled to sweep a wide breadth of country as they traveled. On their return they spread into Hamilton, gathering up and taking out of the country an immense amount of stock, together with a large amount of supplies and household plunder.

In their course north, their right wing passed not more than three miles west of Cleveland. Col. Keiffner, of the 149th Illinois, was then in command of the post at Cleveland. Capt. Norwood and other officers of the 5th Tennessee Cavalry, were anxious to take a command and cut the rebels off on their return into Georgia. Notwithstanding the desirableness and practicability of this proposed measure, Col. Keiffner overruled their request and sent Capt. Norwood, some time after the rebels had passed Cleveland, with an insignificant force to meet them at Georgetown. As was expected by Capt. Norwood, before he reached Georgetown the raiders had been absent from that place two or three hours on their return out of the county. Thus Capt. Norwood's expedition was not only rendered a failure, but he and other Union officers of the post, and the Union people of the county generally, suffered the mortification of having less than two hundred rebels devour and lay waste the country almost within sight of about a thousand of our troops then at Cleveland.

These raids were not confined to Bradley county alone. Hamilton, Polk, McMinn, and other counties east of these suffered also. The Union people of these counties, especially Bradley county, felt the scourge of these raids to be equally intolerable with the reign of rebel rule, before our forces took the country. All the Union men who fled from these counties, except those who were in the Federal army, had returned and were now at home. The raiders were principally rebels who had been raised in the country—men of the worst class, those who had fallen off from Johnston's army as he retreated south before Sherman, and who were now taking advantage of the absence of our army to despoil the Union people. Individual rebels among these raiders would wreak their vengeance on those Union families and those Union men whom they considered their particular enemies. Thus, as it was before our armies took the country, rebels whose homes were in these counties, were again persecuting and destroying their Union neighbors. Notwithstanding the presence of our troops at the principal stations on the railroads, the scourge became so intolerable that the Union people appealed in various ways to our authorities for relief. Some of our commanders at

Cleveland urged that they were placed there to defend the post, not to institute offensive or even defensive operations against the rebels at a distance. The Union people of Bradley county, and possibly those of other counties, finally applied to Gen. Steadman, commander of the district, whose headquarters were at Chattanooga, proposing to defend themselves if he would supply them with arms. This proposition, however, was as unsuccessful as the others. Gen. Steadman did not, it appears, consider that his position endowed him with authority to grant the request. The only alternative, therefore, as a general thing, left the Union people of these counties, was to bare themselves to the storm, and with the best grace they could, allow it to spend its fury upon them.

It ought to be stated, however, in this connection, that, Princessam, Col. of a Michigan regiment, who was in command at Cleveland in the spring of 1865, manifested a disposition to rid Bradley county and other parts of the country of these raiding rebel thieves and cut throats. He encouraged the officers of the 5th Tennessee Cavalry, most of whom, perhaps, were from Bradley and adjoining counties, to prepare themselves to meet and to ferret out these rebel raiders; and promised to furnish them with troops on all occasions for these purposes. Though the help of this officer came too late, being appointed to the command at Cleveland perhaps the first of March, 1865, yet the good effects of his policy in Bradley were soon perceptible. The last attempt of the raiders to enter the county was made during the first days of April following the appointment of Princessam. The band was met by Capt. Norwood near the southern line of the county, and effectually scattered; and had it not been for the mismanagement of one of his Lieutenants, nearly the whole company must have been killed or captured.

In addition to the names given of those engaged in the Gatewood raid into Polk county, the following are the names of a few of those among the raiders into Bradley.

Wm. Stanton, leader; Wm. Rogers, leader; Abram Tate, leader; Wm. King, leader; Martin McGriff, John Tucker, Bloom Upton, Gillihan, Henry Stafford Wm. Bussey, Seth Gregory, Bud Wooton, James Sugart, James Gregory, George Hughes.

SHOOTING OF ELLSBERRY CASEY.

Mr. Casey was shot in Cleveland, Bradley county on the 21st of August, 1865 by a soldier of the 11th Michigan, the Regiment then stationed at that place. Casey had served three years in the Union army, and having just been discharged was keeping a saloon in Cleveland. A soldier of this Michigan Regiment, entered his saloon and called for a glass of liquor. Casey informed the soldier that his own Col., Col. Kegan, had issued an order, prohibiting dealers in Cleveland from selling liquor to soldiers. The soldier, however, insisted on having the liquor, but being still refused, began to curse and abuse Casey, threatening, if he did not comply with his wishes, to tear down his building. Casey then ordered him to leave his store, repeating the order the third time. This still more enraged the soldier, who, drawing his bayonet from its scabbard by his side, began to stab with it over the counter at Casey. Casey drew his revolver and fired upon the soldier, wounding him in the wrist. The Provost Marshal, immediately arrested Casey, and took him to Col. Kegan's head quarters, preparatory to trying him for the offence. The citizens of Cleveland, petitioned Col. Kegan, to deliver Casey for trial, to the civil authorities, which, without much hesitation was complied with, Casey was tried by the civil authorities and acquitted.

By order of Col. Kegan he was immediately arrested the second time, and the second time taken to his headquarters. From the bearing of the Col. towards him —the Col. telling him that he now had him just where he desired to have him — and from the expressions of others around him, companions of the soldier whom he had wounded, Casey feared his life and attempted to flee. He reached the street, but was fired upon by Col. Kegan's men and brought down by a bullet that completely severed his thigh bone. Another soldier who was in pursuit attempted to bayonet him as he lay upon the ground. This was prevented by other soldiers, or by citizens, or perhaps by both. The citizens again petitioned for Casey's release, and their request being complied with, he was taken to a public house and cared for by his friends till he recovered.

No punishment was inflicted upon the soldier who shot Casey, and the unavoidable inference is that, if Col. Kegan did not himself order Casey to be shot, the act was, nevertheless, in accordance with his feelings. Complaint was made to Gov. Brownlow by the citizens against Col. Kegan, and the Governor dispatched an officer to Cleveland to investigate the affair. The investigation, however, such as it was, if it resulted in anything positive, resulted favorable to Col. Kegan, and thus the whole matter terminated, at least so far as authoritative action was concerned.

Although Col. Kegan escaped, perhaps even without censure by his superiors, for his action in this matter, yet serious prejudices were left on the minds of the citizens of Cleveland against him and his Provost Marshall, Capt. Stout—prejudices that will not soon be effaced; and the conduct of these officers in this particular case, as well as their policy in regard to rebels and Union people in Bradley, when properly and conscientiously weighed, undoubtedly justify this prejudice to the full extent of its existence.

The following is taken from the Report of the Adjutant General of the State of Tennessee, James P. Brownlow, of the military forces of the state from 1861 to 1865.

The Report shows the following number of troops raised in Tennessee for the United States service, and which very efficiently aided in putting down the rebellion, viz: eight infantry regiments, eight mounted infantry regiments, twelve cavalry regiments, five batteries of light artillery.

In addition to the above there were enlisted in this State, by U. S. recruiting officers, 17,770 colored troops, which were not reported to this office, and are not included, accordingly, in this record.

From various sources believed to be perfectly reliable, it is estimated, also, that some 7,000 Tennesseeans enlisted in the Kentucky federal regiments, and were credited to that State.

GENERAL AND STAFF OFFICERS FROM TENNESSEE IN U. S. ARMY.

MAJOR GENERALS BY BREVET.—Samuel P. Carter, Alvin C. Gillem, Joseph A. Cooper.

BRIGADIER GENERALS.—Andrew Johnson, Samuel P. Carter, Joseph A. Cooper, Wm. B. Campbell, Alvin C. Gillem, James G. Spears.

BRIGADIER GENERALS BY BREVET.—James P. Brownlow, George Spalding, Wm. J. Smith.

GOVERNOR AND STAFF.—William G. Brownlow, Governor, and Commander-in-Chief of State Forces.

James P. Brownlow, Brig. and Adj't Gen'l. Date of commission, March 6th, 1865; resigned Dec. 27th, 1865.

John H. James, Brig. and Q. M. Gen'l. Date of commission March 6th, 1865; resigned June 30th, 1865.

H. H. Thomas, Brig. and Q. M. Gen'l. Date of commission July 1st, 1865.

Edward Maynard, Col. and A. D. C. Date of commission March 6th, 1865.

Milton C. Wilcox, Col. and A. D. C. Date of commission March 6th, 1865; resigned July, 1865.

THE WINAMAC PROPHECIES.

Truxton Chittenden, of Winamac, Pulaski county, Indiana, being duly sworn, deposes and says: That on or about the 7th of April, 1865, David Myers, of Winamac, made the following statements and predictions, to-wit: That Abraham Lincoln would not live six months, that he would be assassinated; and he, Myers, refused to give his reason for making these statements, further than that he, just previous, returned from church, and sat down to read from his Bible; and as he was reading, heard distinctly the report of a pistol—sprang from his seat, impressed that Abraham Lincoln was assassinated. He also stated that for three mornings in succession, after this, he came to the depot to get a paper, expecting to see the report of the assassination, but failed then to find it; but was firm in the belief that it was or would prove true, and Andrew Johnson would turn traitor and would be hung for participation in the assassination of Lincoln within three years; and thus he would not serve out his time. After the news of the assassination reached us, in Winamac, he Myers, on the 20th of April, said to me: "You would not believe what I told you about Lincoln, but you now see that it was true, and you will not believe that Johnson will be hung within three years, but you will find that true also. I have no doubt of it, and am as sure of it as I can be of any thing." TRUXTON CHITTENDEN.

Subscribed and sworn to this the 10th day of November, 1866. I also certify that the above affiant, Truxton Chittenden, is to me well known as a creditable person. [SEAL.] J. N. INGRIM, N. P.

WINAMAC, Ind., Nov. 10th, 1866.

D. A. Farley, being duly sworn, deposes and says: That some time previous to the assassination of President Lincoln, he, D. A. Farley, had a conversation with David Myers, of the town of Winamac, Pulaski county, Indiana, who stated that Abraham Lincoln would be shot, and that Andrew Johnson would take his place and **turn traitor** to the Republican party, and that before the expiration of his term **of office he, Andrew Johnson, would be hung.**   D. A. FARLEY.

Subscribed and sworn to, this 10th day of November, 1866. **I also certify that the above affiant is to me well known as a** credible person.

          [SEAL.]   J. N. INGRIM, N. P.

WINAMAC, Ind., Nov. 10th, 1866.

Charles A. Meeker, be**ing duly** sworn, deposes and says: **That David My**ers, of Winamac, stated to him **immediately** after the election of Abraham **Lincoln**, in 1860, that he, Lincoln, **would not** live three months after his inauguration. He also stated on the morning **of the** 15th of April, 1865, that Lincoln was assassinated—this statement being **made** before we in Winamac received the news that Mr. Lincoln was shot. Myers **also** stated that he heard the report of the pistol; also, that Andrew Johnson **was** at the bottom of the affair; Myers also stated that Andrew Johnson would yet be hung for treason, and that before his term of office expired. I asked him how he knew these things. He replied that they were spiritual manifestations.   CHARLES A. MEEKER.

Subscribed and sworn to this 10th day of November, 1866. I also certify **that the above affiant, Charles A. Meeker, is well known to me as a** credible **person.**

          [SEAL.]   J. N. INGRIM, N. P.

WINAMAC, IND., Nov. 10th, 1866.

Byram T. Lane—Being duly sworn, deposes and says: That on the 16th day of **April, 1865, learning that certain** statements and predictions had been made by **David Myers, of Winamac, Pula**ski county, state of Indiana, relating to the assassination of **Abraham Lincoln—he (Lane) at that time acting Deputy** Provost **Marshal for the county of Pulaski—arrested said Myers on suspicion** (Myers being **a violent opposer of the administration of Abraham Lincoln) of compli**city in **the plot to assassinate President Lincoln, or of being in possession of know**ledge **of said plot before its consummation. Lane supposing this knowledge** of **Myers to have been derived** through a secret organization that he believed **to exist in the State of** Indiana, before making the **arrest, Lane** requested **Richard Taylor, of Winamac,** to accompany him to the house of Myers. Taylor **accompanied Lane to the house of** Myers, when Lane arrested Myers and took **him to his own (Lane's) house, where** the following conversation ensued:
Lane—**Mr. Myers, the reason that I** have arrested you is this: I learned from **Mr. Wm. H. Ryley, that you stated in** the post-office last night that you knew six **weeks ago that Abraham Lincoln was to be killed, and** that Ryley asked you *how* **you knew, and you replied that that was best known to yours**elf. Did you make **that statement?**
Myers—I did.
Lane—**Now, Mr. Myers, I wish you to tell me how you knew that Abraham** Lincoln **was to be killed.**
Myers—**I don't know as I** have any right to tell you.
Lane—**You can do as yo**u choose, **Mr. Myers**, about giving me the information; **but if you do not do so, I** shall take you **to Col.** Shryock, at Michigan **City, who is** Provost Marshal of the District, and he **can do with you as** he pleases.
Myers reflected some time, then said he **did** not know **as** he could explain, so as **to be understood; but stated that** the knowledge came to **him** something like a **dream, although he was not asleep** at the time.—**That he was** sitting in his room **one night reading his Bible, when** he heard **the report of a** pistol. He sprang to **his feet, and it came to him** that **Abraham Lincoln was** shot, and that Johnson **was to take his place; and that** before **Johnson had served** three years he would **turn traitor to his party.—That he** (Johnson) **would be** arrested for, and tried and **found guilty of the murder of** Abraham **Lincoln, and** be hung **for the** crime. **Myers said that he felt so** certain that **Lincoln was k**illed, that **he came to** the **train every morning for a week**, expecting **to find the** death of Lincoln announced **in the** papers. **I** then **asked** Myers if he knew **or** believed **that such a thing would** take place, why **he did** not notify Mr. Lincoln of the fact. He replied **that he did** not know as **it was his** business to **do so.** I then enquired of him if he **had not** received this knowledge in some secret meeting—if he had not been in **some** secret meeting and there heard that Mr. Lincoln was **to** be assassinated? **He replied that he had not. I** then asked him if he had not made this statement **at some** secret meeting? He answered that he had not. I then said, Mr. Myers, **I shall** release you, **but** be cautious in future, when any one asks you how you **know these** things, tell him, and not say that that is best known to yourself. I

then went out to my gate, and there met Sheriff Korner and others. I asked the Sheriff what he wanted? He replied that he came to ascertain why I had arrested Myers. I told him in effect that it was none of his business; and if he came there with the mob to take Mr. Myers out of my hands, I would send to Col Shryock and have men enough come down, not only to take Myers if I wished, to Michigan City, but to take him and the whole of his party there also.

B. T. LANE.

Subscribed and sworn to this 10th day of November, 1866. I also certify that the above Byram T. Lane is well known to me as a credible person.

[SEAL.] J. S. INGRIM, N. P.

WINAMAC, IND., Nov. 10th, 1866.

Truxton Chittenden—Being duly sworn, deposes and says: That on Sunday, the 16th day of April, 1865, he saw from the window of his warehouse in Winamac, a crowd gathered in front of John Dean's saloon—the said warehouse being about four rods from said saloon. That he (Chittenden) lowered the window of said warehouse, and heard persons in the crowd say that they were going to release David Myers from the custody of the Deputy Provost Marshal, B. T. Lane.—That he saw the crowd leave the saloon and go to the residence of Lane, which was within sight. He (Chittenden) then followed the crowd in hearing distance to the residence of Lane. The Sheriff (Mr. Korner) said to Lane, that he (Lane) had no business to arrest Myers; and the purport of the conversation seemed to be that they (the persons of the crowd) intended to take Myers out of Lane's hands. Lane told Korner, the Sheriff, that if they interfered with his business, he would have men enough sent to take them all to Michigan City.

TRUXTON CHITTENDEN.

Subscribed and sworn to this 10th day of November, 1866. I also certify that the above affiant is to me well known as a credible person. I further certify that the above David Myers never has, to my knowledge, had any connection whatever with, or to any extent professed the faith of, modern spiritualism, but is a member in good standing of an Orthodox Church.

[SEAL.] J. S. INGRIM, N. P.

NAMES OF UNION PERSONS, UNION SOLDIERS, REBELS AND REBEL SOLDIERS, IN BRADLEY COUNTY.

LEADING UNION PERSONS IN THE FIRST DISTRICT.—John Boyer, Preston Bedwell, William H. Bryant, A. J. Cate, G. B. Cate, James Coke, Geo. W. Castellow, Matthew Corn, James Corn, A. J. Carson, W. F. Clark, J. H. Harwood, John Hambright, Isham Julian, R. P. Julian, Wm. Kyle, Geo. C. Kyle, Henry Kyle, P. C. R. Lawson, Wm. Longwith, James J. Lauderdale, —— Mason, F. M. McAllister, Jackson McAllister, George McCoy, S. D. Outlaw, H. H. Purvines, A. J. Parker, William Parker, John Pearce, William Pursley, Jack Petty, Gilbert Randolph, Gillmore Randolph, C. H. Rice, Elisha Smith, R. T. Weatherly, William Weatherly.

UNION SOLDIERS FROM THE FIRST DISTRICT.—Capt. F. W. Baker, Capt. W. L. Cate, Maj. S. C. Hambright, Lieut. James Kyle, Lieut. Nelson Lawson, Lieut. Marshall Lawson, Lieut. Samuel Weatherly, Lieut. William Weatherly, Capt. C. P. Simons, G. R. Ashley, James Ashley, William Ashley, H. L. Baldwin, Robert Brookshear, Joseph Bedwell, John Bedwell, Isaac Bedwell, Leroy Bedwell, W. H. H. Baker, Marshall Buster, Lafayette Boyer, John A. Carson, George Carson, John L. Cate, Jackson Cooper, Robert Cooper, John Cooper, Charles Castellow, John C. Foyster, Vincent Garner, William Gold, —— Holmes, John M. Julian, Robert Keeny, John Kyle, John D. Long, Riley R. Long, Reuben Longwith, Isaac Longwith, Isham Lawson, John Long, Daniel McBrien, Lewis Pearce, Allen Pearce, Robert Pearce, Blackburn Pennell, James Pennell, Joseph V. Purvine, Richard Parker, Frank Parker, Thomas Pursley, David Purkins, Ball P. Petty, James Petty, Joseph Petty, William Smith, James Stevenson, William Swinford, Wesley A. Simmons, Isham C. Simmons, William H. Simmons, James Sparks, James Star, Julian E. Thomas, James Templeton, Henry Weatherly.

LEADING REBELS IN THE FIRST DISTRICT.—H. L. Baldwin, Robert Baldwin, George B. Billingsly, W. P. Colwell, Charles Donahoo, Horace England, John Evans, S. C. Gold, P. W. Green, James Hunt, Timothy Hadey, Christopher Knox, Thomas Kinderick, F. M. Lee, John Mee, J. F. Mee, James Pearce, James Pierce, Washington Routh, M. T. C. Royston, B. S. S. Royston, Bird Scroggins, George Wear, John Wilson.

REBEL SOLDIERS FROM THE FIRST DISTRICT.—Robert Baldwin, William Clark, Henry C. Carrol, Richard Clark, Joseph Donahoo, Charles Donahoo, Horace England, John England, Jacob Edwards, Martin Gold, Jacob Gold, P. W. Green, James H. Hampton, Lieut. Timothy Haney, John Keeny, Lieut. Henry Knox, Christopher Knox, Lieut. F. M. Lee, Isham Long, John Long, Bush Long, W. I. Long, Robert Melton, Capt. Joseph Mee, Wilson Price, Benjamin Parker, William Reynolds, Ralph Reynolds, Lieut. Washington Routh, James Stanson, John Smith, F. Triplit, Jonas Tucker, Geo. N. Weir, John Weir, John Villyson.

LEADING UNION PERSONS IN THE SECOND DISTRICT.—C. W. Allen, James Armstrong—son in U. S. A.; Isaac Armstrong, James Brannon, Jefferson Brewer—two sons in U. S. A.; Wm. B. Ballinger, Hiram Bacon, Samuel Brannon, Martin Brannon, Robt. Barnet, Wm. O. Barnes, Robt. Brookshir, Mrs. Rebecca Climer—son in U. S. A.; Thomas Cowden—son in U. S. A.; Smith Carson, Jackson Copeland, L. P. Carpenter, George Clark, Wm. Clark, A. W. Chilcott—son in U. S. A.; Robert Campbell, sr., Alfred Dixon, John Dixon, S. A. Dixon, S. E. Dixon, Esq., E. S. Gibson, P. B. Gibson, Wm. Gibson, A. J. Goodner, Geo. W. Goodner, John Gowans, Wm. Guinn, James Gowin, Alex. Gray, Wm. Hamentree, Isaac Hicks—son in U. S. A.; Wm. Horn, Ake Henry, John Harmon, William Horton, Timothy Haney—son in U. S. A.; Daniel Johnson—son in U. S. A.; Joel Johnson, sr., Emanuel Johnson, Matthew Johnson, Larkin Johnson, Joel Johnson, Benjamin John, Samuel John, Jacob Kinser—two sons in U. S. A.; Enoch Kincheloe—son in U. S. A.; Peter Lawson, John Lay—soldier; H. K. Lawson—three sons in U. S. A.; Henry Laudon, Mrs. Jane McClennin—son in U. S. A.; Newton McKinney, Mrs. Elizabeth McKinney, Matthew McCollister, James McCollister, Charles Patty, S. B. Palmer—son in U. S. A.; Jonathan Parsons—two sons in U. S. A.; Jacob Routh, Jonathan Routh, Asa Stamper, Wm. Smith, Anthony Smith, Jacob Tappin, Mrs. Prudence Triplet, Philip Trozier, Isaac Varnel, Mrs. Margaret Varnel—son pressed into C. S. A.; Martha York.

MEDIUM MEN OF THE SECOND DISTRICT.—Wm. Blair, Esq., Henry Barr, Daniel Gowan, John Lauden, Julius McClary, Philip Newberry, Josepher Staper, Louis Triplit, Doct. Walker, Geo. T. Parker, Wm. A. Wright, Abram York.

UNION SOLDIERS FROM THE SECOND DISTRICT.—Samuel Brewer, John Brown, Amos Brewer, S. Brannon, Sterling Brannon, Lieut. Walker Baker, S. E. Broils, Wm. Barnes,—died in Ky.; Smith Carson, Jackson Copeland,—killed at Atlanta; Wm. Climer, John Chandler, James R. Chilcott, Wm. Crowden, George Crowden, dead; E. F. Gibson, Wm. Horn,—died in Nashville; John Harmon, Wm. Hicks, Robert Haney,—died at Vicksburg; Doct. Hamentree, Henderson Hamentree, Z. L. John, Andrew Johnson, John Y. Johnson, James Johnson, Capt. John F. Kincheloe, John Lay, H. K. Lawson, Wm. N. Lawson, Isham Lawson, John J. Simmons, Isaac Varnal, John Varnal,—pressed into the rebel ranks and died.

MEDIUM LIST.—John Kinser, T. T. Mclennan, Joseph Barnes, Lewis Triplit, John Louden, Clay Kinser, James Harden.

LEADING REBELS IN THE SECOND DISTRICT.—Isaac Agee, D. Blankenship, Braziel, A. Casson, Mrs. Sarah Carson—widow; Johnson Crews, Jonathan Cry, And'n Campbell, J. W. Cox, Jackson Finnel, John Gatlin, Gilford Gatlin, Wm. Gowan, Hugh Gowan, T. S. Haney, F. Haney, Esq., Lazarus Haynes, James Hunt, J. I. Helms, John Hunt, Jacob Kinser, John Kinser, Reynolds Lawson—two sons in C. S. A.; Wilson Lewallen, Capt. Garner Landermelt, A. H. Lawson—two sons in C. S. A.; Mrs. M. J. McClellan—son rebel bushwhacker; Samuel Montgomery, Matthew McKnabb, Andrew Miller, Wm. Mathas, Robert Melton, Wm. Norris, David Parsons, James Richie, John Richie, Bird Scroggins, Lieut. Franklin Triplit, James Talley, Sterling Talley, Hiram Woods, Silas M. Wan—four sons in C. S. A.; Isaac Wan, James Wan, Wm. W. Whittenburg, Geo. Willis.

REBEL SOLDIERS FROM THE SECOND DISTRICT.—John Agy, Creed Brown, Tom Brown, Joseph Barnes, Jack Barnes, Wm. Braziel, —— Blankenship, Columbus Barnet, John Barnes, Wm. Barnes, James Barnes, Clark Barnet, Crack Barnet, Johnson Crews, Jonathan Cry, Wm. R. Crews, James Chandler, Jackson Finnell, Hugh Gowen, Isaac Gillian, Wm. Gowen, Lewis Gatlin, Jacob Gatlin, Stewart Gatlin, Little Tim Haney, Timothy Haney, Wright Haney, Hewson Harden, J. E. Helms, Wm. Kinser, John Kinser, Jacob Lawson, Edward Lawson, Lewis Lawson, Kin. Lawson, Frank Lowery, Timothy Lowery, Abraham Lowery, Garner Loudermelt, James Loudermelt, George Loudermelt, James Lawson, Charles Lewallen, Clay Loudon, Andrew Miller, Samuel Montgomery, —— Matthias, Robert Marr, Lafayette McClelland, Robert Melton, Philip Newberg, Wm. Norris, David Parsons, Isaac Perry, John Ritchie, Eli Ritchie, James Ritchie, Isaac Stamper, Bird Scroggins, Van Scroggins, Wm. Singleton, Wm. Stamper, James Wan, Marion Wan, Wm. Wan, Isaac Wan, John Wright, Wm. Whittenburgh, John Willis.

LEADING UNION PERSONS IN THE THIRD DISTRICT.—Ephraim Ash, James Armstrong, J. R. Bates, Wm. Burns, jr.—soldier; Wm. Burns, sr.—son in U. S. A.; Charles Bacon—son died in Ky.; James Cry, Daniel Carpenter, Robert Carson, Martin Carpenter, D. C. Cowan, Adam Carpenter, S. Y. Colville, John Cowden—killed at Atlanta; W. J. Duggan, J. N. Duggan, Dawson Deford, Isaac Perton, James Dabbs, Wm. Deford—soldier; S. H. Duggan—soldier; G. Deford, William Dodd—died in Nashville; Robert Dixon, N. W. Epperson—soldier; J. R. Epperson, Thomas Epperson—five sons in U. S. A.; Widow Epperson—three sons in U. S. A.; H. H. Fisher—two sons in U. S. A.; W. M. Felker, Elijah Fair, John Felker,

J. G. Felker, Henry Foster—two sons in U. S. A.; Edward Goode, G. C. Gilbert—two sons in U. S. A.; G. E. Grubb, Jeremiah Green, Stephen Hughes, Leander Hughes, W. A. Helterbrand, J. L. Hughes, John Hughes, Wm. D. Humberd, A. R. F. Hambright, Wm. Humberd, Esq., Anthony Hughes, Orlander Hughes, W. J. Hansford, James Helterbrand, W. H. Hannah, A. J. Hicks—soldier; Thomas Hughes, William Johns, Thomas Jenkins, H. L. Kerby, W. Keith—son in U. S. A.; J. H. Keith, A. C. Keith, Thomas Kimbro—two sons in U. S. A.; James Lauderdale, S. W. Lee—army employee; John Lacy, sr.—soldier; J. A. Lacy, E. G. Long—son in U. S. A.; Joseph Loftice, sr.—son in U. S. A.; Jesse Moyer—son in U. S. A.; A. Melsom—soldier; John McClure—soldier; Pleasant Morrison—two sons in U. S. A. lost on Sultana; J. R. Moreland—son in U. S. A., another pressed into C. S. A. and died; A. H. Mitchell—soldier, died at Knoxville; R. Nixon, D. P. Pettit, Jacob Phillips—five sons in U. S. A.; George Phillips, James Parsons, Oswell Phillips—soldier; Williamson Parks, Thomas Poindexter—soldier, killed in Polk county; Henry Ramins, G. Randolph—two sons in U. S. A.; William Rasor, John Rasor—son in U. S. A.; George Roland—son in U. S. A.; John Roland—son in U. S. A.; S. D. Richmond—four sons in U. S. A.; Michael Roland—single; Isaac Richmond—single; Edmund Ramsey—two sons in U. S. A.; J. H. Ramsey—soldier; W. C. Richmond—soldier; W. R. Richmond, Eli Shearland—son in U. S. A.; John Stonecypher, Phillip Stonecypher, E. H. Southerland—son in U. S. A.; Jos. Stonecypher—two sons in U. S. A.; Henry Stonecypher—two sons in U. S. A.; John Smith, sr, W. M. Samples—soldier; A. M. Southerland, A. P. Wiggins, Adam Wattenberger, Martin Webb—soldier; Enoch White—pressed in C. S. A. and died; David White, William White.

UNION SOLDIERS FROM THE THIRD DISTRICT.—Henry Armstrong, Jacob Bacon—died in Ky.; Captain James E. Colwell, John Cowden—killed near Atlanta; Edward Colville, Elmore Colville, Edward Colwell, S. H. Dugan, Wm. Dodd—died at Nashville; Wm. J. Duggan, Robert Duggan, Prior Duggan, Isaac Denton—died in Knoxville; J. N. Duggan, J. C. Duggan, N. W. Epperson, J. N. Epperson, J. D. Epperson, W. P. Epperson, R. C. Epperson, (sons of Thomas Epperson,) Thomas Epperson, Arthur Epperson, Joseph Epperson, (sons of widow Epperson,) George Edwards, Joseph G. Felker, Wm. Fisher, Wm. Finnell, Thomas Foster—died near Nashville; Russell Foster—died near Nashville; H. C. Fisher, Absalom Giles, James Goode, Jr., James Goode, sr., Larkin Giles, John Humberd, Jacob Humberd, Thomas Hickey, Sam. H. Humberd, A. J. Hicks, George Humberd, John A. Hicks, James Hawkins, Charles Harvey, John Helterbrand, Asbury Helterbrand, Elijah Havey, Cornelius Hooker, Wm. Hyde, Mark Irvin, John Jenkins, Fayette Jorden, Michael Keith, John Kimbro—died in Tenn.; John Kinnamon, Samuel Lemmons, S. M. Lea, Greenville Long—died at home; Samuel Long, David Loftice—killed at Nashville; Joshua Loftice, S. W. Lee, John Lacy, Washington Moreland, William Melton, John Moyers, John McClure, G. W. Moreland—died at Knoxville; John Moyers—killed on Lookout Mountain; Washington Mitchell—dead; James Melsom, Gilford Morrison—lost on Sultana; Isaac Morrison—lost on Sultana; James Moreland, Isaac Moreland, Timothy Mitchell, Samuel May, Nelson Norton, Anderson Nelson, Alexander Norton, George Phillips, Aaron Phillips, Marion Ponder, Williamson Parks, Marion Parks, Oswell Phillips, Reuben Phillips, Isaac Richmond, Wm. C. Richmond, John Richmond, James Ramsey, Russell Ramsey, George W. Rasor, John Roland, Daniel Rogers, Garrett Randolph, Earl Randolph, Jackson Rogers, Samuel Rogers, Absalom Stonecypher, John Stonecypher—died at Knoxville; Elijah Sutton, Thomas Sutton, Philip Stonecypher, Samuel Simmons, Harvey Sanders, Joseph P. Southerland, Wm. Samples, John White, jr., Enoch White, John White, sr., John White, jr., George W. Webb, Martin Webb, John Watters, Washington Westmoreland.

LEADING REBELS IN THE THIRD DISTRICT.—John Airhart, Ambrose Bearsden, Moses Britton, John K. Boyd, J. B. Britton, Wm. A. Britton, John Britton, L. C. Cagler, J. H. Davis, A. A. Davis, Hiram Gillian, James Guisan, R. W. Grant, Jotham Gregory—one of the worst of men; Tapley Gregory, Harrison Hughes, Rice Hughes, G. C. Highberger, G. W. Hughes, Francis Hagler, Pinckney Hawkins, M. R. Hamilton, Lemuel Jones, W. W. Johnson, George Kinser, David Kerr—three sons in C. S. A.; Abner Logan, J. H. Logan, C. H. Livingston, Joseph S. Loftice, G. L. Miller, Doct. Price, J. E. Ross—soldier; P. W. Rogers, Robert Smith, David Stewart, David Stewart, jr., W. H. Taff, Wm. H. Tibbs.

REBEL SOLDIERS FROM THE THIRD DISTRICT.—John Ayerhart, Stephen Bearden, William Bearden, Dr. Bearden, L. C. Cagler, James R. P. Davis, William Davis, Benjamin Davis, (brothers,) D. G. Fry, Wiley Foxtenor, Stephen Gregory, Seth Gregory, James Gregory, Gregory Tapley, Rice Hughes, John Hughes, George Hughes, G. C. Highberger, G. W. Hughes, Francis Haggler, George Kinser, Jesse Kerr, Williamson Kerr, Mack Kerr, John Kerney, Joseph S. Loftice, J. H. Logan, Samuel Lemons, J. L. Miller, David Stewart, E. F. Southerland, Ben Satterfield, Casuel Shields, Peter White, L. L. White, S. H. White.

LEADING UNION PERSONS IN THE FOURTH DISTRICT—Peter Ayerhart—son in U. S. A.; W. A. Coe, W. B. Cowan, Mrs. Elizabeth Campbell—son in U. S. A.; Mrs. Mary Cheek, Samuel Cook, Andrew Cowan, B. A. Davis, J. H. Dearmond—two sons in U. S. A.; Robert Delzell, Capt. John T. Dearmond, Marion Hardin, Eli Hardin, Miss Margaret Howard, J. N. Henry, S. H. Hickman, Elias Henderson—soldier; Benjamin Hambright, Jemima Hannah—widow; W. J. Horner,

Lucy Horned—widow; George Henderson, J. W. Iagon, Jeremiah Johnson—son in U. S. A.; B. A. Johnson, David Lee, Mary Lawson—widow, son in U. S. A.; O. W. Leonard—son in U. S. A.; Joseph Lusk—three sons in U. S. A.; Samuel Maroon—two sons in U. S. A.; A. J. McCallie, Capt. P. W. Norwood, John Posey, P. N. Roberts, W. F. M. Rice, Rev. Elijah Still—son in U. S. A.; William Smedley, A. B. Smedley, Ananias Thatch, W. H. Weatherly, Daniel White, W. M. Willhoit.

UNION SOLDIERS FROM THE FOURTH DISTRICT.—James Ayerbart, John Birchfield, Samuel Boil, Wm. J. Collit—died in Tasewell, Tennessee; Lieut. John O. Cobb, James Carroll, Wm. W. Campbell, Mansel Cornwell, Geo. W. Coley, Samuel H. Duggan, Albert G. Duggan, Capt. John T. Dearmond, Samuel Dearmond, Watson M. Duggan, Jacob W. Everett, George Furguson, John Faris, Stephen Greenfield, Andrew Greenfield, Peter Greenfield, J. D. Higgins, Elias Henderson—died in Nashville; S. J. Holden, Samuel Henry, James R. Henry, C. S. Hooker, W. B. Hyde, Hardy Hughes—volunteered at 50 years of age; Stephen Hughes, William Hughes, Jefferson Hughes, (three brothers,); John Hughes, James T. Iagon, Jacob Irvin, S. E. Johnson, Lieut. J. M. Johnson, W. K. James, John Jordon, Arthur Johnson—died at Nashville; Harry James, Wm. Kimbro, John Knight, Wm. B Kirkpatrick, R. F. Lawson, James A. Lawson, Samuel I Lusk, Lavander C. Lusk, Lieut. J. N B. Lusk, J. R. Leonard, George F. Lampson, John B Landin, George F. Lawson, Peter G. Maroon—died in Ky.; Lieut. Samuel W. Maroon, G. C. Montgomery, Samuel May, Capt. P. W. Norwood, Lieut. James R. Perry, Martin Palmer, Wm. Roberson—died at Nashville; James Roberson, James Roberts, G. W. Rasor, Joseph Still, James Still, C. L. Smedley, George Smedley, Allen Tuell, Jonathan White, Washington Westmoreland, R. W. Weatherly, John Waters, W. M. Willhoite.

LEADING REBELS IN THE FOURTH DISTRICT.—Hinson Ellerson, M. F. Fyllerton, W. H. Fulton, Thomas Hannah, Hardy Hughes—three sons in the U. S. A.; W. W. Johnson, Eli V. Morlock, David May, James Parsons, Wiley Ragsdale, F. A. Sloan, Melson Siner, Alfred Tilley, Wm. P. Tracey, Green Weatherly.

REBEL SOLDIERS FROM THE FOURTH DISTRICT.—H. H. H. Hambright, Charles Hicks, Tate Lawson, M. M. Leonard, Jacob Parsons, James Parsons.

LEADING UNION PERSONS IN THE FIFTH DISTRICT.—Joseph Anderson, Welcome Atchley, G. W. Brooks, Abram Brooks, —— Bonny, John Blackburn, John Bene, Wm. Bene, Widow Barkley—son pressed in the C. S. A and died; George Courtney, Isaac Cooper, George Colville—son in U. S. A.; J. M. Coppis, Calvin Davis, Uriah Hunt, Dudley Hoxey, J. R. Humphreys, Widow Henderson, James Felterbrand, G. R. Hambright—two sons in the U. S. A.; Russell Lawson—son in U. S. A.; J. H. Lee—two sons in U. S. A.; Andrew McCormack, Joel McMitt, Joseph Manes—son in U. S. A.; W. H. Manes, Rev. Louis Mitchell—son in U. S. A.; D. G. McCulley—son in U. S. A.; Henry Maples, Widow Manes—three sons in U. S. A.; John McGriff, Walker McGriff, T. L. Ramsey, John Reed—son in U. S. A.; Isaac Smith, Hiram H. Smith, John R Smith, John Scott, Silas Sisk, John Sisk, Blackburn Sisk, Rev. A. F. Shannon, Samuel Tague, M. Tague—two sons in U. S. A.; Wm Trewhitt, J. M. Trewhitt, Levi Trewhitt, jr., Levi Trewhitt, sr.—murdered at Mobile; Thos. T. Trewhitt, Jabue Whitten, two sons in the U. S. A.; William White, Jacob Wattenberger—two sons in U. S. A.; Wiland Wattenberger, Samuel Wattenberger.

MEDIUM MEN OF THE FIFTH DISTRICT.—Martin Langston, George Morelock.

UNION SOLDIERS FROM THE FIFTH DISTRICT.—Joseph Anderson, Harrison Bacon, Moses Barger, Zachariah Burson, Jacob Bacon—killed at Franklin, Tenn.; Richard Carter—once pressed in C. S. A.; John Davis, John Davis, Benjamin T. Hambright, Joseph Howell, J. R. Hambright, Jerry Lawson, Wm. Langston, John Lee—died at Nashville; S. W. Lee, William McHolland—last seen on the ground dead or dying, with rope marks around his neck; Amos Manes—shot at home by J. M. Henry; Wm. Manes, John Mitchell, James McCulley, Harrison Manes, D. H. Murphy, L. B. McNabb—hospital surgeon; John L. Reed—assistant surgeon; Thomas L. Reed, John Stuart—died in Ky.; James Stuart, Kendrick Stuart—four brothers; Newton Stuart, George Templeton, George Teigue, Samuel Teigue, James L. Taylor—killed by rebels near Cumberland Gap; Wilson Wattenbarger, Willard Wattenbarger, James Whitten, John Whitten.

LEADING REBELS IN THE FIFTH DISTRICT.—John Atchley, Amos Allison, Thos. Atchley, S. D Bridgeman, John Beaty, Robert Boyd, Wm. L. Brown—son a guerrilla; James Donahoo, John Forest, Rev. John Gilbert, James Henkle, Charles Hess, Joel Hess, —— Janes, Captain John Kuhn, Wm. Logan, Hiram Lomans—son in C. S. A.; Wm. Medaris, John Osment, John Reid, Doct. Lemuel Sugart—son a guerrilla; Robert Stuart, Wm Smith, Wm H. Tibbs—two sons in C. S. A—one a guerrilla; George Tucker—son in C. S. A.; Nicholas Upton—two sons in the C. S. A.—one a guerrilla.

REBEL SOLDIERS FROM THE FIFTH DISTRICT.—Thomas Atchley, John Atchley, Rufus Allison, Capt. Bill Brown, Samuel Brown—guerrilla; Ben Bridgeman, John Forest, James Henkle, Ben Holtscloth, Frank Hess, —— Janes, John T. Kuhn, Captain John Kuhn, Lieut. Nathan W. Kuhn, G. W. Langston, Wm Logan, Wm Medaris, Joseph Osment, Mell Osment, Robert Simpson, Lilburn Sugart, Livingston Sugart, James Sugart, Wm Sugart, Charles Tibbs, John Tibbs—guerrilla; George Tucker, L. B. Upton—guerrilla; Isaac Upton.

APPENDIX.

LEADING UNION PERSONS IN THE SIXTH DISTRICT.—Washington Alexander, John Atchley, M. F. Anderson, John Bower, R. G. Blackburn, Doct. B. Brocker, Mrs. Sarah Brown—widow; Doct. J. G. Brown, James Batt, Marek Black—two sons in U. S. A.; J. R. Beckner, J. H. Boyd—son in U. S. A.; A. E. Blunt, John Banks, James Baker, J. C. Coffman, Arthur Coffman, H. M. Collins, Joseph Carson, James Chilcott, F. A. Carter, R. J. F. Calaway, Leonard Carouth, Andrew Chilcott—son in U. S. A.; Wm. Cate—son in U. S. A.; Andrew Campbell, Wm. I. Campbell, James Campbell, Jacob Collit, Edward Cooper, W. H. Craigmiles, D. H. Carson, P. M. Craigmiles, James Coffman, John Coffman—soldier; A. W. Davis, Joseph H. Davis, Wm. L. Dearing, Mrs. W. J. Delano, W. R. Davis, M. E. Dodson, Woodson Davis—son in U. S. A.; Wm. C Davis, Rev. Wm. H. Daily, H. B. Davis, A. W. Davis, W. P. Foster, John Forget, Judge Gaut, C. M. Gallagher, S. Grigsby, J. H. Gaut, S. P. Gaut, John Goodner, John Glaze, Masten C. Henry, Harrison Henry, James H. Henry, Robert Hayne—son in U. S. A.; Baldwin Harle, Joseph Harle, J. P. Hacker, James Hassell, Ake. E. Henry, Wm. W. P. Hancock, S. Hunt, J. Henderson, W. S. Hays, John F. Hays, Clayburn Haggard, Alfred Hayner, F. E. Hardwick, Green Henry, E. M. Ingle, Benjamin Johess, F. P. Kelley, Elijah Kibler, Patrick Lane, Rev. J. B Lawson—died in U. S. service; Isaac Low—sheriff; Wm. H. Low—son in U. S. A.; Mrs Mary A. Leapier—widow; M. M. Leonard, M. W. Legg, S. F. Larrison, D. C. McMillen—son in C. S. A.; W. S. Montgomery, S. N. Montgomery—son in U. S. A.; Jesse Maples, L. B. Miller, Wm. Minnis, Thomas Maroon, Dr. A. McNabb, James McGee, J. H. Norman, C. A. Norman, D. B. O'Neil, L. L. Osment, M. B. Prichard, L. G. Purtle—soldier; Capt. E. J. Purtle, Elijah Purtle—two sons in U. S. A.; Samuel Parks, J. F. Price, A. N. Pendergrass, Williamson Parks—son in U. S. A.; John Pierce—son in U. S. A.; A. J. Parks—three sons in U. S. A.; A. C. Parks, J. N. Rucker, James S. Robison, J. E. Robt, L. G. Ross, Capt. Thomas Rains, G. W. Rollins, F. G. Robisson, J. C. Steel, Maj. Wm. P. Story, Wm. Samples—son in U. S. A.; Matthew Samples, Rev. Eli H. Sutherland—son in U. S. A.; A. J. Trewhitt, Esq., Wm. R. Trewhitt, G. B. Thompson—three sons in C. S. A.; J. C. Tipton, Isham Vest, J. H. Walker—soldier; A. J. White, E. C. Williams, W. C. Walker, Henry Wooden, W. G. Weatherby, William Welcher, M. M. Willhoit, M. A. White, G. P. Welcher, Thomas Young, Doct. Wm Hunt.

UNION SOLDIERS FROM THE SIXTH DISTRICT.—Surg. J. B. Brown, Joseph Boyd, Reuben Boyd, James Beagles, Zachariah Burson, Wm. H. Black, Geo. W. Black, Capt. F. A. Carter, Wm. Cooper, Thomas Cooper, Marion Choat, Isaac Collit, Jos. Chadwick, J. H. Callahan, David Cooper, Lieut. Wm. B. Davis, Charles Davis, James Davis, Col. M. R. Edwards, Henry Hayes, Lafayette W. Hicks, N. B. Hicks, Gideon Horn, Bradford Hague, Geo. M. Hayes, Major S. Hunt, Gilp Harvey, John Hague, Samuel Harvey, Capt. Robert Hague, Wm. H. Jones, Rev. Jacob Lawson, Powell H. Low, John McDaniels, C. G. Montgomery, Jackson Maples, Henry Parks, Robert Parks, Bud Parks, Wm. M. Parks, Charles Pearce, James Pearce, John Parks, Jesse Parks, Elijah Parkle, Wm. Parks, Capt. Thomas Rains, Ben Robisson, F. G. Robisson, Daniel Robisson, Charles Reynolds, Robert Samples, William Samples, Joseph Southerland, William Southerland, Charles Thompson, G. B. Thompson, Richard Thomas, M. M. Tucker, Ben Thompson, C. G. Traynor, J. D. Traynor, Hugh Weee, Samuel Weee, Orlando White, William White, Capt. James Ware, Wm. Williams, James E. Walker, Capt. Robert Wooten, Surgeon Wm. Hunt.

LEADING REBELS IN THE SIXTH DISTRICT.—John A. Black, Robert Boyd, S. Y. Brown—soldier; S. D. Bridgeman, Ezekiel Bates, T. L. Bates, C. Y. Brown, John N. Cowan, Rev. W. E. Colwell, John H. Craigmiles, Matthew Carter, Paschal Carter, Mrs. Mahala Cannon, John P. Campbell, Joseph Coble, James M. Craigmiles, Henry Cate, James M. Cowen, Wm. R. Demore, S. E. Dixon, Thos. Dodson, P. J. R. Edward, F. W. Earnest, J. S. Fry—son in C. S. A.; J. A. Francisco, Jos. Fry, Dr. G. W. Ford, Louis Guthman, Isaac Guthman, Wm. B. Craddy, Wm. H. Grant, William Grant, C. L. Hardwick, Wm. J. Hughes, James H. Huff, James Hoyle, L. M. Jones, S. E. Johnson, James M. Johnson, Josiah Johnson, Campbell Johnson, E. F. Johnson, David Kincannon, L. W. Keeling—soldier; J. J. Kennedy, A. H. Lawson, Caswell Lee, Dr. G. A. Long, J. E. M. Montgomery—Major in C. S. A.; J. L. Morisson, Robert McNelly—Editor of *Cleveland Banner*; Preston Maples—two sons in C. S. A.; Rev. Wm. McNutt, C. H. Mills, Thos. McMillen, Allen Nipper, John Osment—two sons in C. S. A.; W. H. Pete, J. H. Payne, A. B. Russell, B. F. Ragsdale, J. L. Swan, S. A. R. Swan, R. M. Swan—son in C. S. A.; J. E. Surgine, David Straty, Joseph K. Taylor—soldier; Wm. H. Tibbs, M. C. C.—two sons in C. S. A.; Wm. C. Tibbs, J. A. Tibbs, G. W. Tucker, Wm. H. Underwood, John Wood—two sons in C. S. A.; Davis Whitman, Euclid Waterhouse, J. C. Wood.

REBEL SOLDIERS FROM THE SIXTH DISTRICT.—Capt. Alvin Beagles, Matthias Beagles, W. A. Camp, Robert Cook, J. A. Davis, Solomon Guthman, Manuel Guthman, Robert Grant, John B. Hogle, T. L. Hogle, Doct. Hogle, Charles Hardwick, James Irwin, Brad Irwin, James K. Johnson, E. F. Johnson, A. H. Lawson, John Lauderdale, Lewis V. Lawson, Jacob Lawson, James Lauderdale, John Lea, Jos. Lea, Wm. McGhee, Theodore Mountcastle, Martin Magriff, Jefferson Magriff, Allen Nipper, John H. Parker, Wm. Pasley, C. L. Reynolds, S. A. R. Swan, David Straley, Joseph R. Taylor, Larkin Taylor, John Traynor, James Traynor, C. C. Tibbs, John Tibbs, George Tucker, John Woods.

LEADING UNION PERSONS IN THE SEVENTH DISTRICT.—Abram Burdit, J. W. Barnet, Melson Bacon, Samuel Burton, —— Bird, —— Bird, —— Bird, J. F. Cleveland—son in U. S. A.; Berry Collins, T. L. Cate—Tuscaloosa prisoner; Widow Caywood—son in U. S. A.; Alfred Castiller, George Cooper, T. J. Collier, James Curry, Jefferson Eldridge, Geo. Ezell—soldier; Minton Garrett—soldier; Widow Hall, Wm. Hancock, Benj. Jimison, Young Kibler, Montgomery Kibler, Fountain Larrison—son in U. S. A.; John More, George More, Rev. Richmond Parks, Rev. R. T. Parks, N. J. Peters—son in U. S. A.; M. H. Purviance—son in U. S. A.; Wm. Simpson—son in U. S. A.; John Swinney—soldier; Campbell Steed, W. B. Simmons, Widow Taylor—son in U. S. A.; Willson Thomas—son in U. S. A.; Andrew Thomas—three sons in U. S. A.; J. E. Willson, John Winkle—soldier; Samuel Wooden.

MEDIUM LIST.—Campbell Ackerson, N. Hayes—three sons in C. S. A.; Thomas Knox, Wm. Day, Isaac Day—three sons in C. S. A.; C. Collins, Jacob Casey, John McReynolds.

UNION SOLDIERS FROM THE SEVENTH DISTRICT.—Abel Burdit, George Burdit—killed; W. F. Bell, Elbert Bacon, Jacob Collit, Chester Collins, Franklin Caywood, Jacob Collier—died at home; Eli Cleveland, Jacob Casey, George Ezell, Mintor Garrett, Joseph Garrett—died at Nashville; Moses Harmon, Frank Haywood, Napoleon Hall, David Jack—died in army; Clinton Jack, Henderson Jones, Sam'l Kebler, Benjamin Lane—died at Camp Dick Robisson; John Lambert—died at Nashville; Robert Larrison, James Marr, John Hee, Benjamin Pruitt, John Purvians, J. N. Peters, Joseph Purvians, John Swinney, John Simpson, Jos. Spenrs, Wm. Taylor, David Thomas, Albert Thomas, John Thomas—three brothers; Wm. A. Thomas, John Winkle, Robert Wooten.

LEADING REBELS IN THE SEVENTH DISTRICT.—Lorenzo Alexander, Samuel Billingsly, H. Collins—one son in each army; Captain Simon Eldredge, Henderson Finley, Wm. Gault—soldier; Wm. Kelley, Jacob Lawson, Widow Lee, Col. Lee, Russell Lawson, E. Morrison, Hiram McCasther, Wm. McMillen, Joseph McMillen, S. H. Parks, R. T. Parks, G. W. Parks, Susan Parks—widow, six sons in C. S. A.; Brice Robbins—son in C. S. A.; M. D. L. Spriggs, Ezekiel Spriggs, Robert Wooten.

REBEL SOLDIERS FROM THE SEVENTH DISTRICT.—Samuel Billingsly, James Brown, John Collins—Union at heart; John Collins, George Day, Samuel Day, Jonas Day, Jackson Day, Eldridge Ezekiel, Capt. S. W. Eldredge, James Eperson, Tobe Eperson, S. D. Eperson, Stephen Eperson, J. W. M. Eperson, Henderson Finly, John Finly, Enoch Finly, Wm. Gault, George Hayes, Wm. Hayes, James Hayes, Thomas Hoyle, Thomas Henderson, Samuel Hickman, Jacob Lawson, L. K. Lawson, R. C. Lawson, Col. R. Lawson, Nelson Lawson, Wellington McClellan—rebel Captain, one of the worst of men; G. W. Parks, T. J. Parks, C. M. Parks, R. C. Parks, R. T. Parks, S. H. Parks, (six brothers,) Samuel Pickle, James Robbins, M. D. L. Spriggs, John Shipman.

UNION SOLDIERS FROM THE NINTH DISTRICT.—Solomon Belvin, T. Breedwell, Wm. Bracket, Jacob Carter, Jesse D. Carter, James Cavett, Andrew J. Cole, John Cuffie, Joseph D. Duncan, James Dennis, John Everett, sr., John Everett, jr., Lucas Everett, Andrew Everett, James Everett, Warren Eaton, Newton Eaton, Robert Eaton, A. J. Furguson, Richard Farmer, J. L. Farmer, James Farmer, Samuel Farmer, Wm. D. Farmer, D. D. Foster, James Francisco, John Francisco, H. C. Francisco, Wm. Farmer, Lieut. Eli Fitzgerald, Squire Fitzgerald, Archy Fitzgerald, Merriam Graham, Samuel Graham, Landon Graham, Lewis Gregsby, James Gregsby, J. K. Green, Wm. Green, Wm. Grissom, Joseph Grissom, Wilford Grissom, Lieut. Richard Grissom, Joseph Hyden, F. A. Holt, Jackson Harvey, Pleasant Harper, Alfred Hyden, John Hooper, Wm. Hooper, Jabue Hooper, R. C. Hooper, Robert D. Hayes, Lieut. James Hooper, Lieut. Pleasant Harper, Minton Houser, Lieut. F. C. Johnson, Wm. King, James King, Francis King, Isaac Kirkpatrick, Alex Liles, Andrew D. Leopard, Green Lawson, John D. McPherson, Lieut. R. H. McPherson, James McDowell, Silas Morgan, John Morgan, William McDuffee, Newton McDuffee, Samuel McInturff, Hugh Murphy, James Murphy, Robert Murphy, Wm. Marr, Nathan Marr, James Marr, Samuel McCracken, John McCracken, R. F. McPherson, Wm. Murphy, Edward Murphy, Robert McEwen, H. A. McEwen, Gardner McEwen, Kane Millard, Henry Newbury, Wm. Perren, Squire Perren, James Perren, Robert Prichet, John D. Prichet, Wm. D. Ross, James Ross, T. J. Ross, Alex D. Rogers, Thomas D. Rains, James Romaines, Jas. Rives, Captain W. C. Shelton, Van Seaburn, James Scroggins, Omiller Shiply, Thos. Spurgen—U. S. recruiting officer and Tenn. pilot; Wm. Stanfield, Joseph Stanfield, Hardy Stanfield, Charles D. Swafford, Howard Swafford, Dallas Shelton, E. N. Taylor, T. J. Taylor, Lafayette Tucker, T. H. Tucker, Merrien Tucker, John Tucker, Elijah Tudor, John Wrinkle, Wiley Wrinkle, D. D. Wrinkle, —— Witt, John Wilson, R. D. Wilson, George Wilson, Wm. Wyrick, Samuel Wright, Irvin D. Wood, Albright Wyrick, T. W. D. Wyrick, James Young.

UNION MEN PRESSED INTO THE C. S. A.—Benjamin Grissom—died at Cumberland Gap; Elbert Graham—died at Taswell, Tenn.; Isham Guinn—died at Taswell, Tenn.; John Lawson—died at Knoxville, Tenn.; Robert McEwen—died at Knoxville, Tenn.

REBEL SOLDIERS FROM THE NINTH DISTRICT.—John Basket, John Everett, Christopher Graves, James Willson.

UNION SOLDIERS FROM THE TENTH DISTRICT.—James O. Beard—lost on the Sultana; Nicholas Baty—died at Nashville; John Baty, Thomas Baty, Lieut. Col. Stephen Beard, Henry Barger, John Barger, James B. Brooks, George W. Black, Wm. H. Black, George Bradshaw—died at Louisville; Major James S. Bradford, Doct. Campbell, Hugh Campbell—lost on the Sultana; James Capp, Sam'l Cheak, Alex. Carson, Capt. Charles Champion, Joseph Collins—lost on the Sultana; Jas. Collins—escaped from the Sultana; Michael Capp, Judge K. Clingham, Jas. Clingham—died at Nashville; Capt. J. R. Clingham, Loran Davis—died at Nashville; Elam Dean—dead; Thomas Dean, —— Debralkum, George Debralkum, John Everett—died at Nashville; Jackson Furguson, George Furguson—died South; Samuel W. Grigsby, John Garner, John Gonce, Elias Guinn—died at Nashville; James Goodwin, Amos Goodwin, Hartford Goole, Isham Guinn—died at Taswell, Tenn.; Wm. Grigsby, Marion F. Grigsby, Wm. Gammon, John Gearin, Thomas Gearin—died at Resaca; Jackson Hays, Andrew Hickman—killed on Chattahoochie, near Atlanta; William Hickman, William Holden, Anderson Hyden, Jackson Henkle, Madison B. Hysinger—lost on Sultana; Washington Henkle, Benj. F. Hysinger, Lieut. Pleasant Harper—died at Nashville; Walter L. Haskins—killed on Lost Mt., Ga.; Reece Ingle—killed at Resaca; Elbert Ingle, Geo. Ingle, Jackson Irvin, William Irvin—dead; Stephen Johnson, Joseph Lane, Ben Lane, Thomas Lane, Jesse C. Lee, Burrill Lee, Wm. Lacewell, Westly Mowry, Samuel George Marlo, James K. Polk Marlo—accidentally killed with his own gun; Wm. Miller—died in rebel prison; Jacob Miller, John Miller, Isaac McCamis, George McCamis, Wm. Mowry, Jackson Mowry, John Miller, Leander Mowry, Lieut. Isaac B. Newton, Melvin Ormes, Joseph Ormes, Thomas Ormes, John Owensby, Andrew Overhuleer, Wm. H. Oliver, Douglas Ottinger, James Prater, Jas. Poindexter, Lafayette Panter, John Peak, John Parker, Geo. Parker, Thomas Prater, Bud Roberts, Daniel Rogers, James Rains—accidentally killed by pistol shot; Samuel Ralston—died near chattanooga; Robert Ray, Quiller Shiply—lost on Sultana; John Simpson—died at Louisville; Charles Swafford—died in Andersonville prison; Butler Seaburn, James Swafford, Biles Swafford—died at Andersonville, Ga.; Aaron Swafford—died at Louisville; Henry Smith, James Smith, Enoch Shipley, James Sears, Abner Stults, Vanburen Seaburn, James Turner, Lavater Taylor, Joseph Thompson, Lafayette Thompson, Isaac A. Thompson, Jackson Thompson, David Wright, Samuel Wright—died at Nashville; Stephen Willhoite, Charles Weatherly, Luke L. Wrinkle, James Wooden, Thomas Wooden—killed at Resaca; William Wooden—died at Nashville of smallpox; T. J. Weir, John L. Weir—died at Andersonville; Samuel H. Weir—died at Nicholasville, Ky.; Wiley Wrinkle—died at Nashville; Mark Wrindle, Wm. Wrinkle, Sidney Wise, Joseph Young, Jas' Newell, Wm. Norton, John Wooden—died at Nashville.

HEADS OF FAMILIES IN THE TENTH DISTRICT, WHO WITH THEIR SONS JOINED THE FEDERAL ARMY.—Dr. Campbell, Joseph Collins, Stephen Beard, John Thompson, J. A. Thompson, each one son; Thomas J. Weir, two sons.

UNION PERSONS IN THE TENTH DISTRICT. — Welcome Beard, Stephen Beard, Mrs. Joseph Collins, Dr. Campbell, Mrs. Elizabeth Cheat, Moses Carson, Benjamin Franklin, John R. Gonce, Joel Hall, Felix Hice, D. D. Halkum, Jacob Hysinger, Jesse Haskins, Wm. Johnston, Robert Lee, Barbery Lee, Caroline Mowrey, Wm. Peck, John Poindexter, Alexander Shipley, Peter W. Swafford, Mrs. Mary Swafford, R. C. Seaburn, Isaac A. Thompson, John Thompson, Elishn Wise—each one son in the U. S. A.; James L. Bargar, Andrew Capp, Mrs. A. A. Clingan, Thos. Dean, Jonathan Erwin, Mrs. Elizabeth Goodwin, Joseph Hicks, John Hickman, Allen Marler, Thomas Praytor, Abner Stults, Thomas J. Weir—each two sons in U. S. A.; Beaty James, Mrs. Elizabeth Furguson, John Ingle, Anderson Lane, Andrew McAmis, Samuel Mowry, Noah R. Smith, Wm. Wooden—each three sons in U. S. A.; John E. Grigsby, Mrs. Elenor Miller—each four sons in U. S. A.; Miles G. Davis.

HEADS OF UNION FAMILIES IN THE TENTH DISTRICT, WHO HAD NO SONS IN THE FEDERAL ARMY.—A. M. Allen, Mrs. Elizab'h Beaty, Asa Bean, Elijah Beard, Jacob A. Barger, Mrs. Bennet Collins, Joseph Carter, Joseph Cheek, Joseph Cobb, Thomas Cooper, Bennet Cooper, Thomas H. Calaway, Albert Davis, Alex. Dancy, James P. Dean, Henry Davis, Elijah Fortner, George Gibson, Jacob Goodner, Coswell Goodner, John Goodner, S. S. J. Gilliland, Wm. Gilliland, Lewis Griffin, James Gaut, Mrs. Mary Hale, William P. Hase, Samuel Henkle, Joseph Henkle, G. W. Hawk, Mrs. Mary G. Hanes, Wm. Ingle, Robert Johnson, C. M. Johnson, J. G. Johnson, Burrell Lee, Russell Lee, Wm. E. Lee, Thomas Lee, Aaron Lee, Peter Lacewell, Hamrick Marler, James Maury, Joseph Oldham, Wm. Poindexter, Uriah Potter, John Purvance, J. W. Pangle, Lorenzo Tipton, John Thompson, Alfred Smith, Franklin Suttles, T. J. Smith, John Underwood, Merrill Witt, Gideon Williams, Jackson Williams, Rufus Wrinkle, Jesse Wooden.

WIDOWS WHOSE HUSBANDS DIED OR WERE KILLED IN THE FEDERAL ARMY.—Mrs. Nicholas Beaty, Mrs. Jos. Collins, Mrs. John Everett, Mrs. Jackson Hanes, Mrs. Barry Hames, Mrs. Madison Hysinger, Mrs. Rice Ingle, Mrs. Andrew Overhuleer, Mrs. Samuel Raulsson, Mrs. Aaron Swafford, Mrs. John Wooden, Mrs. Wiley Winkle.

SINGLE UNION MEN IN THE TENTH DISTRICT NOT SOLDIERS, —— Davis, Jas. Goodner, Joseph Gardner, John Halcum, Freeling H. Haskins, Daniel Kibler, Wm. Lee, John Lee, Robert Lee, James Peck, Harrison Thompson.

LEADING REBELS IN THE TENTH DISTRICT.—Russell Allen, Joseph Barksdale, Rafe Barksdale, Edward Browder, Gideon Brannom, Andrew Carson, William Carr, Joseph E. Dyke, Alfred Davis, J. D. Funderburk, C. S. Grigsby, James P. Harris, Stephen L. Harris, Doct. C. A. Legg, Dallas Miller, Sam'l Maxwell, John Minnis, Robert Minnis, Wm. Potter, Thomas Potter, Romulus Roberts, William Runyans, J. H. Reeder, Thomas Renfrow, James Seaburn, Miles W. Seaburn, Richard Seaburn, J. H. Thompson, Wiley Thompson.

REBEL SOLDIERS FROM THE TENTH DISTRICT.—Edward Allen, Joseph Barksdale, Edward Browder, John Brannom, Gideon Brannon, Sterling Brandon, G. G. Grigsby, Thomas Goode, Obadiah Harris, Alfred Legg, Isaac W. Legg, Meredith Legg, Dallas Miller, John Minnis, Robert Minnis, Felix Purviance—bushwhacker; Thomas Potter, Richard Potter, James Roberts, George Roberts, Hiram Roberts, Polk Runions—bushwhacker; Wm. Renfrow, Henry Renfrow, Henderson Renfrow, Thomas Renfrow, Romulus Roberts, John Seaburn, Miles W. Seaburn, Richard Seaburn, Wiley Thompson, Richard Thompson.

UNION SOLDIERS FROM THE ELEVENTH DISTRICT.—Daniel Atchley, Green Boon, —— Bradford, Micager Brooks, Dock Brooks, James Denton, Dock Denton, Martin Fan—died at Nashville; Robert Fan, Joseph Gass, Benjamin Hall, Morgan B. Hall—died at Chattanooga; Curran Harris, Joseph Harris, Elwood Harris, Marion Harrold, Leonard Harrold, Luke Harrold—four brothers; D. M. Harvey, Lieut. D. N. Kelly, Lieut. Wm. Kelley, Lieut. James Kelly, R. M. C. Lewis—died at Columbus, S. C.; Joseph Lacy—died in Cincinnati; M. H. H. Lacy—died in N. C.—Thomas Lary—died in Ky.; three brothers; Joseph Lambert—died at Nashville; Daniel McAndrew—died in Ky.; Samuel McAmy, John McAmy, —— McDaniels—died at Murfreesboro; Joseph Pair, Sam'l Pair, D. Stephenson—died at Louisville, Ky.; Jackson Swafford—died at Nashville; Ezekiel Swafford, Howard Swafford, Wm. Swafford, Wm. Selvidge, Wm. Thomas—died in Louisville; Wm. Talent, John Trotter, Joseph Talent, Jerry Triplet, Meredith Wolf.

REBEL SOLDIERS FROM THE ELEVENTH DISTRICT.—Samuel Browder, Wm. Blanton, James Blanton, Bird Browder, Francis Barksdale, Joseph Barksdale, Samuel D. Barksdale, Gale Gabit, John Gwin, James Gwin, Albert Hannah, Alex Leamon, James McKegham, Samuel McKegham, —— McKegham, Rob't Parks, David Russell, Wm. Russell, Egleton Russell, Asbery Taylor, Jeptha Talent, Poney Talent, Erby Thomas, John Tucker, Wm. Willis, Dock Woods.

LEADING REBELS IN THE ELEVENTH DISTRICT.—Samuel Browder, William Brown, Rafe Barksdale, Michael Bough—killed, it is supposed by the Miller boys; Thomas Hall, John Hall, John Hannah, James N. Johnson, Marshall W. McDaniels, Stewart Russell, William Triplit, William Tucker—killed; Jeptha Talent, David Thompson, William Woods.

LEADING UNION PERSONS IN THE TWELFTH DISTRICT.—Henry M. Allen—son in U. S. A.; Jefferson Bridges, R. B. Bridges—two sons in U. S. A.; W. R. Bradley—son in U. S. A.; Joseph Brown, Solomon Bell, John W. Bell, R. H. Brown, Aaron Bennet, Israel Boon, John Bloon—son in U. S. A.; John Bottoms, Wilford Chapman—son in U. S. A.; James Davis, E. F. Dawn, Thomas Early, Leander Frazier, Peter Greenfield—four sons in U. S. A.; Lewis Hale, John Harris, Henry Hall, W. L. Howard, Lee Huffacre, Wiley Huffacre, C. P. Howard, S. P. Howard, Hamilton Howard, Samuel Howard, Ephraim Hutline, Perry Howard, George W. Heaslet, Nathan Hinch, John Howard, Crawford Jones, Mrs. Cynthia Jones—widow; Riley Keyton, Samuel Kelley, Elijah Kelley, Henry Lynton, A. J. Lynton—son in U. S. A.; —— Langston—died in Nashville; Isaac Lee, P. M. Lee, Jefferson Lewis, James Mason, Mrs. Mary McSpadden, J. L. Metzer, J. B. Mitchell, James Mitchell, W. D. Mitchell, William Mitchell, B. F. Mitchell, Mrs. Martha Mitchell—son in U. S. A.; Mrs. Jane McCarty—son in Government employ; Joseph Melton, Jacob McDaniel, F. S. Miller, Austin McDonald, E. B. McCord, Perry McSpadden, Samuel McSpadden, Benjamin McSpadden, R. P. McSpadden, A. P. Miller, Munroe Miller, Thomas Miller, Henry Nicholson, Alfred Worth, Widow Price—son killed in U. S. A.; Mrs. Mary Pesterfield, Joel Parker, Andrew Pair—two sons in U. S. A.; Amos Potts—son in Government employ; A. K. Potts, Albert Potts, William Potts, James A. Rubed, William Sanders, J. H. Smith, Early H. Scrimpsher, Thomas Schnoggins, Jos. Smith, John Smith, A. S. Swanson, James Taylor—son in U. S. A.; Stephen Thatch—son in U. S. A.; William Talent, Esq.—son in U. S. A.; George Varnel, Marion Wolf, Mrs. Mary Willholte, Alfred Willholte—Government employ; Abraham Winkler—four sons in U. S. A.; W. L. Willis, Mrs. Nancy Wolf, James Wolf, David Wolf, Montgomery Williams, Willis White, Riley Waters.

UNION SOLDIERS IN THE TWELFTH DISTRICT.—Henry M. Allen, Capt. Andrews, John Bell, Andrew Bridges, John Bridges, A. C. Bradly—dead; Judson Boon, James Beloin, John W. Bell, Lieut. Samuel Chapman, William Crum, Jasper Carden, Newton Carden, J. D. Carter, William Gillet, John Greenfield, Wiley Hammonds—died in service; Jesse Huffacre, Campbell Hicks, Alexander Hall, Wiley Huffacre, Bartlet Johnson, Franklin Johnson—died at Chattanooga; Russell Johnson, Stephen Johnson, Wm. Lynton, Samuel McAmey, James Miller—died at Nashville; Perry Mitchell, James McCarty, Jonathan McNare, Robt. Mohon—died in the service; Jonathan Miller; —— Miller; Charles North, Preston North, Gabriel North, Zachariah Nicholson, Jesse Prince, Jos. Pair, Samuel Pair, George Price, Wm. Robison, James Roberts, Samuel Smith, Robert Smith, Jeff. Taylor,

John Thatch, Allen Tuell, Samuel Talent, Thomas Winkler—died at Nashville; Wm. Winkler, S. N. Winkler, Hiram Winkler, John Wolf, David Wolf, George Wolf.

LEADING REBELS IN THE TWELFTH DISTRICT.—Rev. John Burke, Henry Bennet—horse thief; Doct. F. L. Blair, Geo W. Bennet, Maze Blackburn, R. M. Chestnut, James B. Caywood, Thomas Gardner—son guerrilla; J. H. Gibson, Michael Howell—son in C. S. A.; William Hale, Perry Hawkins, J. W. Hawkins, Campbell Johnson, M. M. McDonald, Marion More, John D. Nesl, John Philips, Stephen B. Philips, Wm. Scott, James Smith, Mrs. Mary Tucker, Fleming T. Wells, James Willson, Capt. Wm Wheeler.

REBEL SOLDIERS FROM THE TWELFTH DISTRICT.—Lafayette Blackburn, Henry Bennet—horse thief and guerrilla; John Bennet, Wm. Bennet, Jesse Bennet, Jas. Burke, George Burke—guerrilla; Hugh Blair, Wm. Blackburn, Jesse Blackburn, Abram Blackburn—guerilla; John Brown, Alex. Bennet—guerilla; Wm. Carden, Henderson Gardner, James Hawkins, William Hawkins, John Hawkins, Joseph Howell, Campbell Johnson, Zachariah Johnson, Lowery Johnson—guerrilla; Luke Lea, John McCoy, James McCoy, Louis McSpadden, Alfred Martin, Isaac Martin, John Martin, James Martin, Thomas A. Miller, B. Neil, J. Neil, Edward Philips, William Philips, John Philips, Tate Shull, Wm. Stradler, Jefferson Murphrey, Joseph Willson, William Willson, William Wheeler.

UNION MEN PRESSED INTO THE REBEL ARMY AND SOON AFTER DIED.—Boon Huffine—died at home; Mock Smith—died near Knoxville; Isaac Winkler—died at home.

LEADING UNION MEN IN THE THIRTEENTH DISTRICT.—Isaac Armstrong, J. Armstrong, James Armstrong—two sons in U. S. A.; Henry Brown—three sons in U. S. A.; Jefferson Brewer—two sons in U. S. A.; Robert Coffey—forced into rebel service and soon died; P. L. Carden—two sons in U. S. A.; Mrs. Mahala Cartwright—son in U. S. A.; George Carson—soldier; Martin Frazer—four sons in U. S. A.; O. G. Frazier, Hamilton Fox, S. L. Griffith, Lynch Goode—son in U. S. A.; Mrs. Griffith, widow—two sons in U. S. A.; George Ghan—son in U. S. A.; Wm. Howell, Wm. Horton, Martin Hannah, Wm. Johnson—soldier; John Lawson, Nelson Lawson, Lafayette More, Washington More—son in U. S. A.; Jackson Million, John Million, S. W. Officer, Nathan Osment—son in U. S. A.; Nathaniel Philips, Jesse A. Pritchet, Benoul Pritchet—two sons in U. S. A.; Gilmore Randolph—two sons in U. S. A.; Redferin Routh, Gabriel Ragsdale, David W. Stuart, Jasper Stuart, William Taylor, James M. Thompson.

WAVERING UNION MEN OF THE THIRTEENTH DISTRICT.—Levi Civils, Buck Guinn, John Griffith.

UNION SOLDIERS FROM THE THIRTEENTH DISTRICT.—Jefferson Brewer, Amos Brewer—died near Murfreesboro; Jacob Bacon—killed near Nashville; Harrison Bacon, Elbert Bacon, Samuel Brewer, Tillman Burns, Thomas W. Brown—died at Nashville; Wm. H. Brown—died at Trenton, Tenn.; Lieut. James L. Brown—died at Camp Dennison, Ohio; John Barnet, Riley Caygler, Thomas S. Caywood, Washington Copeland, Elbert Copeland, Andrew Copeland—killed near Atlanta; Calvin C. Copeland, J. F. Cartwright, Marion Carden, Wright Carden, George Carson, Thomas Copeland, Capt. John C. Duff—died in prison in N. C.; George Edwards, Riley Fox, George Fox, John F. Fox, Marion Fox, Wm. Finnel, Wesley Finnel, O. G. Frazier—Federal recruiting officer; G. E. Frazier, Thomas G. Frazier—died; John N. Frazier, John Griffith, Solomon Griffith, Daniel Glen, Jasper Guinn, Marion Goode, Hanson Griffith, Haywood Gillian—died; Joseph Howell, Henry Hayes, Wm. Johnson, Louis Milburn—died; John More, Stephen Nelson, Jeff Officer, Henry Osment—killed near Nashville; Nathaniel Philips—died a prisoner at Andersonville; Joseph Pritchet—died a prisoner at Richmond, Matthew Boynalston, Wm. H. Rucker, Garet Randolph, Earl S. Randolph, Marion Routh, James M. Shannon—died; Wm. Siegler, James Armstrong.

LEADING REBELS IN THE THIRTEENTH DISTRICT.—Mathew Baswell, Wm. Barnet, Thomas Brown, Mrs. Adarine Davidson—two sons in C. S. A.; Richard Dean, J. Detherough, Alex. Dean, A. Etter, —— Ellison, —— Ellison, G. W. Finnel—two sons in C. S. A.; John Fagan, James Ferguson, Newton Griffee, Lock Griffee, John Gibson, Isaac Hope—son in C. S. A.; Robert Hope, Peter Kinser, John Kinser, John Kennady, Henry Kinser, Lazarus Lawson, James Officer, Robert Penny, Edward Roberts, George Siegler—son in C. S. A.; Wm. Shelton, James Smith, Moses Spruakles, George Willis, John Wooten, Robert Wooten, Wm. Webb.

REBEL SOLDIERS FROM THE THIRTEENTH DISTRICT—Wm. Airhart—guerrilla; Jas. Airhart—guerrilla; Isaac Barnet, Robt. Barnet, Thos. Barnet, Wm. Barnet, Isaac Bruce, Jesse Bruce, Hezekiah Bruce, Creed L. Brown, Thomas Brown, James Carson, John Copeland, Parton Davidson, Young Davidson, Jacob Detherough, Lieut. A. J. Dean—turned guerrilla; B. M. Ellerson, Alex. Ellerson, Thos. Ellerson, Samuel Ellerson, Andrew Etter, James Furguson, James Fagan, John Gibson, L. Y. Griffee, Ira Griffee, Jesse Howell, Thomas Howell, L. C. Howell, Nathaniel Howell, James Howell, (five brothers,) Jonathan Hope, James Henkle, Samuel Hampton, Thomas Howell, Kane Howell, (two brothers,) Thomas Hickey, Wm. Kennady, John Kinser, Louis Kinser, Samuel Kinser, Lazarus Lawson, Wm. Mount—guerrilla; Nichols Witcher, John C. Routh, Wm. Routh, Alex. Boylston, Thomas Scot, Polk Scot, Samuel Swan, Wm. Shelton, Bud Wooten—guerrilla; Robt. Wooten, Wm. Webb, George Willis.